The BACKCOURT

BY MÁRQUEZ PRICE

Copyright ©2025 by Márquez Price

All rights reserved.

Published in the United States by Márquez Price of Teach One Publishing

No part of this book may be reproduced or used in any manner without written permission of the copyright owner except for the use of quotations in a book review. Any attempts to amend, sell, distribute, paraphrase, or quote the contents of this book, without the consent of the author or copyright owner can and will result in legal action. This book is copyright protected.

For more information,

Contact: marquez_prc@yahoo.com or www.mpricebooks.com

First paperback edition February 2024

Edited by: Fiona Fenix

DEDICATION

This book is dedicated to quintessential backcourt:
Delano Price and Hoegie Simmons

TABLE OF CONTENTS

Acknowledgements..................................7

Preface 11

Foreword by Ernie McCray 15

Chapter 1: Foundations Of Brotherhood...............19

Chapter 2: A Season for The Ages 77

Chapter 3: From The Courts to The Streets 101

Chapter 4: The Rise of a Legend at Texas A&I 114

Chapter 5: The Double-Edged Legend of
          Hoegie Simmons 156

Chapter 6: The Rise of Bear Down Gym and the
          Impact of Bob Elliott.................174

Chapter 7: Hoegie's Descent – The Game Slips Away....204

Chapter 8: The Lean on Me Era at
          Catalina High School..................239

Chapter 9: Honoring Legacy 259

Chapter 10: Connections to Greatness. 288

Chapter 11: Hoegie Simmons: The GOAT of
                Tucson Hoops?. 301

Chapter 12: A Reunion of Legends 311

Epilogue: Márquez Price 320

Epilogue: Delano Price 327

ACKNOWLEDGEMENTS

This book would not have been possible without the players, both former and present, who were willing to share some of the most precious details of their stories with me. Some shared their names; others remained anonymous or were represented by pseudonyms due to the sensitive nature of the information provided. I am eternally grateful for their trust, humor, love, and vulnerability. I would also like to thank the Tucson basketball community, many of whom went out of their way to discuss pertinent pieces of this book. I am particularly indebted to Delano Price, my father, and Hoegie Simmons, my "uncle," for being "The Backcourt" of this book, just as my parents are the backcourt of my life.

The following represents the people I want to personally recognize and salute for taking the time to interview with me for the book, as well as those who inspired me indirectly or vicariously through their participation:

Ernie McCray – The value of who you are and what you represent to the city of Tucson, Tucson High School, The

Acknowledgements

University of Arizona, the Dunbar neighborhood/school, my family, and this book is ineffable. We all aspire to be like "Ernie McCray." Simply put, thank you for being you. The Price family loves you like no other. Your contributions go far beyond the borders of this book. Much love!

Fat Lever – Your timing was impeccable, and I'll never forget how you showed up for this legacy piece. Interviewing you was a highlight; you conducted the interview exactly as you managed the floor in your playing days as an extraordinary point guard. Both my father and I have always held you in unwavering esteem, and we will continue to do so. It was also cool that you remembered my father introducing me to you as a kid at the camp you did at Pima College!

Kenny Ball – Another "uncle"! Thank you for your interview. Only you could provide the insights you gave because you were there with my father and Hoegie. I wanted to make sure you were highlighted in this book, not only because you were a huge part of that '69 State Title Team and one of the all-time Tucson greats but also because my father and Hoegie have the utmost respect for you. You three on the same team were a cheat code; the original "Big 3." Much love from the family.

Sean Elliott – I was privileged growing up to be around you and spend time with you through my father. The times you would come into town and play two-on-two with my father, Monday Rios, Val Hill, and your brother were priceless. I threw my first assist to an NBA player for a dunk when you let me get in those games! I still have the tape! (LOL) The Sean Elliott basketball camps at Cholla and Pueblo, and the Boys and Girls Banquet where you brought Grant Hill to Tucson, are all cherished memories. You also brought David Robinson to one of those camps, which was neat. My father deeply values your timeless bond with him and keeps your glowing reviews of him framed in his room of accomplishments.

Paula Dotson – Sweet P! You've always been and will always be a champion in the eyes of the Price family. My father and Hoegie love you, and you'll always be the best to lace 'em up on the women's side. I soaked up a lot of "game" from you and you were ahead of your time.

Bob Elliott – Your interview was paramount and allowed me to delve into the era of Bear Down through a lens of immaculate perception. Thank you for sharing your story. One of a student-athlete with a long-term plan that needs to be passed down for the survival of future generations.

Larry Demic – Thank you for your interview. You brought a levity that allowed me to add depth to the human side of this story. It was a pleasure meeting you. Gary, Indianans!

Eric Money – I thoroughly enjoyed our conversation for this interview. I can see how and why you and my father are so close. It was a necessary punctuation to the years of "Eric Money" storytelling my father instilled in me. He made sure I knew that you were the real deal on the basketball court. Thank you also for being a stand-up guy. You made me feel welcomed instantly with your genuine disposition.

Deron Johnson – You gave one of the top interviews for this book, brother. Your sharp insights and witticisms were on point and invaluable. As a kid, seeing you play at Sunnyside while my father was an administrator allowed me to dream big with that basketball. You were the first larger-than-life ballyhooed sensation I witnessed in Tucson, good enough to rival anyone nationally. It goes without saying what you were and continue to be.

Michael Luke – Thank you for being the "spark" that helped me change my literary world. I'll forever be indebted to the gadfly who galvanized my pen. That first article you wrote about my father and Hoegie helped plant the seed that has now grown into the fruition of this story.

PREFACE

I was born to tell the story of Delano Price and Hoegie Simmons. A story I am uniquely qualified to share. Delano Price is my father, an unflinching presence who has been by my side my entire life. Hoegie Simmons, though not a blood relative, is like an additional uncle to me. During the first twelve years of my life, I saw him at least three times a week, followed by a twenty-year hiatus. Since then, our bond has been reassembled and continues to be strong to this day.

Unknowingly, I began preparing to write this story as early as I was four or five years old. At the time, my father, Delano Price, and Hoegie Simmons, both in their early thirties, were still thriving at the peak of their basketball prowess. I was immersed in their narrative from the beginning, spending countless hours in the dank and dimly lit gyms of the Downtown YMCA and Bear Down Gymnasium in Tucson, Arizona. From the sidelines, I watched them monopolize the court, and between pickup games, I'd dart onto the hardwood to mimic the artistry I'd just witnessed them perform against hapless defenders.

Preface

As the regulars in those gyms recognized me as Delano's son, always by his side, they began sharing nostalgia-filled stories about the renowned backcourt of Delano Price and Hoegie Simmons. Their anecdotes became my education, and those gyms became my classroom.

With a basketball in my small hands, its weight and size almost overwhelming, I started to dribble, shoot, and dream. What I didn't realize at the time was that, like the ball itself, I was being launched on a predetermined trajectory. One that would rise, arc, and eventually return to deliver a legacy worth preserving.

As the years passed, I found myself traversing the same gyms where my father and Hoegie once reigned, shaping my own contribution to the backcourt legacy. With my cultivated basketball repertoire as my tools, I carved my place in that lineage. Wearing the same Badger red-and-white uniform they had donned decades before; I often looked up at the '69 state title banner hanging in the Tucson High gymnasium. It was a poignant, transitional moment, linking me to a cherished lineage. Playing with the same passion for basketball as my father and Hoegie, I began to realize that I was continuing to author a story that was yet to be fully written.

The material for this book seemed to find me as naturally as my love for the game. Former players, coaches, journalists, and spectators enthusiastically shared countless versions of the backcourt story. My father and Hoegie themselves became storytellers, recounting their experiences as I meticulously asked questions and pieced together their narrative. Even when unprompted, others offered anecdotes that illuminated the duo's impact on and off the court.

Preface

Before I became a standout basketball player in Tucson, my father and Hoegie had already been written about in newspapers for as long as I can remember. During my own high school career, as I earned recognition in city and state basketball rankings, their story accompanied me like an ever-present shadow. It was during that time, as a teenager, that I discovered I was equally skilled in basketball and writing. I instinctively knew that one or the other would become my lifelong pursuit.

Their story remained constant, even as I matured and moved beyond the court. A eureka moment later revealed what I had overlooked for years: these stories, connections, and serendipitous encounters were not coincidences but signs. I was being summoned to write their story. The Backcourt.

FOREWORD BY ERNIE MCCRAY

There's nothing more satisfying to my soul than a good read and I most assuredly classify "The Backcourt" by Marquez Price in that category. When I first heard of Marquez, from Delano Price, his dad, I got the distinct impression that this young man, indeed, possessed an old soul. Then, after reading some of Marquez's poetry I knew my assessment of him was right on, that he's in tune with what's going on in the world and dares to try to change it for the better. Such human instincts are as old as humanity.

I felt these traits in him as I found myself relating to his eloquent narrative in a number of ways: as a native Tucsonan where the bulk of the story takes place; as a Black man since so much of it is about race; as an athlete considering that I, like Delano and Wallace "Hoagie" Simmons, the book's main characters, once wore the red and white uniforms of the Tucson High Badgers. With immense pride. As Badgers they were two of the greatest backcourts in Arizona's high school basketball history and I can give myself a little pat on the back for being, in my day, the go-to guy. Basketball transformed our lives, and I have high regard for the way Marquez captures how this metamorphosis came to be, how he painted a picture of what it takes for people to overcome obstacles, breathing life into the adage: "Where there is a will, there is a way."

He has crafted a story from his family's history that is a mirror to the bygone days of myriads of Black folks. His portrayal of how his father's grandfather, his great-grandfather, grew up in the savage world that was the Old South, reminded me of my grandfather, coping with the coldhearted masters of a sharecropping plantation in Hawkinsville, Georgia, dreaming of, and determined to, someday, live a life of dignity as opposed to feeling as though he was some kind of subhuman species of human beings. These men resisted such dehumanizing conditions and raised besides their resolute wives, children who, because of the way they were brought up by these strong god-fearing hard-working fathers and mothers, guided their progeny to seek more hopeful lives, to become decent and learned and wise.

Marquez's family, like mine, ended up in Tucson eventually as part of the Great Migration wherein African Americans fled the cruelties of the South to seek a better life in the North, Midwest, and West. Elaborating on that, Marquez conveys how, once settled in these new settings, his family launched into being treated with dignity immediately and relentlessly and found ways to be appreciated. Never looking back. Ditto that for my family too, with basketball playing a large role in making some of our dreams come true, opening a door for us to become part of something in which we could work with others towards a common purpose, practicing and conditioning with undying passion to become the best we, collectively and individually, could be.

Marquez couldn't help making this story shine because he's a good baller, too, influenced by his dad, who was influenced by me and others in the Tucson basketball community, and I was influenced by Arizona Wildcat greats beginning in the 40's. And the beauty of it all is that from sport and ongoing and unflinching family support, we went on to earn college degrees and take leadership roles in our communities. Oh, Marquez has weaved such a wonderful read that is tied together throughout by bits and pieces of the relationship between Delano, his dad, and Hoagie, his dad's more than gifted backcourt teammate. Based on the ups and downs of what they go through, one puts this book down having witnessed a story wrapped in the spirit of Black love: an account of overcoming, of accepting differences, of the enduring power of friendship.

The Backcourt overflows with the contents needed for creating a better world.

CHAPTER 1

FOUNDATIONS OF BROTHERHOOD

Delano Price's story begins with the roots of his family tree, deeply embedded in the soil of Warren, Arkansas, where his father, A.D. Price, was born on November 11, 1905. It was a time when the scars of slavery were still fresh, and the echoes of oppression reverberated through every corner of the South. A.D., or "Daddy" as he was affectionately called by his children and grandchildren, carried the legacy of those who had endured the brutal reality of a system that refused to see them as fully human. Even his name, consisting of only initials, reflected a painful historical truth: Black Americans were often denied the dignity of a full name, reduced to mere letters in the eyes of a society that sought to strip them of their identities.

Despite this, A.D. embodied strength, flexibility, and discreet pride. He grew up in a world that demanded more of him than it offered in return, but he persevered. A tall, wiry man with a

Chapter 1

compelling presence, A.D. had an air of steadiness about him that his family would come to rely on. His hands, large and strong, were tools of labor and love, and his gait, deliberate and firm, symbolized a man who moved through life with purpose. To his son Delano, A.D. was larger than life, a figure whose silent strength spoke volumes without the need for many words.

On the other side of this storied lineage was Delano's mother, Mattie C. Pickett, born in Gillett, Arkansas, on August 30, 1918. Known later as "Motha," Mattie was a woman who defied her diminutive stature with a personality that was nothing short of formidable. Standing just five feet tall, she carried herself with an authority that could command respect in any room. Her green eyes, piercing and vibrant, seemed to see straight through a person, and her sharp wit along with a capacious storage of recited sayings often left others scrambling to keep up. "I weigh 160 pounds, and you can have all of it," she'd declare unapologetically to anyone foolish enough to cross her. It was a statement of confidence as much as it was a warning.

Mattie's strength wasn't confined to her words. Her physical capabilities were just as striking. She had a peculiar and awe-inspiring skill: the ability to crack three or four Brazil nuts, known at the time by the racially charged term "nigger toes," in the palm of her bare hand with a simple squeeze. It was a feat that symbolized her strength and her defiance of societal expectations. In her emerald-green eyes, there was a fire that could intimidate even the most daring adversaries. Her fists, used periodically, were a last resort that many knew better than to provoke.

Beyond her physical strength and commanding presence, Mattie possessed a remarkable talent in the kitchen. She was a

Chapter 1

culinary artist who could take the simplest of ingredients and transform them into meals that not only satisfied hunger but also nourished the soul. Feeding her family was more than a duty; it was an act of love, a ritual that brought everyone together. Her cooking was a cornerstone of the Price household, a tradition that celebrated determination and resourcefulness. Yet, she guarded her recipes with fierce obstinacy, treating them as family heirlooms not to be shared with the outside world.

Mattie's role as the matriarch extended far beyond the kitchen. She was a protector, a disciplinarian, and a source of unwavering support for her family. When she walked the streets of Sugar Hill in her Sunday best, she carried herself with regal air, exuding confidence and authority. Hidden within her immaculate clothing was a concealed blade, which was a subtle but powerful reminder of her willingness to defend her loved ones at any cost. Mattie's sharp tongue and bold demeanor ensured that few dared to challenge her, and those who did quickly learned the error of their ways.

Together, A.D. and Mattie formed a partnership that was as complex as it was enduring. Their marriage reflected the times and was marked by both love and the struggles born from systemic oppression and economic hardship. A.D.'s quiet demeanor often balanced Mattie's fiery personality, creating a dynamic that held their family through the toughest of times. Their home was a sanctuary, a place where the values of hard work, resolution, and community were instilled in their children.

For Delano, his parents were providers as well as the embodiment of strength and perseverance. A.D.'s steadfastness and Mattie's boldness served as guiding lights in his life, shaping his character and inspiring him to aim for greatness. The stories of their lives, their struggles, and their triumphs became a part of Delano's identity, a legacy that he would carry with him on his journey.

In every interaction, in every moment, A.D. and Mattie left an indelible mark on their children and grandchildren. They were a living testament to the power of intention, a reminder that even in the face of systemic oppression, love and determination could build a foundation strong enough to withstand any storm.

It wasn't uncommon for ten or more people to gather around Mattie's table. Feeding a crowd was routine for her, a challenge she embraced with grace and determination. Her kitchen was a bustling hub of activity, the aroma of simmering stews and baking bread drawing family, friends, and neighbors like moths to a flame. Each meal she served was a communal experience, a moment of togetherness that reinforced the bonds of family and community. Yet, despite the generosity with which she shared her cooking, Mattie was fiercely protective of her methods. Her recipes remain hers alone, unwritten and untouchable. To share them would be to give away a piece of herself, and that was a line she would not cross.

But Mattie's authority extended far beyond the kitchen. Her presence was felt wherever she went, a force of nature wrapped in elegance and determination. She walked with confidence that left no room for doubt, a queen surveying her domain. To the women in the neighborhood, her message was clear: Mattie C. Pickett was not to be trifled with. She was a protector, not just of her family, but of the respect they commanded. Any slight against her husband, her children, or her household was met with swift and decisive action.

Chapter 1

Her blade, though rarely used, was a symbol of her readiness to defend what was hers. It wasn't just a weapon as it was an extension of her fierce spirit, a tangible representation of the strength and self-respect that defined her. With her blade in hand, she could peel a Granny Smith apple with a precision that was almost hypnotic. The peel would fall away in a single, continuous ringlet, shedding like the skin of a snake. It was a quiet but powerful display of her dexterity and control, a subtle reminder that she was a woman who could handle herself in any situation.

Mattie's disposition and ferocity called to mind Sophia, the indomitable character from Alice Walker's The Color Purple. Like Sophia, Mattie was unmercifully intrepid, a woman who refused to be diminished by the oppressive forces around her. Her defiance wasn't loud or showy. It was woven into the fabric of her being. She stood tall against the expectations of a society that sought to subjugate Black women, asserting her worth with every step she took. Her strength was both a shield and a sword, protecting her family while carving out a space for them in a world that often sought to erase their existence.

Much like Sophia, Mattie's strength was rooted in love for her family, her community, and herself. She understood the value of self-respect and passed that understanding on to her children. She taught them to hold their heads high, to stand firm in their convictions, and to never accept less than they deserved. Her lessons were often unspoken, communicated through her actions and the way she carried herself. In every interaction, she modeled the importance of dignity, leaving an indelible mark on her family's identity.

Mattie's fierceness wasn't limited to confrontations or displays of strength; it also showed in her approach to life's challenges. She had a way of turning adversity into opportunity, using her resourcefulness to overcome obstacles and create a better future for her family. Whether it was stretching a meal to feed an unexpected guest or finding a way to make ends meet during tough times, Mattie's ingenuity was unmatched. She was a problem-solver, a strategist, and a visionary, always thinking several steps ahead.

Her role as the matriarch of the Price family was one she embraced wholeheartedly. She was the glue that held everything together, the anchor that kept the family grounded. Her home was a sanctuary, a place where love and laughter thrived despite the hardships they faced.

In the years to come, Mattie's influence would ripple through her family, shaping their values and guiding their choices. Her lessons in resilience, self-respect, and love would become the foundation upon which Delano built his life. As he grew into the man who would become a basketball legend and a pillar of his community, he carried with him the indomitable spirit of his mother. Every time he stepped onto the court, every time he faced a challenge, he drew strength from the woman who had shown him what it meant to be fearless, determined, and unstoppable.

Mattie C. Pickett was utterly tenacious in a time when the world expected Black women to shrink. Her personality was rooted in an unshakable sense of self-respect and an innate understanding of her worth with qualities that were both her armor and her weapon. She carried herself with the kind of confidence that turned heads and commanded attention, a stark contrast to the deference society often demanded of women, particularly Black women. For Mattie, submission was not an option, especially not to the oppressive societal structures that sought to control her every move. She had inherited a legacy of resistance, one forged in the crucible of slavery and tempered by the harsh realities of Jim Crow. To survive, she had to be bold; to thrive, she had to be defiant.

Her pugnacious nature was most evident in her confrontations with anyone who dared oppose her will. Mattie did not tolerate disrespect, whether it came from a neighbor, a stranger, or even a member of her own family. She had a way of making her boundaries clear, her sharp tongue and even sharper wit leaving no room for misunderstanding. To her, every act of resistance, every refusal to bow to societal expectations, was a small victory, a reclamation of power in a world designed to deny her agency.

This defiance extended to her role as a wife and mother. Mattie was a trailblazer in her time, challenging the deeply entrenched belief that a woman's place was to be subservient. Her marriage to A.D. Price was a partnership of equals in theory, though not without its share of turbulence. A.D., or "Daddy" as he was lovingly called, was a laconic man, slow to anger and deliberate in his actions. He carried the weight of his family's survival with quiet dignity, rarely complaining about the burdens that life placed on his shoulders. But even the most stoic of men could find their resolve tested, and A.D. was no exception.

Financial hardship frequently visited the Price household, as it was for many Black families navigating the systemic inequities of the early 20th century. The pressures of making ends meet often created tension between Mattie and A.D., their differing temperaments clashing in moments of stress. Their arguments were a mirror of the times, a reflection of the frustrations that arose from living in a world that seemed determined to break them. Like Sophia and Harpo in Alice Walker's The Color Purple, Mattie and A.D.'s relationship was marked by moments of combative passion, the result of two strong-willed individuals navigating the complexities of love under oppressive circumstances.

Mattie's response to disrespect, whether from A.D. or anyone else, was invariably blunt and forceful. She didn't believe in holding her tongue or suppressing her emotions for the sake of peace. "If I don't stand up for myself," she'd often say, "who will?" Her confrontational nature wasn't born out of a desire for conflict but rather a deep-seated need to assert her humanity in a world that constantly tried to deny it. For Mattie, respect was non-negotiable, and she demanded it from everyone around her, including her husband.

A.D., on the other hand, preferring to let his actions speak for him. His silence wasn't a sign of submission but rather a deliberate choice, a way of conserving his energy for the battles that truly mattered. He was the steady rock to Mattie's fiery storm, a grounding force that balanced her passionate intensity. Together, they created a dynamic that was as complex as it was effective and endured as a partnership forged in struggle but sustained by love.

Their marriage reflected a broader historical truth: Black partnerships in the aftermath of slavery were often steeped in frustration and ambivalence. The legacy of slavery had left deep scars, both visible and invisible, on Black men and women, shaping their relationships in ways that were sometimes difficult to navigate. The systemic dehumanization of slavery had stripped

Chapter 1

Black men of their ability to protect and provide for their families, while Black women were forced to shoulder immense burdens, often as the sole pillars of their households. This imbalance created a tension that lingered long after emancipation, influencing the dynamics of love and partnership for generations to come.

In the Price household, this tension manifested in moments of conflict but also in acts of adaptation. Mattie and A.D. had developed a mechanism of survival, a way of weathering the storms that life threw at them. They understood that their struggles weren't just their own; they were part of a larger narrative of Black survival in America. Their ability to endure, to keep moving forward despite the odds, was a testament to their strength and their love for each other.

For Mattie, love was not a passive emotion but an active force. She loved fiercely, with a ferocity that could be both nurturing and overwhelming. Her love for A.D. was evident in the way she supported him, even when their disagreements seemed insurmountable. She respected his role as the head of the household but never allowed that respect to undermine her own sense of self. To her, marriage was a partnership, not a hierarchy, and she refused to be relegated to a position of inferiority.

A.D., for his part, admired Mattie's strength, even if it sometimes tested his patience. He understood that her boldness was a necessary defense, a way of protecting not just herself but their entire family. In his quieter moments, he would often reflect on how much he had learned from her, about resilience, about self-respect, and about the power of standing firm in one's convictions. "She's the fire," he once told a friend, "And I'm just here to keep it burning." For Delano and his siblings, their parents' marriage was both a source of inspiration and a blueprint for navigating their own relationships. It showed them that love wasn't always easy, but it was always worth fighting for.

In many ways, Mattie and A.D.'s relationship encapsulated the duality of Black love during their time. A love that was both tender and tumultuous, shaped by external pressures and internal complexities. It was a love that bore the weight of history, carrying the scars of a painful past while striving toward a brighter future. And through it all, Mattie's boldness and A.D.'s quiet strength remained the pillars of their partnership, a foundation that would sustain their family for generations to come.

To this day, the legacy of Black love remains a complex, evolving story. Black Americans continue to heal and rediscover what it means to love each other in a way that is healthy, whole, and unburdened by the weight of history. It is a process of reclaiming tenderness and vulnerability after generations of systemic oppression have sought to fracture and suppress them. The enduring strength of Black love, however, is not merely a story of survival but a story of transcendence. Despite the traumas inherited from centuries of enslavement and discrimination, Black love has persisted as a shining exemplary of pliability, creativity, and mutual care.

Mattie C. Pickett embodied this love in all its complexity. She wasn't perfect, but she was steadfast, determined, and unapologetically devoted to her family. For ninety months of carrying ten children, she held the mantle of matriarch with pride, pouring her energy into her children, her household, and her community. Raising ten children was no small feat, especially in a world that often sought to diminish the contributions of

Chapter 1

Black mothers. Yet Mattie approached the task with the same fierce determination that defined every aspect of her life.

"I was a breeding woman," she would say with a wry smile, reflecting on her role within the family. "Always the queen bee, buzzing around my hive." The image was a fitting one. Like a queen bee, Mattie commanded respect and devotion from those around her, creating a tight-knit community that revolved around her strength and guidance. She was the nucleus of the Price family, the force that held everything together even in the most challenging times.

"Nobody messes with Mattie Price," her children would say, a statement that was as much an observation as it was a rule. Mattie's reputation as a fiercely protective mother extended beyond her family and into the wider community. If someone dared to mistreat one of her children, they were sure to face her wrath. She had no patience for bullies, bigots, or anyone who underestimated the strength of her family. Her children knew that they could rely on her to stand up for them, no matter the cost.

But Mattie's protection wasn't limited to physical or verbal confrontations. She protected her children's spirits, ensuring that they grew up with a sense of pride and self-worth. In a world that often sought to tear them down, Mattie was their first line of defense, teaching them to hold their heads high and never let anyone make them feel less than they were. She reminded them daily of their value, their potential, and their ability to overcome any obstacle.

Her role as the queen bee extended beyond her immediate family. Mattie was a pillar of her community, a woman whose influence could be felt far and wide. She took it upon herself to look out for the children in her neighborhood, ensuring that they had food to eat, clothes to wear, and someone to turn to when times got tough. Her home became a haven for those in need, a place where love and generosity flowed freely.

This generosity, however, was always tempered by Mattie's no-nonsense approach to life. She didn't coddle anyone, not even her own children. Her love was rooted, a recognition that the world could be harsh and unforgiving. She prepared her children for this reality, teaching them the importance of hard work, perseverance, and self-reliance. "If you want something," she'd say, "you'd better be ready to work for it."

Mattie's sense of humor was another key part of her personality; a tool she used to lighten the load of her many responsibilities. She had a way of making people laugh even in the darkest of times, her quick wit and sharp tongue cutting through tension like a knife. "I might be small," she'd joke, "but I'm mighty." It was a statement of fact, one that everyone who knew her could attest to.

Her humor was often laced with wisdom, a way of imparting lessons without preaching. She had a knack for turning everyday moments into teachable ones, using her sharp observations to drive home important points. Whether it was reminding her children to be kind to one another or encouraging them to stand up for themselves, Mattie's words carried weight. She spoke with authority, her voice a blend of love and discipline that left a lasting impression.

Mattie's father, Morandi Pickett, known to the family as "Big Poppa," was a man who loomed as large in the family's legacy as his nickname suggested. Born into an era rife with racial

Chapter 1

violence and systemic oppression, his life was a testament to both the resilience and the complexities of Black survival in the Jim Crow South. Big Poppa's indomitable spirit was forged in tragedy and tempered by an unwavering dedication to his family, a combination that made him both revered and complicated in the eyes of those who knew him.

Big Poppa's childhood was marked by one of the most devastating acts of violence that could befall a Black family during that time. His father was lynched; a heinous act of racial terrorism meant to instill fear and suppress resistance. The trauma of this event was seared into the memory of the family, especially for Big Poppa and his oldest son, Eli. Big Poppa had to go and identify his father's body, a harrowing experience that left Eli with a lifelong hatred of white people. "I'll never care for a peckerwood," Eli would say, his voice tinged with the bitterness of a wound that would never fully heal.

This experience shaped Big Poppa in profound ways. His mother remarried, but the relationship between Big Poppa and his stepfather was fraught with tension. This conflict only reinforced Big Poppa's need to rely on himself, cultivating a will that would become legendary within the family. He was a man who would not bow, even in the face of overwhelming odds. His life was a constant battle for dignity, a struggle that played out in both dramatic and everyday moments.

Big Poppa's tenacity found outlets in his work and his faith. As a surveyor at the Smith Rice Mill and a pastor, he balanced the physical demands of labor with the spiritual responsibilities of guiding his community. He was a man who walked with God, though not always in the ways one might expect. His relationship with the divine was as bold and unyielding as the rest of his personality. In the middle of the worst thunderstorms, when others would seek shelter, Big Poppa would walk outside and shout to the heavens, "If you want to take somebody, take me. Just not my family." Family legend has it that the storms would stop at his command, the thunder retreating in deference to his unshakable faith.

But Big Poppa was no passive man of faith. He carried a Winchester shotgun with him, a symbol of his refusal to be a victim in a world that often sought to victimize Black men. This shotgun played a pivotal role in one of the most defining moments of his life. During a heated altercation with a white man over an owed debt, the man threatened Big Poppa with a whip. "I'm going to give you a reason to remember me," the man sneered, raising the whip to strike. Big Poppa, unmoved by the threat, warned, "Don't hit me with that whip." When the man ignored the warning, Big Poppa's response was swift and decisive. With one shot, he killed the man, demonstrating a marksman's precision. It was an act of self-defense, but in the racially charged South, it was also an act of defiance with a Black man standing up to white aggression.

The consequences were immediate and severe. In that time and place, such an act was almost certain to result in a lynching. Big Poppa's life was spared, but he was sentenced to two and a half years at Cummings Prison in Arkansas, a facility notorious for its brutal treatment of Black inmates. The prison operated as a modern-day plantation, where Black men were subjected to backbreaking labor and inhumane punishments, including being whipped over barrels, cruel echoes of slavery.

To defend Big Poppa, the Pickett family had to put up their land, a painful sacrifice that underscored the precarity of Black property ownership in the South. Land was an asset as well as it was a symbol of autonomy and a rare means of security in an otherwise hostile world. Losing it would have been a devastating blow, but the family's commitment to Big Poppa's survival was unwavering.

Despite these hardships, Big Poppa's larger-than-life persona endured. He was a man of contradictions, capable of immense love and moments of jealousy and infidelity. He loved his wife deeply, but his roving eyes often led him into trouble. His wife's beauty was a source of pride and tension; he admired her radiance but bristled when others did the same. On one occasion, a man complimented her, and Big Poppa responded by knocking him into a nearby ditch. It was a reminder that his love, though complicated, was fiercely protective.

His infidelity was another layer of his complexity. He would often disappear with other women, leaving the family to speculate about his whereabouts. Yet, despite his flaws, he remained a pillar in their lives. His charisma, strength, and unwavering dedication to his children earned him their respect and love. For all his imperfections, he was a man who stood tall in the face of adversity, a figure who inspired as much as he frustrated.

Big Poppa's love for his family extended beyond his immediate household. When Mattie's son Leslie, affectionately called "Mickey," needed guidance, Big Poppa stepped in. He raised Mickey as his own, providing him with the stability and support that every child deserves. His role as a father figure was a role he took seriously, even as he juggled the complexities of his own life.

Chapter 1

Big Poppa's passions also reflected his larger-than-life personality. He was an ardent admirer of Joe Louis, the legendary Black boxer nicknamed "The Brown Bomber." Before Louis won his first title, Big Poppa would tell anyone who would listen, "There's a boy coming out of Detroit that a person is going to have to be born to whoop him." His admiration for Louis wasn't just about the sport; it was about what Louis represented which was a Black man rising to greatness in a world that tried to keep him down.

Big Poppa's connection to boxing extended to his grandson Delano. He often called young Delano "Joe Louis," a nickname that reflected his belief in the boy's potential and his striking resemblance to Joe Louis. Big Poppa's influence was evident in the way he carried himself, walking around with newspapers like The Pittsburgh Courier and The Chicago Defender, two prominent Black publications that symbolized pride and empowerment in the Black community. He understood the importance of staying informed, of knowing your history and your place in the world.

Despite his flaws, Big Poppa's legacy was one of fortitude and grit. He was a man who lived boldly, loved deeply, and fought fiercely for his family. His life was a microcosm of the broader Black experience in America and was a story of struggle, survival, and the relentless pursuit of dignity. For Mattie and her children, Big Poppa was both a source of inspiration and a reminder of the complexities of love and family.

His influence would ripple through the generations, shaping the values and aspirations of his descendants. In his defiance, his faith, and his love, Big Poppa left a legacy that would guide the Price family for years to come. He was a legend not just because of what he did, but because of how he lived, he was a man who refused to be broken, even in the face of unimaginable odds.

Mattie and A.D. Price's love story was forged in a time of profound social upheaval and personal challenges. When they met and married on January 1, 1939, their union marked the beginning of a partnership that would endure trials both externally and internally. Mattie brought with her a son, Leslie Sims, from a previous relationship. A.D., too, had a past as he had been married once before to a woman named Verna. Their separation was not finalized when he and Mattie began their life together, a complication that would follow them like a shadow. Verna's presence, though distant, loomed over their marriage in the early years.

Every time Mattie traveled to Kansas City, Missouri, Verna would find a way to taunt her, stirring a fire in Mattie's soul. Mattie, never one to back down from a challenge, wanted nothing more than to confront Verna and settle the matter once and for all. However, the practicalities of life forced them to take a different path. A.D. and Mattie eventually had his previous marriage annulled, freeing them from Verna's grasp and allowing them to solidify their union. This episode, though resolved, was emblematic of the larger struggles they faced as a couple navigating life in a world that often seemed determined to pull them apart.

To young Delano, his father was a giant, a figure whose mere presence filled the room. "Daddy would say, 'I'm six feet even,'" Delano recalled, "and I believed every inch of it." A.D.'s movements were deliberate, his arms swinging side to side as he walked, giving him an air of quiet authority. Delano loved to watch his father come down the street, a silhouette of resilience and dignity against the backdrop of a world that sought to diminish him.

Mattie, by contrast, was fiery and outspoken, a force of nature who complemented A.D.'s quiet strength. Their partnership was not without its tensions, but it was built on a foundation of mutual respect and a shared commitment to their family. They learned to navigate their differences, drawing on each other's strengths to weather the storms of life. These storms were many, as the societal pressures of the time bore down on Black families with relentless force.

One of the most defining aspects of their journey together was their participation in the Great Migration, a transformative period in American history that saw millions of Black Americans leave the South in search of better opportunities. For Mattie and A.D., this meant leaving the familiar fields of Arkansas for the industrial city of Gary, Indiana. Their migration was both a physical and a symbolic journey, one that reflected the broader movement of Black Americans taking control of their destinies in a country that had long denied them agency.

The Great Migration, which unfolded in two major waves between 1910 and 1970, was one of the largest domestic migrations in U.S. history. For Mattie and A.D., as for so many others, the decision to leave the South was driven by a combination of push and pull factors. The South, with its entrenched system of racial segregation and economic exploitation, offered little in the way of opportunity. The lingering effects of slavery were evident in every facet of life, from the sharecropping system that trapped Black families in cycles of debt to the violence perpetrated by groups like the Ku Klux Klan.

Chapter 1

Jim Crow laws ensured that Black Americans were segregated in life and in death, denied access to resources that could improve their circumstances. Even cemeteries were segregated, a grim reminder that the dehumanization of Black people did not end with their passing. For many, the South was a place of unrelenting hardship, where daily survival often depended on navigating a landscape fraught with danger and injustice.

Against this backdrop, the North held the promise of opportunity. Stories filtered back to the South of Black men earning five dollars a day in the steel mills and auto factories of cities like Gary, Chicago, and Detroit, a stark contrast to the 75 cents a day they could expect in the fields. These tales of economic mobility, coupled with the allure of urban life, created a powerful pull for families like the Prices.

However, the journey north was not without its challenges. For many, it meant abandoning the land that had been both a source of sustenance and a place of profound pain. The land was part of their lineage, a tangible connection to the generations that had come before them. Leaving it was an act of both desperation and hope, a decision that carried with it the weight of history and the promise of a better future.

When Mattie and A.D. arrived in Gary, they found a city that, like so many urban centers in the North, was both a beacon of opportunity and a reminder that racism was not confined to the South. Gary was hyper-segregated, with Black families clustered in neighborhoods that, while vibrant and close-knit, often lacked the resources available to their white counterparts. Despite these challenges, the Prices made a life for themselves, drawing on the persistence and ingenuity that had carried them through so many trials.

A.D. found work at Republic Steel, a job that demanded long hours and backbreaking labor. He never owned a car, relying instead on his legs and the generosity of neighbors to get to work. If he missed a ride, he would simply walk, embodying the determination that defined his character. His commitment to providing for his family was unwavering, a silent testament to his love and dedication.

Mattie, meanwhile, continued to be the heart and soul of the family. Her role extended beyond the walls of their home, as she became a pillar of the community, offering support and guidance to those in need. Together, she and A.D. created a sanctuary for their children, a place where unity flourished despite the challenges they faced.

Their story was not unique as it illustrated the broader Black experience during the Great Migration. For families like the Prices, the move north was not just about escaping the South, it was about reclaiming their lives, identities, and destinies in a country that had long sought to strip them away.

The Great Migration was nuanced and complex, a story of both triumph and struggle. It gave rise to the bustling urban centers that became hubs of Black culture, producing some of the greatest artists, writers, and musicians of the 20th century. But it also exposed the persistent inequalities that plagued Black communities, even in the so-called Promised Land of the North.

Mattie and A.D. Price's family grew steadily, a testament to their resilience and love in the face of life's challenges. Each of their ten children carried with them the legacy of their parents, shaped by the values and lessons passed down in a household filled with both discipline and affection. Their children's lives reflected the times and places in which they were born, from the rural South to the bustling urban landscapes of the North.

In Arkansas, Mattie gave birth to Doris, Alex, affectionately known as "Lil' Brother," Maxine, Bertha, called "Lil' Sister," and Pearl. All of them were delivered by midwives, reflecting the era's common practice, particularly in rural Black communities where access to hospitals was limited or nonexistent. These were the children of the South, born into a world shaped by the remnants of slavery and the harsh realities of Jim Crow. Despite the challenges, Mattie and A.D. created a home filled with love and purpose, preparing their children for the journey ahead.

The Price family's move to Gary, Indiana, brought about a significant shift in their lives, not just geographically but culturally and economically. It was a journey that began with a moment of defiance. A.D.'s encounter with the bull that repeatedly destroyed his garden. The garden was a patch of land with deeper meaning; it was a source of sustenance and pride, a tangible representation of A.D.'s efforts to provide for his family. When he came upon the bull one day and decided to put an end to its destruction, it was an act of both necessity and resolve. Throwing a pitchfork with precision, A.D. killed the bull, knowing full well the repercussions that might follow.

The value of livestock in the South often exceeded the perceived value of Black lives, and A.D. understood the gravity of his actions. When a white man came looking for the bull, A.D. had no choice but to go into hiding. Mattie, ever the protector and strategist, took the children and moved to Gary, Indiana, to join A.D.'s brothers, Sam and Hugo, who were already established there. It was a calculated decision, one that reflected the broader migration patterns of Black families seeking safety and opportunity in the North. A.D. joined them later, completing the family's transition from the rural fields of Arkansas to the industrial streets of Gary.

Gary, Indiana, was unlike anything the Price family had known in Arkansas. It was a hyper-segregated city, but within its Black neighborhoods, there was a sense of community and self-sufficiency that was both comforting and empowering. For young Delano, Gary felt like a world where Black people were the majority, their presence woven into the fabric of everyday life. From the milkman to the fire chief, from grocery store workers to local sheriffs, Delano's childhood was steeped in the Black experience. It was a world where Black excellence and grit were on full display, a sharp contrast to the oppressive realities of the South.

The Prices settled at 2592 Jackson Street, a house that became synonymous with their family name. "The Prices of 2592 Jackson Street" was how they were known in the neighborhood, a proud Black family building a life for themselves in a city of opportunities and challenges. Their neighbors included the Jackson family. Yes, that Jackson family. Michael Jackson and his siblings lived just down the street, and the two families knew each other well. It was a time before fame had taken hold of the Jacksons, when they were simply another family on Jackson Street, navigating the challenges of life in Gary.

The Price household was a bustling hub of activity, filled with the sounds of children playing, the smells of Mattie's cooking,

Chapter 1

and the steady hum of family life. The house itself was adjoined by a store owned by Tim and Bula Dixon, where Mattie worked as a butcher. It was a fitting role for a woman who had long mastered the art of providing for her family through skill and resourcefulness. Her work at the store was an extension of her role as the family matriarch, ensuring that her children always had food on the table and a sense of security in their lives.

For A.D., life in Gary meant long hours at the steel mill, a job that was as grueling as it was essential. The steel industry was the lifeblood of the city, providing jobs for thousands of Black families who had migrated from the South. A.D.'s work ethic was unmatched, and his commitment to providing for his family never wavered. When he wasn't at the mill, he took on odd jobs, painting houses and doing handyman work to make ends meet. His determination to support his family was constant, a quiet but powerful force that shaped the lives of his children.

Delano and his siblings grew up in a world that was both vibrant and challenging. Gary's Black neighborhoods were close, filled with the sights, sounds, and smells of a thriving community. There were barber shops and beauty salons, churches that rang with gospel music sang by Mahalia Jackson, and corner stores where neighbors gathered to share news and laughter. It was a world where everyone looked out for each other, where the struggles of one family were shared by the community.

The Price children, like so many others in Gary, navigated a city that was both a haven and a battlefield. The opportunities provided by the North were tempered by the realities of systemic racism and economic inequality. Schools were often underfunded, and jobs, while more plentiful than in the South, were still hard

Chapter 1

to come by for many Black families. Yet, within the walls of 2592 Jackson Street, the Prices found solace and strength.

For Delano, these years were formative. He was born in Gary, Indiana on February 19, 1951, one of the only Price children to be born in a hospital. His brother Michael being the other. By then, the family had begun to establish themselves in Gary, building a life that balanced the traditions of the South with the opportunities of the North. Delano's earliest memories were of his father's towering presence and his mother's unwavering determination. He grew up watching A.D. walk to work, his lanky frame and swinging arms, a symbol of hardiness. He saw Mattie at the butcher counter, her hands deftly slicing meat while her sharp tongue kept customers in line. These images were etched into Delano's memory, shaping his understanding of strength, love, and responsibility.

The years on Jackson Street were some of the happiest for the Price family. Despite the challenges they faced, there was a sense of unity and purpose that defined their lives. The house was filled with laughter, music, and occasional argument which served as a testament to the spirited personalities that made up the Price clan. It was a place where traditions were honored, where meals were shared, and where lessons in determination were taught every day.

For Delano and his siblings, growing up in Gary meant living at the intersection of history and progress. They were part of a generation that was beginning to redefine what it meant to be Black in America, drawing on the strength of their parents and the legacy of the Great Migration to chart a new path forward. Their journey from Arkansas to Indiana was more than just a move; it was a transformation, one that would shape their lives and the lives of generations to come.

A.D. Price, known as "Daddy," to his children, was a man whose life was shaped by hardship, sticktoitiveness, and unwavering love for his family. His story was not just his own but part of a larger narrative about Black survival and perseverance in America. A.D. carried the weight of his family's legacy on his shoulders, and his sacrifices and struggles left an indelible mark on those who knew him, especially his son, Delano.

A.D. came from a large family, with siblings who each carried their own burdens and triumphs. His older sister, Elen York, was a strong figure in her own right, and he had a half-brother, Alonzo Martin, whom he loved as if they shared the same mother. Alonzo's life, however, was marred by tragedy. A group of men attacked Alonzo, accusing him of stealing a cow, and in the brutal altercation, they knocked out one of his eyes. For A.D., this incident was a source of enduring pain and frustration. He often lamented that had he been there, things would have turned out differently. That sense of protective responsibility, ingrained in A.D.'s character, would later define his role as a father and husband.

A.D. also had sisters Beatrice and Amy, as well as brothers Hugo and Sam. Their lives intertwined in a tapestry of shared experiences and struggles, their bonds tested and strengthened by the harsh realities of life in the segregated South. One particularly poignant memory for Delano was a family outing to see the movie Sounder with his wife, Jacque, and his parents. As they watched the story of a Black family's struggle during the Great Depression, A.D. grew emotional. The film brought back memories of his own childhood, a time when he and his siblings worked together as an economic unit to survive. They made their own sorghum syrup and learned to ride horses, skills that were both practical and symbolic of their resilience. For A.D., those memories were a reminder of the hardships he had endured and the strength he had drawn from them.

A.D.'s father, Alec, was a towering figure in his life, both literally and figuratively. Standing 6'4", Alec was a deacon in the church, a man of faith and principle. But his life was cut tragically short under circumstances that reflected the brutal realities of being Black in the South. According to A.D., Alec's death was officially attributed to an accident with runaway horses on a Sunday; a day of rest when no work was supposed to be done. But the truth was far more harrowing. Alec had been killed by a white man who had been exploiting his wife, taking advantage of her under the constant threat of stealing their land. When Alec discovered the man at his home, his imposing presence provoked panic, and the man shot him through the heart. In the scuffle, Alec's fingers were also shot off as he tried to shield himself.

A.D., still a boy at the time, was the only family member who attended Alec's funeral in Warren, Arkansas. The Price family blamed Alec's wife, Beatrice Slater, for his death, and their once-stable household descended into poverty. Beatrice, overwhelmed and unable to care for her children, walked as far as 25 miles with them before telling her sons, A.D., Hugo, and Sam, that she could no longer take care of them. At just 13 years old, A.D. found himself on his own.

The years that followed were marked by a relentless struggle for survival. A.D. hopped trains, worked in logging camps, and during the Great Depression, found work with German farmers. He often spoke of those times, describing the black flour sacks that came to symbolize President Hoover's failure to address the economic crisis. One vivid memory involved a man at a logging camp accusing young A.D. of cheating during a card game. The man held a knife to A.D.'s throat, a stark reminder of the dangers he faced daily. Despite these hardships, A.D. survived, driven by a determination that would later define his role as the head of his own family.

Delano remembered following his father around as a child, marveling at his strength and work ethic. A.D. had hands like iron and stamina that seemed unbreakable. Delano recalled watching his father move a refrigerator by himself, a feat that underscored his physical power. But A.D.'s strength was physical, emotional and moral. He taught Delano practical skills, such as building a fire with a back log and kindling. He also imparted lessons about responsibility and perseverance.

A.D. married Mattie when he was 32 years old, and their life together was a testament to the sacrifices they both made for their family. A.D. worked at the Smith Rice Mill, often taking a boat across the river to get to work. He had a fondness for Coca-Colas, drinking two at a time when the formula was still "pure and uncut," but the habit eventually led to an ulcer. A.D.'s childhood had been cut short by necessity; he was, as Muddy Waters would sing, a "Mannish Boy," forced to grow up too soon.

For all his strengths, A.D. was not without flaws. He gambled frequently, treating it like the stock market; a risky but potentially lucrative way to improve his circumstances. Often, he lost his paycheck, creating tension and stress within the family. However,

Chapter 1

as he aged, A.D. reformed, leaving gambling behind and dedicating himself fully to his family.

A.D.'s skill as a marksman was illustrious. Though he never served in the military, his precision with a gun was unmatched. One memorable moment came when A.D., then older, shot a beer can from the length of a football field which was something Delano and his brothers Michael, Raymond, Alex, and Randle had repeatedly failed to do. Hunting was essential for A.D., who often brought home squirrels, raccoons, and possums for Mattie to cook. These meals, born of necessity, became the foundation of what would later be celebrated as "soul food," a cuisine that turned scarcity into nourishment and love.

The family's move to Tucson, Arizona, was a pivotal moment in their lives. Overwhelmed by the pressure of providing for ten children, A.D. left for Tucson ahead of the family, seeking a fresh start. Mattie, ever resourceful, tracked him down with the help of a hawkshaw and found him working in a cotton field. A.D. apologized and sent for his family, reuniting them and recommitting himself to his role as their protector and provider. He worked the graveyard shift at the University of Arizona, securing a job after repeatedly returning to ask for work until a Black foreman named Homer Townsen gave him a chance.

A.D.'s influence on Delano was profound. During Delano's junior year of high school, A.D. struggled with the noise of the crowds at basketball games. One game saw Tucson High losing until Delano went on a scoring spree that turned the tide. Hearing the roar of the crowd, A.D. returned to the gym, proud of his son's performance. Delano often described his father as his hero, a man who had overcome insurmountable odds to provide for his family. One of Delano's fondest memories was walking into the house after winning the state championship and seeing A.D. reading the newspaper headlines about the game.

A.D.'s life was a miracle of continuous determination. Despite suffering a heart attack when Delano was just 11 years old, A.D. rallied and lived into his seventies. His strength and love left an enduring legacy, shaping Delano's life and the lives of generations to come. A.D. was more than just a father; he was a symbol of perseverance, a man who faced the world's hardships and emerged unbroken.

Delano Price's early education took place in the segregated schools of Gary, Indiana, a city that served as both a sanctuary for Black families and a crucible of systemic challenges. While his older siblings attended Theodore Roosevelt High School, a K-12 institution that was entirely Black, Delano's formative years in elementary school revealed the deeply entrenched racial divides of the time. At Roosevelt, the school wasn't just an educational institution; it was a cultural hub, a place where the community gathered to celebrate achievements and support one another in the face of adversity. For Delano, these early experiences of segregation laid the groundwork for his understanding of both the limitations imposed by society and the boundless potential of Black excellence.

The Price family's connection to Roosevelt High School would have been reason enough for pride, but the school's historical legacy added another layer of significance. Decades after Delano left Gary, Roosevelt would produce one of Indiana's most celebrated basketball players: Glenn "Big Dog" Robinson. Robinson's journey from Roosevelt to becoming the first overall pick in the 1994

Chapter 1

NBA draft was emblematic of the state's deep-seated love for basketball and its ability to elevate individuals to legendary status. Known for his dominance on the court, Robinson's achievements included being named Indiana Mr. Basketball, earning multiple college accolades at Purdue University, and securing an NBA championship in 2005. For young athletes growing up in Indiana, Robinson's career served as proof that the dream of greatness was attainable even for those from humble beginnings.

Indiana's basketball culture was unlike anything else in the country. Often referred to as the "basketball capital of the world," the state's obsession with the sport was deeply rooted in its history. For Delano, who grew up surrounded by this fervor, basketball was a way of life as much as it was a game. The sport had woven itself into the fabric of Indiana's identity, functioning as both a unifying force and a stage for individual brilliance. This passion for basketball stretched back to the early 20th century, when the game was introduced to small towns and rural communities across the state. It quickly became a unifying pastime, bringing people together in school gymnasiums and outdoor courts, where competition was fierce, and skill was revered.

The Indiana High School Boys Basketball Tournament, first held in 1911, played a significant role in solidifying the state's basketball tradition. The tournament's "David vs. Goliath" narrative captivated audiences, as small-town teams often rose to challenge and defeat much larger schools. Perhaps the most iconic moment in the tournament's history was the 1954 victory of tiny Milan High School, a story that later inspired the classic film, Hoosiers. For players like Delano, this history served as both inspiration

CHAPTER I

and aspiration, a reminder that greatness could emerge from even the most unlikely places.

Indiana's love affair with basketball extended far beyond high school gyms. The state's college basketball programs, particularly at Indiana University and Purdue University, became national powerhouses, producing legendary players and unforgettable moments. Under the leadership of iconic coach Bob Knight, Indiana University won multiple NCAA championships, including a perfect season in 1976 that remains unmatched in men's college basketball. These achievements elevated the state's reputation and cemented its place in the sport's history.

For Delano, the pervasive culture of basketball in Indiana was impossible to ignore. Outdoor courts dotted the landscape, from city parks to barnyard hoops in rural areas, where pickup games became a daily ritual for players of all ages. These courts were places to play along with being crucibles of competition and community, spaces where friendships were forged, and rivalries were born. It was on these courts that players honed their skills, learned the value of teamwork, and developed the resilience needed to succeed in life.

The influence of the American Basketball Association (ABA) and the National Basketball Association (NBA) further solidified Indiana's reputation as a basketball mecca. The Indiana Pacers, founded in 1967 as part of the ABA, became a source of pride for the state's fans. When the Pacers joined the NBA in 1976, their competitive spirit and commitment to excellence kept Indiana basketball at the forefront of the professional scene. For fans like Delano, the Pacers represented the pinnacle of what Indiana

CHAPTER 1

basketball could achieve, becoming a professional team rooted in the state's enduring passion for the game.

The cultural impact of basketball in Indiana extended far beyond the court. Sport has become a central thread in the state's identity, influencing everything from local traditions to the architecture of high school gymnasiums. Many of these gyms were among the largest in the nation, reflecting the community's unwavering support for the game. Films like Hoosiers and documentaries about the state's basketball history further immortalized its legacy, ensuring that the stories of players, teams, and communities would continue to inspire future generations.

In February 2024, the NBA on TNT aired a special program titled Basketball Stories: Indiana Glory, featuring legends like Larry Bird, Reggie Miller, and Isiah Thomas. The episode celebrated Indiana's unique relationship with basketball, offering insights from players who had experienced it firsthand. For viewers like Delano, the program was a powerful reminder of the state's basketball piety that became a phenomenon that Bird described as "bringing people together like nothing else."

Isiah Thomas, who left Chicago to play at Indiana University, spoke about the reverence for basketball in the state. "There's a religious spirituality about the game that you have to honor," he said. "In Indiana, everybody can shoot. People do not miss open shots." His words captured the state's collective dedication to skill, a sentiment echoed by Reggie Miller, who marveled at the passion of high school crowds. "For some of those kids, this was their NBA championship," Miller said, highlighting the stakes and intensity of every game.

For Delano, these stories were distant reflections of the state's basketball culture and something more personal; they were a part of his own experience. Growing up in Gary, he witnessed firsthand how basketball brought communities together, cultivating a sense of pride and belonging. The game transcended the boundaries of race and class, offering a common ground where players and fans alike could unite in their love for the sport.

Basketball in Indiana was a pastime woven into the culture. It was a tradition passed down from generation to generation. For Delano, this tradition was both a privilege and a responsibility. The lessons he learned on the court; discipline, perseverance, and teamwork, would serve him well in every aspect of his life. The game taught him to dream big and to believe in his ability to overcome obstacles, a mindset that would shape his journey long after he left Indiana.

As he reflected on his childhood, Delano understood that basketball had given him a strong sense of purpose. It had also given him a connection to something larger than himself. Whether it was playing pickup games with friends or watching legends like Glenn Robinson and Larry Bird, basketball was a constant source of inspiration. It was a reminder of the survivability and creativity that defined his community, a testament to the power of the game to uplift and unite.

Delano's journey through Indiana's basketball culture was a defining chapter in his life, one that shaped his identity and instilled in him a deep appreciation for the game. It was a journey that began on the segregated courts of Gary and carried him forward, connecting him to a legacy that spanned generations.

Chapter 1

For Delano, basketball was a tradition that embodied the spirit of Indiana and the unyielding inner strength of its people.

Moving to Tucson, Arizona, marked a turning point in Delano Price's young life. For the first time, he encountered the realities of integration and the challenges of navigating a multicultural world. Coming from Gary, Indiana, a city deeply shaped by the Great Migration and characterized by strong Black community networks, Tucson felt unfamiliar and "odd." His first day of school in Tucson, as a second grader, was one of those moments that stayed with him forever.

The classroom felt different. In Gary, his schools were segregated, with an overwhelming majority of Black students. In Tucson, Delano was introduced as "the new student from Gary, Indiana," and as he looked around the room, he saw a mosaic of faces that were Latino, Native American, White, and Black. It was a cultural shift that initially left him feeling disoriented. Delano had grown accustomed to a community where nearly everyone shared his experiences and identity, but now, he found himself in an environment that reflected the broader tapestry of America.

Recess offered its own lessons in cultural differences. Delano noticed the other boys going to the bathroom, wetting their combs under the sink, and running them through their hair. His friend Genie Diaz, whose cold black hair seemed almost alive in its sleekness, caught his attention. Curious, Delano asked Genie if he could use his comb. When he wet the comb and ran it through his own hair, he was startled to see no change as his thick, coiled hair remained unaffected. This small moment was emblematical to the larger adjustments Delano would need to make as he navigated this new environment. Along with the rules of the classroom and playground, he had to grasp the cultural rhythms of his peers.

Despite these differences, Delano's natural charisma and innate ability to connect with others allowed him to form friendships. He quickly bonded with classmates like Paul and Rene, whose warmth and curiosity mirrored his own. However, not all interactions were positive. One day, as Delano walked home with Paul and Rene, they invited him into their house. But when their mother saw Delano, she refused to let him inside upon realizing he was Black. It was a stinging reminder that even in this seemingly integrated world, the specter of racism remained ever-present.

Fortunately, Delano's family had settled in Sugar Hill, a predominantly Black neighborhood in Tucson. Sugar Hill became both a refuge and a source of identity for Delano as he adjusted to life in Arizona. The neighborhood, rich in cultural heritage, was a community bound by shared history and mutual support. The origins of Sugar Hill can be traced back to the late 1940s and early 1950s, when Tucson's Black population began to grow significantly, fueled by post-World War II migration and the pursuit of economic opportunities. The name "Sugar Hill" was a nod to the affluent African American community in Harlem, reflecting the aspirations and pride of its residents.

Sugar Hill, a collection of homes, thrived as a hub of activity and independence. Its residents, despite facing systemic racism and segregation, built a self-reliant community that thrived in the face of adversity. Churches served as spiritual and social anchors, schools provided education and opportunity, and local businesses offered both goods and a sense of economic independence. The neighborhood's tight-knit nature meant that everyone looked out for one another. If a family needed help, neighbors were there to provide it, whether it was childcare, a hot meal, or simply a listening ear.

During the mid-20th century, Sugar Hill also became a focal point for civil rights activism in Tucson. Local leaders worked tirelessly to address issues such as housing discrimination and educational inequities, advocating for broader social change. These efforts didn't go unnoticed, contributing to significant advancements in the city's inclusion and equity policies. Yet, as with many Black communities across the country, challenges persisted. Systemic barriers and economic inequality remained a reality, but Sugar Hill's residents refused to let these obstacles define them.

Delano found comfort in the community's warmth and vitality. The neighborhood's culture and history offered him a sense of belonging, even as he continued to grapple with the unfamiliarity of integration. The spirit of Sugar Hill's residents inspired Delano, teaching him the importance of perseverance and solidarity. He began to see himself not just as an individual but as part of a larger legacy of strength and determination.

Life in the Price household was another source of stability and identity for Delano. With so many siblings, his family often felt like two separate families within one. His older siblings, many of whom had helped raise him, acted as surrogate parents, while he and his younger brother Michael shared in the daily adventures of childhood. Delano's brother Randle served as a bridge between the two "families," helping to unite their diverse experiences and perspectives. "Sometimes older siblings never see you beyond the child they helped raise," Delano observed, "and birth order helps define a lot of what people become."

The dynamics of his family life reinforced the values of responsibility and interdependence. Growing up in a household bustling with activity taught Delano how to navigate relationships and manage conflicts, which was a skill that would serve him well in the larger world. His family's unity mirrored the solidarity of the Sugar Hill community, creating a dual foundation of support and flexibility that anchored Delano as he navigated his new environment.

The lessons Delano learned in Sugar Hill extended beyond the confines of the neighborhood. The area's history as a center for activism and cultural pride instilled in him a sense of purpose and responsibility. He began to see himself as part of a broader narrative, one that connected the struggles and triumphs of his ancestors to his own voyage. This perspective shaped Delano's approach to life, fueling his ambition and deepening his appreciation for the sacrifices made by those who came before him.

As he continued to grow and adapt to life in Tucson, Delano carried the spirit of Sugar Hill with him. The neighborhood's legacy of buoyancy and cultural pride became a source of strength, reminding him that even in the face of adversity, it was possible to thrive. The experiences he gained during these formative years would go on to shape his identity and values, laying the groundwork for the man he would become.

Today, Sugar Hill remains a mark of the enduring strength of Tucson's Black community. Although the neighborhood has undergone changes due to urban development and gentrification, efforts to preserve its historical significance continue. Community initiatives and oral histories highlight the contributions of Sugar Hill's residents, ensuring that their stories are not forgotten. For Delano, Sugar Hill was a home, a sanctuary, and a testament to the power of community.

In reflecting on his early years in Tucson, Delano often returned to the lessons he learned in Sugar Hill. The neighborhood taught him the importance of pride and solidarity, values that would guide him throughout his life. It was in Sugar Hill that Delano began to understand the power of identity and the strength that comes from knowing who you are and where you come from. These lessons, rooted in the rich cultural heritage of Sugar Hill, became the foundation upon which Delano built his future.

Basketball found Delano Price through an unassuming door at the YMCA, a place where he would forge his identity and build a lifelong love for the game. Introduced to the facility by his friend Archey Douglas, Delano's initial visits were furtive; sneaking into the building to gain access to the courts, the gym, and the camaraderie of the other boys who also sought refuge there. They were caught more than once, their boldness tempered by the stern glances of the YMCA staff. Yet Delano's persistence and passion for the game drew the attention of C.S. "Chick" Hawkins, a white man who managed the facility. When Delano asked Hawkins if he could work in exchange for membership, Hawkins recognized something special in the boy.

Chick gave Delano a menial job, an arrangement that proved transformative. With free membership secured, Delano spent nearly every waking moment at the YMCA. He'd leave home after breakfast and wouldn't return until the facility closed at 9:30 PM, often walking home exhausted but exhilarated. The

CHAPTER I

YMCA was more than just a gym; it was a haven for Delano and countless other kids whose families couldn't afford luxuries like club membership. For many, it was a place where dreams began to take shape.

Delano's dedication to basketball became all-consuming. With several baskets scattered throughout the gym, he would spend hours playing imaginary games, moving from hoop to hoop as if orchestrating his own championship. The isolation didn't deter him; rather, it sharpened his focus. Basketball became an outlet for creativity and a vessel for self-discovery. By the sixth grade, his commitment to the sport translated into tangible success. He began playing organized basketball and won his first trophy in the seventh grade, emerging as the junior league scoring champion at the YMCA. It was a proud moment, the first of many milestones that would solidify his connection to the game.

Summers at the YMCA were particularly vibrant. The neighborhood kids flocked to the facility, spending their days boxing, swimming, and, of course, playing basketball. Their meager resources were pooled for snacks, or when desperation struck, they resorted to theft which reflected the economic challenges many faced. Despite these hardships, the bonds forged during those summers were unbreakable. The gym was their stage, the court their proving ground, and the friendships formed within those walls became a cornerstone of Delano's youth.

As Delano's skills developed, so did his signature weapon: the jump shot. Widely regarded as one of the greatest shooters to come out of Tucson, Delano's jump shot was a marvel of precision and elegance. His journey to mastering it began with observation. With limited access to footage in the 1960s, Delano studied still images of players like Oscar Robertson and mimicked their form. He analyzed the mechanics of Hal Greer and Walt Frazier, emulating their movements until they became second nature. Players like Nate Archibald, John Havlicek, and Sam Jones also left an impression, their styles blending into the tapestry of Delano's unique approach.

Imitation didn't define his jump shot; relentless practice did. Day after day, Delano refined his technique, ensuring every element, hand-eye coordination, footwork, and follow-through, was in perfect harmony. His dedication turned repetition into artistry. Unlike today, when countless trainers and YouTube tutorials dissect every aspect of the game, Delano was entirely self-taught. His skill developed organically, like a prodigy jazz trumpeter who learns by ear rather than formal training.

Locally, Delano idolized shooters like Junior Douglas and Chester Willis, who had been key players on Tucson High's 1962 state championship team. While their form was graceful, Delano's accuracy soon surpassed theirs. His ability to generate perfect rotation on the ball captivated onlookers. It was said that if you closed your eyes near the court, you could identify Delano's presence by the sound of the chain or nylon net snapping crisply as the ball swished through. His shots were so precise that the ball often became tangled in the net, a testament to the force and accuracy of his release.

When Delano entered Roskruge Junior High, he faced the challenge of proving himself on the team. As an underclassman, he started at the bottom of the depth chart, ranked 17th. Without even a proper tank top uniform, Delano wore an old shirt with a faded number from the 1950s. His frustration was palpable, especially when his friend Bobby Morris, physically imposing in his shared class, started over him. Despite his limited playing time, Delano refused to let discouragement define him.

One pivotal moment occurred during a Christmas tournament. Delano's older brother Alex, who was home on leave from the Marines, came to watch the game. Delano didn't play a single minute, sitting on the bench as the clock ticked down. Alex, undeterred, cheered enthusiastically for Delano and his team, a gesture of unwavering support. That moment stuck with Delano, a quiet reminder of the importance of persistence. Years later, when Delano stood dribbling the clock out during the state championship game his senior year, he thought back to that night, a testament to how far he had come.

Fueled by determination, Delano returned to the YMCA after his seventh-grade season and dedicated himself to improvement. With guidance from Raul Villanueva and a 6'5" peer named Chucko Miranda, Delano honed his skills. By the following year, he was not only starting but captaining the team. He earned a spot on the all-city team and led Roskruge to the championship game, where they narrowly lost to Utterback Junior High. That loss, though painful, fueled an indomitable resolve within Delano to push himself even further.

High school marked the next chapter of Delano's basketball journey. As a freshman at Tucson High in the fall of 1965, he quickly made an impact, helping his team win the city championship and setting a record for most points scored by a freshman team. It was during this time that Delano first heard of "Hoegie Wolf," a rising star at Pueblo High School. The buzz around Hoegie's talent intrigued Delano, and when the two finally faced off in a game, the hype proved warranted. Hoegie's dizzying speed and remarkable skill left an impression on Delano, but Tucson High ultimately triumphed in an overtime thriller, 65-56.

The following year, Hoegie transferred to Tucson High, adding a new dynamic to the team. While Delano and budding star Kenny Ball played varsity, Hoegie's temperament relegated him to junior varsity despite his prodigious talent. Known for his fiery demeanor, Hoegie often dominated games before being ejected by the third quarter, already having scored 25 or 30 points. Despite Tucson High's struggles that season, finishing with a 6-12 record, Delano's growth continued. He averaged double figures as a sophomore and earned honorable mention all-city.

By their junior year, Delano and Hoegie had formed an unrivaled backcourt duo. Though Hoegie was ineligible for most of the season, he averaged 18 points per game in the final six games. Delano, meanwhile, made second-team all-city, helping Tucson High to a 14-6 record. Although they fell short of the city championship, losing to Rincon High School, the experience solidified Delano's reputation as a fierce competitor and a leader.

Delano's basketball journey was far more than a series of games and accolades. It was a testament to his fierce, competitive nature, his ability to rise above challenges, and his relentless pursuit of excellence. From sneaking into the YMCA to becoming one of Tucson's most celebrated players, Delano's reputation was one of grit, determination, and an unyielding love for the game.

Wallace "Hoegie" Simmons was born in the heart of Monroe, Louisiana, a place steeped in the rhythms and tensions of the Deep South. Life in Monroe was defined by its convolutions as it was a vibrant Black community coexisting within a society riddled with systemic racism and the legacies of segregation. Hoegie's early years were marked by toughness and rebelliousness, traits that would come to define him both on and off the basketball court.

By the time Hoegie was 14, his defiance had drawn the attention of the local authorities. Known for getting into frequent fights, he had become a fixture in the juvenile system. His mother was given an ultimatum: send Hoegie away or see him placed in a farm school until he turned 18. Farm schools were notorious for their brutal conditions, with young Black boys forced into grueling labor, picking cotton, and bailing hay under the watchful eyes of overseers. Even worse, the sentences often extended well beyond their initial terms, with juveniles finding themselves trapped in the system until their late twenties. For Hoegie's mother, the choice was clear that she needed to get her son out of Monroe.

Thus began Hoegie's journey to Tucson, Arizona, a move that would change the trajectory of his life. His mother stayed on the north side of town in the Sugar Hill neighborhood with her sister, while Hoegie was sent to live with an aunt on the south side. This geographical separation placed him in South Park, another one of Tucson's oldest historically Black neighborhoods. For Hoegie, the move was jarring. Monroe had been a homogenous environment, populated almost exclusively by Black residents, including Creoles, Cajuns, and Albinos. Tucson, by contrast, was a melting pot of cultures. Here, Hoegie encountered Mexicans, Indigenous Native Americans, and other groups for the first time, an experience that both intrigued and disoriented him.

Despite its challenges, South Park offered Hoegie a sense of community and belonging. The neighborhood's roots stretched back to the early 20th century, when African American families began migrating to Tucson during the Great Migration. Like many Black neighborhoods across the country, South Park was born out of necessity. Restrictive covenants and housing discrimination confined Black residents to specific areas, but they turned these limitations into opportunities to build thriving communities.

During the 1920s and 1930s, South Park became a hub for African American workers employed in Tucson's railroads, construction, and service industries. By the 1940s and 1950s, it had grown into a self-sufficient neighborhood, with Black-owned businesses, churches, and schools forming the backbone of the community. These institutions provided services along with a sense of pride and solidarity.

South Park was a residential area and a cultural epicenter. Churches hosted events that brought the community together, schools provided education and opportunity, and local businesses served as gathering places where neighbors could exchange news and support one another. It was a neighborhood defined by resilience, where the struggles of systemic racism were met with unwavering determination and creativity.

Yet, like so many Black neighborhoods across America, South Park was not immune to the forces of urban renewal and gentrification. By the mid-20th century, highway construction and city planning initiatives had begun to encroach on the area, displacing families and erasing landmarks that had once been central to the community. Despite these challenges, South Park's legacy endured. Today, it stands as a testament to the struggles and achievements of Tucson's Black community, with ongoing efforts by local historians and organizations to preserve its history and honor its contributions to the city's cultural fabric.

Chapter 1

For Hoegie, South Park was a place of contrast. It offered stability and a sense of identity, yet it also exposed him to the harsh realities of systemic inequality. His time in South Park coincided with his enrollment at Pueblo High School, where he began his high school journey. As a freshman, Hoegie was still adjusting to life in Tucson. The cultural differences he encountered were stark, but they also broadened his perspective and fueled his ambition.

At Pueblo High School his freshman year, basketball became Hoegie's refuge. The sport offered him a way to channel his energy and defiance into something constructive. His natural talent was immediately evident, and it didn't take long for him to make a name for himself on the court. However, his transition to Tucson wasn't without its challenges. The cultural diversity he encountered at Pueblo was unlike anything he had experienced in Monroe. He once remarked on the novelty of seeing Mexicans and Indigenous Native Americans, groups he had previously only known through the distorted lens of television and erroneous labels.

Hoegie's initial encounters with his new peers were often tense. His blistering personality and quick temper led to conflicts, including a memorable incident with a Mexican boy who blew cigarette smoke in his face. True to form, Hoegie warned the boy not to do it again, and when the boy ignored him, Hoegie made good on his promise to "beat the shit out of him." The fight resulted in Hoegie's first suspension in Tucson, a reminder that his transition to this new environment would require more than physical relocation.

Despite these early missteps, basketball became a unifying force in Hoegie's life. On the court, he was a force of nature, combining speed, agility, and an almost preternatural understanding of the

Chapter 1

game. Coaches and teammates alike were struck by his raw talent and unrelenting drive. Basketball provided Hoegie with a sense of purpose and a path forward, even as he continued to navigate the densities of his new life in Tucson.

Wallace "Hoegie" Simmons carried the weight of his upbringing in Monroe, Louisiana, like an indelible mark etched onto his character. Born into a deeply segregated society, his formative years were a paradox of guts and rebellion. Hoegie's world was defined by the rigid hierarchies of the South, a place where every interaction was charged with the weight of systemic racism. Yet even as a boy, his defiance was evident, a spark that would one day define his identity.

"I'm lookin' at ya'll," he would tell other races after moving to Tucson, "but don't pay no attention to me because I had never seen anything else." The world outside Monroe was entirely foreign to him, and the cultural diversity of Tucson, with its mix of Mexicans, Indigenous peoples, and others, was both intriguing and baffling. In Monroe, he had only ever known Black communities, Creoles, Cajuns, and Albinos, and his ideas about others were shaped largely by television stereotypes. "Indians," for example, existed only as characters fighting cowboys in the shows he watched.

Back in Monroe, confrontations had been commonplace. Hoegie attended all-Black schools from first through eighth grade, where discipline was met with physical force. His basketball coaches believed in tough love. If the team lost, every player, regardless of individual performance, was subjected to beatings. "When you messed up, they would hit you with a stick or their fist, then send you to the back of the line," Hoegie recalled. These brutal methods, while harsh, instilled in him a remarkable physical mettle and mental fortitude. His coaches, recognizing his raw talent, nicknamed him "Caveman" for his long arms and uncanny ability to "jump out of the world."

Basketball had always been a family affair for Hoegie. His older sister was a formidable player in her own right, and it was on their backyard goal that Hoegie first honed his skills. Night after night, they would play until midnight, with his sister dominating the games. She was his first rival and his first teacher, pushing him to improve through sheer competition. Their mother's sister, a sports enthusiast, encouraged their love for the game, promoting a family culture that revolved around athleticism.

Yet, even as basketball became a sanctuary, the realities of life in Monroe were never far behind. Segregation was omnipresent, shaping every aspect of daily life. At local convenience stores, instead of mirrors, parrots were perched at the tops of aisles, trained to squawk racial slurs when Black customers approached. "Nigger stealing, nigger stealing!" the parrots would chirp, a chilling reminder of the dehumanization embedded in Southern culture. For young Hoegie, these indignities were both infuriating and formative.

Public transportation offered its own humiliations. If Hoegie and his mother boarded a bus, the driver would often point at her seat, signaling that she needed to stand for white passengers. While his mother complied, Hoegie bristled with non-cooperation, urging her to resist. He couldn't understand why Black adults were expected to refer to white children as "ma'am" or "sir," a practice that rankled his sense of justice. "Coming up in the South, it was tough," he said later. "I was a modern-day slave. They did us bad back then, but it made me stronger."

Chapter 1

Despite the hardships, Hoegie's family connections were a source of both depth and complication. His parents divorced when he was just two years old, leaving his mother, Mary Simmons, to raise him. Hoegie had little respect for his father, W.C. Freeman, who had abandoned the family. "I never cared nothing about him," Hoegie admitted, though he maintained a tenuous relationship with Freeman out of respect for his grandmother, Freeman's mother. She often pleaded with Hoegie to show kindness to his father, but their encounters were troubled.

One particularly painful episode occurred when Freeman's father passed away. At the time, Hoegie was playing college basketball in Kingsville, Texas. Hoping to attend the funeral in Arkansas, he called his father in Houston to arrange a ride. Freeman agreed, only to leave without him. Furious and humiliated, Hoegie returned to Louisiana and told his grandmother, "I love you, but I'll never speak to that dog again in life."

Years later, when Freeman died, Hoegie and his sister traveled from Pasadena to attend the funeral. The gathering, held on a Monday, began with tense anticipation. By the time Hoegie arrived on Friday ahead of the funeral, his anger toward his father was still palpable. During the service, he stood up and declared, "I'm glad he's dead, and if any of you have a problem with it, we can fight right now." A near-melee ensued, narrowly avoided by family intervention.

Freeman's legacy was complicated further by his prolific fatherhood. Nicknamed "Cowboy," a term often used derogatorily for Black men, Freeman had fathered 36 children. At the funeral, all his children were asked to stand together, a moment of surreal recognition for Hoegie. "We all look alike," he said. "His sperm count was strong. They shoulda sent his body to the University because he had all of them kids, and they all look alike."

Among his siblings, Hoegie and his brothers George and Charles were said to resemble Freeman most closely, a comparison that brought him little solace. Born Wallace Charles Freeman Jr., Hoegie had taken his mother's name, Simmons, as a rejection of his father's legacy. This defiance extended to his father's brother, "Diddy," who also had over 30 children. The tangled web of family ties left Hoegie with siblings he had never met, a sprawling network of relatives that underscored the involvedness of his upbringing.

Despite these familial challenges, Hoegie's early experiences fueled his determination to rise above his circumstances. Basketball offered him an outlet, a way to channel his frustrations into something productive. The discipline instilled by his coaches in Monroe, though harsh, gave him the physical toughness and mental grit needed to succeed. His sister's dominance on their backyard court inspired him to strive for excellence, and the support of his extended family in Tucson provided a foundation upon which he could build a new life.

In reflecting on his upbringing, Hoegie acknowledged the duality of his experiences. "Me and my cousins could have killed a lot of white people and put them in the swamp and ran out west somewhere," he said, referring to the violent undercurrents of Southern life. "But our mamas and grandmamas were staying there, and they would have come in the night and burned down their houses and killed them." It was a stark reminder of the generational sacrifices made to ensure survival and stability.

For Hoegie, these sacrifices were not in vain. They instilled in him a hardiness and a drive to succeed, qualities that would define his journey as an athlete and a person. His path from Monroe to Tucson was one of transformation, shaped by the trials of the South and the opportunities of the West. It was a journey that, while riddled with challenges, ultimately prepared him for the heights he would later reach.

When Wallace "Hoegie" Simmons moved to Tucson's northside neighborhood of Sugar Hill, it marked the beginning of a transformative chapter in his life. The neighborhood was a vibrant yet cohesive community, filled with families who had migrated west in search of better opportunities. It was also home to Delano Price and his family, who lived on Lester Street, just a short walk from Hoegie's new residence in Hampton. The proximity proved to be serendipitous, as Hoegie and Delano quickly became inseparable.

Each morning, Hoegie would walk to Delano's house, and together they'd make their way to school. These daily treks were more than just a commute; they were a time for shared dreams, mutual encouragement, and the kind of camaraderie that only comes from a deep, unspoken understanding. Both boys carried the weight of their pasts; Hoegie, the son of a broken home and a product of the harsh South, and Delano, a disciplined young man raised in a household where flexibility and family ties were paramount. Their shared experiences of growing up as Black boys in a world filled with systemic challenges bonded them instantly.

Delano's father, Mr. A.D., became a significant figure in Hoegie's life. Having both lived in the South, Mr. A.D. and Hoegie shared a connection rooted in their understanding of its unique hardships and cultural nuances. For Hoegie, Mr. A.D.

was a steadying presence, a man whose calm forte and wisdom reminded him of what family could be. "I loved Mr. A.D. dearly," Hoegie would later say, reflecting on how much he had admired and respected the man who had quietly welcomed him into the Price family's fold.

The Price family embraced Hoegie, but it was Delano's mother, Mattie, who left the most lasting mark. Known for her fierce love and no-nonsense attitude, Mattie commanded respect. She had a clear sense of right and wrong, especially when it came to protecting her sons. One of her steadfast rules was that her boys, including Hoegie, were not to date white girls. "Take that white girl home," she would tell Hoegie if she ever saw him or Delano with a white girl. Mattie's stance wasn't born out of prejudice but rather a deep understanding of the societal dynamics at play. If white families couldn't accept her sons as equals, she saw no reason to welcome their daughters into her home. It was a principle rooted in dignity and self-preservation; a lesson Mattie passed down with unwavering conviction.

Mattie's protective nature extended to ensuring that Hoegie stayed on the right path, especially when it came to school and behavior. Delano's sister, Pearl, a teacher at Tucson High School, also played a pivotal role in keeping Hoegie in line. She monitored his studies and behavior, ensuring that he didn't stray too far from his academic responsibilities. For a young man like Hoegie, whose rebellious streak was matched only by his charisma, the Prices provided both structure and unconditional support. In many ways, they became the family he hadn't realized he needed.

Chapter 1

Delano and Hoegie's friendship grew stronger with each passing day. They shared everything. Meals, stories, and dreams of basketball glory. Unlike many of their peers, neither Delano nor Hoegie drank or smoked, a testament to their shared discipline and focus. Their bond was built on mutual respect and a shared determination to rise above their circumstances. "Delano and Hoegie became best friends instantaneously," people would say, marveling at the unbreakable connection between the two boys.

For Hoegie, the Prices were his chosen family. He often said that Delano and his biological brother, George, were the only brothers he truly had. The Prices' home became a reservation for Hoegie, a place where he could be himself without fear of judgment or rejection. When life became too chaotic, especially later in his life when he became entangled in the criminal elements of street life, the Prices were always there to offer refuge.

Delano's brother Randle, who worked at the dog track, was particularly instrumental in protecting Hoegie during his darker moments. Whenever Hoegie found himself on the wrong side of the law, it was Randle who hid him at the track, providing him with a safe space until the storm passed. Randle's loyalty was emblematical of the Prices' commitment to Hoegie, a commitment that remained steadfast even as he struggled to find his way.

Despite the challenges Hoegie faced, his bond with the Prices kept him grounded. Mattie's firm, yet loving guidance, A.D.'s quell wisdom, and Pearl's reliable support provided a foundation of stability that Hoegie hadn't known in his own family. For a young man who had grown up feeling abandoned and misunderstood, the Prices offered a sense of belonging that was transformative.

Chapter 1

On the basketball court, Delano and Hoegie's chemistry was undeniable. Their friendship off the court translated into an almost telepathic connection during games. They pushed each other to be better, each recognizing the other's potential and working tirelessly to bring it out. Together, they formed one of the most formidable backcourt duos Tucson High had ever seen.

But their relationship went beyond basketball. Delano's steady presence often served as a counterbalance to Hoegie's intense temperament. When Hoegie's anger threatened to get the better of him, it was Delano who stepped in, offering calm and perspective. Similarly, when Delano needed a spark of passion or a burst of energy, Hoegie was there to provide it. They complemented each other in ways that went far beyond the game, their friendship a perfect blend of discipline and dynamism.

As they navigated their teenage years, Delano and Hoegie learned from each other, grew together, and supported one another through every challenge. Their friendship was a beacon of hope and resourcefulness, an affirmation to the power of connection and community. In a world that often sought to diminish them, they lifted each other up, proving that together, they were unstoppable.

In many ways, Sugar Hill was the backdrop to this extraordinary friendship. The neighborhood, with its rich history and closely connected community, provided the perfect environment for Delano and Hoegie's bond to flourish. It was a place where families looked out for one another, where neighbors became extended family, and where young men like Delano and Hoegie could dream of a future that was brighter than their past.

As Hoegie walked to Delano's house each morning, their trek to school became a metaphor for their shared journey through life.

Chapter 1

One marked by fearlessness, determination, and an unbreakable bond. Together, they traversed the challenges of adolescence, the pressures of basketball, and the intricacies of their identities as young Black men in Tucson.

Chapter 1

Hoegie's father W.C. "Cowboy" Freeman

Chapter 1

Delano's father A.D. Price

Chapter 1

Delano's grandfather Alec

Chapter 1

Big Poppa, Big Momma, and baby Eli

CHAPTER 2

A SEASON FOR THE AGES

The 1968-1969 basketball season at Tucson High School was fated to be immortalized as a pivotal chapter in Arizona's sports legacy. The Badgers, led by the steady hand and sharp shooting of captain Delano Price, set out on a path that would forever etch their names into the legacy of high school basketball history. Averaging an astounding 83.3 points per game in an era without the three-point shot, their offensive prowess shattered records, captivating the city and electrifying gymnasiums across the state. At the center of this juggernaut was a lineup filled with talent, grit, and the unrelenting will to win.

Anchoring the team was a starting five that seemed plucked from the dreams of any coach. There was Delano himself, the consummate leader, averaging 21.5 points per game while setting the tone for his teammates with his unshakeable poise and precision shooting. Alongside him was the fiery and versatile

Chapter 2

Kenny Ball, whose unique combination of skill and intensity made him one of the most formidable players in Tucson High's history. The lineup also featured the diminutive but lightning-fast Hoegie Simmons at point guard, the towering inside presence of 6'8" Elizaro "Chuco" Miranda, and 6'7" Bruce Klewer, whose humor and hustle provided balance to a team brimming with fierce competitors.

Kenny Ball, the 6'3" forward, was a cornerstone of the team's success. A multi-dimensional player, Kenny, could do it all. He could score from anywhere on the court, dominate in transition, and lock down opponents on defense. But what set him apart was his ambidexterity. Whether it was a silky reverse layup with his left hand, or a spin move into a right-handed fadeaway, Kenny's mastery of both hands made him nearly unguardable. His ability to finish with precision from improbable angles left defenders bewildered and fans in awe.

"He was the most complete player of the four years I was at Tucson High," Delano would later say, reflecting on his teammate's impact. Kenny's temperament, however, was what truly defined his game. Fueled by an unrelenting fire, Kenny played with a chip on his shoulder, using his anger as a source of motivation. This intensity came to a head during the city championship game against Rincon High School, where Kenny singlehandedly dismantled the opposition by scoring 22 consecutive points, breaking their will and securing a critical victory for the Badgers. It was a performance that embodied his fierce competitive spirit and solidified his reputation as one of Tucson High's all-time greats.

Kenny's journey to greatness began in his sophomore year when he was named to the Tucson American Newspaper's second-team all-star roster, averaging 18 points per game. By his junior year, he had elevated his game further, earning first-team all-city honors from the Tucson Citizen and second-team all-state recognition from the Arizona Republic. His senior year, however, was the pinnacle of his high school career. Kenny was named first-team all-city, first-team all-state, and honorable mention All-American. He also took home the coveted Bud Doolen Award, given to the team's most valuable player.

In the 1968-1969 season, Kenny was a force of nature. His scoring, rebounding, and leadership were instrumental in the team's record-breaking success. Beyond the statistics, Kenny's contributions were felt in the moments that didn't make the box score. His relentless hustle, his willingness to take on the toughest defensive assignments, and his ability to inspire his teammates to rise to his level of intensity.

"He could get anywhere on the floor," said teammate Joe Petrosus, the sixth man and a standout athlete in his own right. "His footwork, his hands, the way he could finish was something special to watch." Joe, a 6'2" multi-sport star who excelled in football and baseball, was the first player off the bench. Joe's hustle, athleticism, and selfless play made him the glue guy every great team needs. Joe's ability to step in and contribute seamlessly was a testament to the depth and chemistry of the 1969 Tucson High team.

While Kenny's accolades piled up, his journey after high school was filled with twists and turns. He chose to attend the University of Arizona, passing up offers from powerhouse programs like Nebraska and Oklahoma. However, personal challenges led him to leave the university, and he took a job on the railroad to support

CHAPTER 2

his young family. A tragic rail accident in 1973 nearly ended his basketball career, but Kenny's resilience saw him through. While rehabbing, he was approached by Pima Community College coach Patton, who convinced him to return to the court.

During his two years at Pima, Kenny displayed the same dominance that had defined his high school career. In the 1974-1975 season, he was named ACCAC All-Conference second team and led the league in free-throw shooting at 82%. The following season, he earned honorable mention All-American honors, first-team all-conference, and first-team Southwest Region NJCAA recognition. His records for single-game scoring (35 points) and free throws made (15 of 16) at Pima remain benchmarks of his brilliance.

Despite receiving offers from NCAA programs again, Kenny's NCAA eligibility had expired due to procedural issues with his withdrawal from the University of Arizona. It was a cruel twist of fate for a player of his caliber. He had planned to attend Grand Canyon College in the NAIA, but when the railroad called him back to work, he chose the stability of seniority and a steady income over the uncertainty of pursuing basketball further. Reflecting on the decision, Kenny would later say, "I missed a great opportunity. Grand Canyon won the NAIA National Championship in what would have been my senior year."

Through it all, Kenny never lost his passion for the game or his respect for his teammates. "What a shooter," he said of Hoegie Simmons. "So fast. Wow! That behind-the-baseline fadeaway jumper, nobody played like Hoegie. There's only one Hoegie. He and Delano were electric. It was easy to play with them."

Chapter 2

On Delano, Kenny was equally effusive. "Delano was a class act. He was our leader and coach on the floor. He was such a smooth, steady player and the purest shooter I've seen. He held our team together then and still does now. I love him with all my heart. Me and Hoegie played with anger. Delano is a born leader. I'm proud to be his friend. A true gem of the city."

As the Badgers prepared for their historic 1968-1969 season, Kenny's presence loomed large. His ambidexterity, his tenacity, and his unyielding drive were the perfect complements to Delano's leadership and Hoegie's electrifying playmaking. Together, they formed the core of a team that would go down as one of the greatest in Arizona high school basketball history.

With each practice and every game, the bond between Kenny, Delano, and their teammates grew stronger. They were players, brothers, united by a shared purpose and a common dream. For Kenny, the season represented the culmination of years of hard work and sacrifice. For the team, it was a chance to leave an indelible mark on the sport they loved.

As the opening tip-off of the 1968-1969 season approached, one thing was certain: the Tucson High Badgers were a team to be reckoned with, and Kenny Ball was one of its brightest stars.

Tucson High charged into the 1968-1969 basketball season with unmatched energy and determination, their backcourt duo of Delano Price and Wallace "Hoegie" Simmons emerged as the heart and soul of the team. The Badgers were a team on a mission, and much of their firepower came from the unbreakable chemistry between these two guards, who combined speed, skill, and leadership in a way that left opponents scrambling.

Tucson High stormed out of the gate, winning their first 11 games with an astonishing average margin of 22 points. The team, anchored by a devastating offense and a stifling defense, was relentless. At its core, Delano's steady leadership as captain and Hoegie's thrilling playmaking set the tone for what would become a legendary season. But beneath the surface of this early success, tension was simmering.

Coach Tony Morales was a disciplined, old-school leader who expected unwavering commitment from his players. While this approach worked well with some, it clashed with the fiery personalities of Kenny Ball and Hoegie Simmons. Kenny, a passionate competitor, often struggled to contain his anger when pushed too hard. Hoegie, on the other hand, saw Morales' demanding style as a painful reminder of his past in Monroe, Louisiana, where strict authority figures used physical punishment as a form of control.

These dynamics came to a head in a pivotal early-season loss to Rincon High School. Tucson High was up by 13 points in the second half but faltered against Rincon's full-court press, ultimately losing 86-84. The loss was a gut punch to the Badgers, who hadn't beaten Rincon in five years under Morales. Delano took responsibility for the defeat, saying, "We were up by 13 in the second half and should have crushed them." It was a moment of reckoning for the team.

The loss lit a fire under the Badgers, but the real turning point came in their next game against Douglas High School. Down 53-37 at halftime, Coach Morales, seething with frustration, walked out of the locker room. Delano seized the moment to rally his teammates, giving an impassioned pep talk that resonated with the team. "We're not losing again," he vowed, his voice steady but fierce. The Badgers responded with a blistering second-half comeback, ignited by Hoegie's 15-point scoring spree and Delano's 31-point masterpiece. Their aggressive full-court press overwhelmed Douglas, flipping the script and securing a season-defining victory.

The next day, the newspapers proclaimed, "Simmons rescues Badgers from basketball disaster." Hoegie later reflected on that moment, saying, "After we came back and beat Douglas, Delano told us that we were not going to lose another game, and we believed him as our captain. We played harder and didn't lose any more games. The best years of my basketball playing were in high school with Delano."

The rematch against Rincon in February of 1969 was a battle for redemption. The air inside Tucson High's gym was thick with anticipation, the tension palpable as the teams warmed up. Before the game, Morales delivered a fiery speech, pointing to a photo of the undefeated 1962 state championship team hanging on the locker room wall. "The only difference between you and them is your one loss," he declared. The challenge was clear: erase the memory of that earlier defeat and solidify their place in Tucson High history.

Rincon once again tried to impose their relentless press, but this time Tucson High was ready. Fueled by raw emotion and unflappable confidence, Hoegie took control. "I told Delano to give me the ball, and I will break this press myself," he said. With unparalleled speed and dribbling wizardry, Hoegie dismantled Rincon's defense. He motioned for his teammates to run downcourt as he sliced through defenders with a mesmerizing array of crossover dribbles, spins, and lightning-quick cuts. Rincon's press, so effective in their first meeting, was rendered useless by Hoegie's brilliance.

Then came "The Pass." With Tucson High leading in the second half, Chuco Miranda grabbed a rebound and tossed an outlet pass to Hoegie. Without looking, Hoegie delivered a left-handed, no-look, behind-the-back bullet pass the entire length of the court. The ball landed perfectly in Kenny Ball's hands for a layup in transition. The play seemed to defy physics, and for a moment, the gym fell silent in disbelief. Then, as the ball swished through the net, the crowd erupted into a deafening roar. It was the kind of moment that transcended the game, forever etched in the memories of everyone who witnessed it.

Delano led all scorers with 27 points, followed closely by Kenny with 26 and Hoegie with 25. Tucson High's victory was a resounding statement: their earlier loss to Rincon had been an anomaly, and they were now the undisputed kings of the court.

The bond between Delano and Hoegie, already strong, was solidified during these high-pressure moments. Their competitive fire pushed them to new heights, even during practice. In one memorable session late in the season, Morales grew frustrated with their lackadaisical effort during conditioning sprints. "Somebody better win this next sprint!" he barked. Delano and Hoegie proceeded to run five consecutive sprints, each ending in a tie. Hoegie's natural speed gave him an edge, but Delano's relentless drive wouldn't let him lose.

This relentless competition extended beyond practice. When they weren't running drills or playing games for Tucson High, Delano and Hoegie faced off in countless games of one-on-one and H.O.R.S.E. Delano, for all his skill and determination, could never beat Hoegie one-on-one. "We would be tied at game point," Delano recounted, "and Hoegie would drive to the baseline and shoot an impossible fadeaway jumper over the backboard with me draped all over him. The shot would sink every time."

Their friendly rivalry fueled their greatness and cemented their brotherhood. They made a lifetime bet on who would play basketball the longest, a testament to the respect and admiration they had for each other's talent and determination.

By the end of the season, Delano and Hoegie had become the most formidable backcourt in the state. Delano's steady leadership and pure shooting complemented Hoegie's explosive athleticism and creative playmaking. Together, they embodied the perfect balance of discipline and flair, strategy and improvisation. Their partnership began with basketball, but it stood as a tribute to the power of friendship, trust, and shared purpose.

As Tucson High prepared for the state tournament, the bond between Delano and Hoegie was stronger than ever. They were brothers, united by a common goal and an unyielding belief in each other. The 1968-1969 season was a journey to a championship as well as the story of two young men pushing each other to greatness and, in the process, inspiring everyone around them. Their backcourt was the beating heart of a legendary team, and their story was just beginning.

The 1968-1969 Tucson High basketball season had been a dazzling display of athleticism, camaraderie, and grit, culminating in the team's long-awaited state championship victory. From their explosive offensive prowess to their impenetrable defense, the Badgers were a force of nature. But the story of their triumph went beyond the numbers as it exemplified their determination, their coach's vision, and the unyielding bond of a team destined for greatness.

Tucson High closed out their regular season with a statement win, dropping 100 points on Douglas High School in a game that left no doubt about their championship aspirations. The southern region tournament loomed, and Tucson High was ready to prove their mettle once again. They squared off against Rincoln in a rematch that many anticipated would be a battle. But the Badgers had evolved since their narrow loss earlier in the season. Fueled by their past defeat, they dismantled Rincoln with precision and power, cruising to an emphatic victory.

The road to the state championship brought Tucson High to the Phoenix Veterans' Memorial Coliseum, where they faced a nemesis: the two-time defending state champions, Phoenix Union. Historically, Phoenix Union had been a stumbling block for the Badgers in tournament play. Despite Tucson High's 21-1 record, many doubted their ability to overcome the Coyotes, whose reputation as tournament giants was intimidating.

Coach Morales had spent the season quietly preparing his team for this moment. The Badgers entered the semifinals with a chip on their shoulders and an unshakable resolve. Phoenix Union, while talented, was plagued by sloppy play. Their 28 turnovers, including 19 in the first half, spoke volumes about the pressure Tucson High applied.

Delano Price, as always, was the steady hand guiding the Badgers. He led the charge with 26 points, showing the poise and precision of a seasoned leader. Kenny Ball was a force to be reckoned with, contributing 23 points, while the towering presence

Chapter 2

of Chuco Miranda, who added 17 points and 12 rebounds, dominated the paint. Tucson High's relentless full-court press smothered the Coyotes, and by the third quarter, the Badgers led by as much as 22 points. Phoenix Union managed to close the gap slightly, but the outcome was never in doubt. Tucson High triumphed 74-66, exorcising their tournament demons and punching their ticket to the state championship game.

The stage was set for the championship clash against Tempe High School. The stakes were high, and the atmosphere in the Coliseum crackled with anticipation. Tucson High entered the game with the confidence of a team that had overcome every obstacle, but Tempe was no pushover. Their coach, Sam Duane, had devised a game plan to counter Tucson High's press and stifle their scoring trio of Delano, Hoegie Simmons, and Kenny Ball.

From the opening tip, it was clear this would be a battle. Tempe matched Tucson High's intensity early, with both teams trading baskets in a fast-paced first quarter. But the Badgers had an ace up their sleeve: Chuco Miranda. The 6'8 big man played the game of his life, scoring 21 points on 9-of-15 shooting and grabbing 13 rebounds. His hook shots, reminiscent of Kareem Abdul-Jabbar, were nearly impossible to defend. Miranda's dominance in the paint disrupted Tempe's rhythm and provided Tucson High with a crucial edge.

Delano and Hoegie were as reliable as ever, each scoring 24 points. Delano's smooth shooting and ability to orchestrate the offense complemented Hoegie's explosive speed and fearless drives to the basket. Together, they sliced through Tempe's defense, setting the tempo and keeping the Badgers in control.

Chapter 2

Tempe fought valiantly, but Tucson High's full-court press and barrage of offensive on the other side of the ball proved too much to handle. As the clock ticked away, Delano bounced the ball as time waned. He thought back to his 7th grade year at Roskruge when he looked up at the clock having not entered the game in its entirety at. His redemption had come full circle. By the final buzzer, Tucson High emerged victoriously, defeating Tempe 80-76 to claim the state championship.

The victory was a culmination of a season defined by hardiness and excellence. Tucson High finished the year with a stellar 23-1 record, ranked number one in the state prep poll. Their average of 83.3 points per game, achieved without the benefit of a three-point line, was a testament to their offensive firepower. Their scoring outburst of 128 points against Sunnyside High School remained a city record and highlighted the potency of their attack. The record also remained an Arizona state record for 27 years until Mike Bibby's Shadow Mountain High School broke it in 1996.

Delano led the team in scoring with an average of 21.5 points per game, closely followed by Kenny Ball with 21.0 and Hoegie Simmons with 18.4. The trio's chemistry was undeniable, and their contributions extended beyond the stat sheet. Delano's leadership, Hoegie's flair, and Kenny's consistency formed the backbone of a team that will be remembered as one of the greatest in Arizona high school basketball history.

The accolades poured in. Delano and Kenny were named first team all-city and first team all-state, while Hoegie, controversially, was placed on the second team all-city which was a decision widely regarded as a misstep. Basketball enthusiasts speculated that had the trio attended different schools, each would have been a state scoring champion of their own. Delano and Kenny were also named honorable mention all-Americans.

For Coach Tony Morales, the championship marked the end of a storied career. Though he hadn't shared his plans publicly, he knew the '69 season would be his last. Morales had stepped into his role under difficult circumstances, replacing legendary coach Bud Doolen after his sudden passing in 1955. Over the years, Morales had navigated the challenges of increased local competition and shifting dynamics in high school basketball, guiding Tucson High to a 178-113 record during his tenure.

Winning the state championship was a fitting finale for a coach who had dedicated so much to the program. "I don't want to compare them," Morales said when asked how the '69 team stacked up against the undefeated '62 team. "Both of them were really special." His humility underscored the significance of the achievement, not just for him but for the players who had given their all to bring home the title.

A Team for The Ages

The 1969 Tucson High basketball team secured its place in history for its dominance on the court and the legacy it left behind. In 1999, Phoenix Metro Magazine ranked the team among the top 10 in Arizona state history, a testament to their enduring impact. Delano, Hoegie, and Kenny were individually ranked among the top 100 players of the 20th century in Arizona, their contributions immortalized in the annals of high school basketball.

For the players, the championship was a symbol of their collective journey. The bond they shared, forged through countless hours of practice, games, and moments of triumph and heartbreak, was unbreakable. They had come together as individuals and emerged as a team, leaving a legacy that would inspire generations to come.

Tucson High has yet to capture another state basketball championship since the glorious 1969 season. As of 2024, head coach Eric Langford is poised to give the current Badgers a strong shot at adding another banner to the gym. Langford, one of the best players to emerge from Tucson High in the late 1980s and early 1990s, went on to achieve All-American honors at both Eastern Community College and Grand Canyon University. Following his collegiate success, he enjoyed a 13-year professional basketball career in Mexico.

Chapter 2

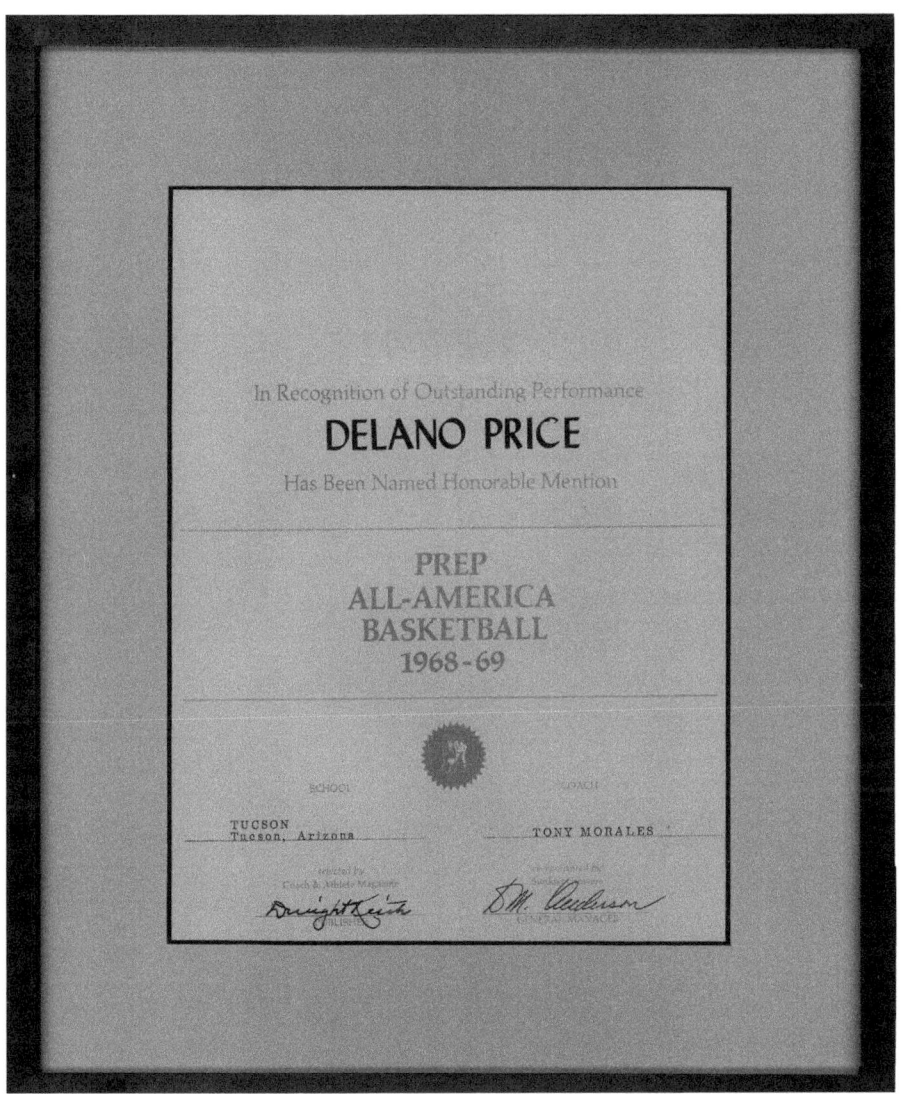

Delano Price Prep All-America Basketball 1968-69

Chapter 2

THS attack too much for Pueblo

Chapter 2

THS ends Palo Verde win streak

Chapter 2

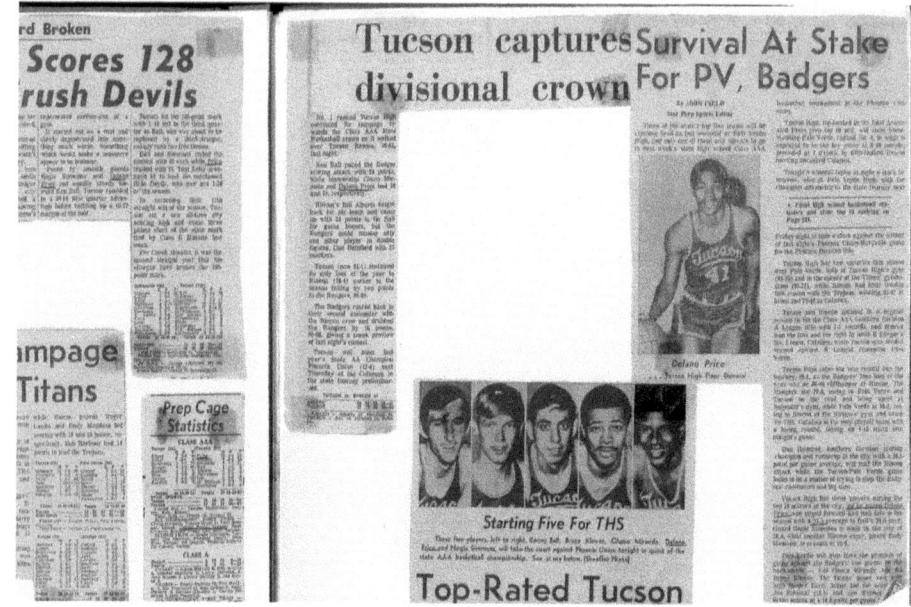

Top-rated Tucson

Chapter 2

THS scores 128 to crush Devils

Chapter 2

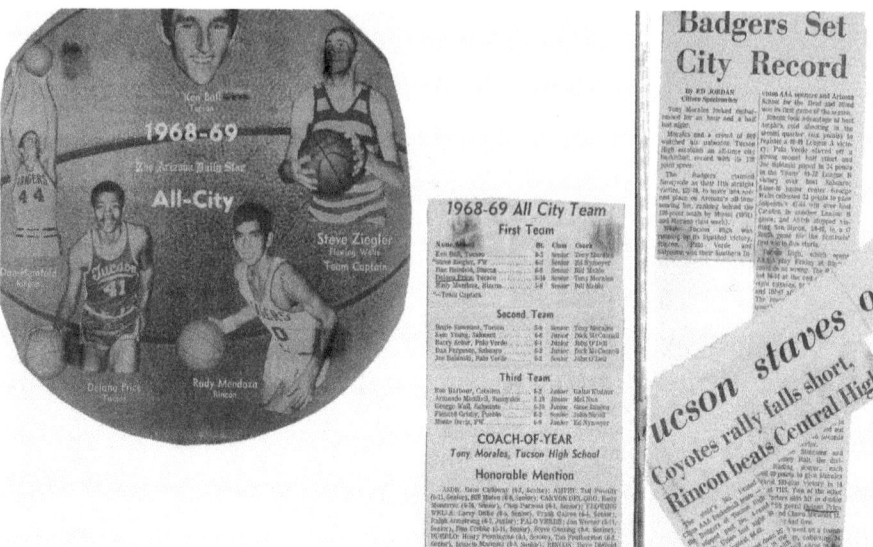

Delano Price and Kenny Ball first team All-City, Hoegie Simmons second team.

Chapter 2

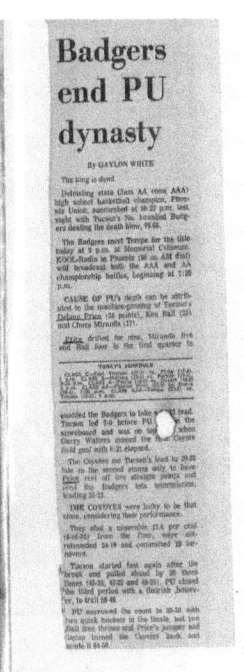

Delano Price and Kenny Ball first team All-State

Chapter 2

AAA picks

CHAPTER 2

Delano's signature jumper

Delano driving towards the opposition

CHAPTER 3

FROM THE COURTS TO THE STREETS

When Delano Price left Tucson High School in 1969, he carried with him the legacy of a state champion and the aspirations of a small-town athlete stepping into a larger arena. At 5'10, Delano wasn't the tallest or flashiest recruit, but his pure shooting, leadership, and competitive edge made him a standout. Phoenix College, one of the top junior college basketball programs in the country, offered him a scholarship, and its proximity to home was an added comfort. However, the transition from the close-knit world of Tucson to the vibrant and expanding city of Phoenix would be life-changing, in no small part due to a teammate who would become both mentor and enigma: Art Weathersby.

CHAPTER 3

Arriving at Phoenix College

Delano's freshman year began with cautious optimism. Phoenix College was a powerhouse program, boasting a roster of players with impressive high school pedigrees. Among his new teammates were Charles Flemmings, a former star at Flagstaff High School destined for Northern Arizona University, and Steve Zapello from Camelback High School, a skilled all-around player. Louie Santacruz, hailing from Arizona high school powerhouse Carl Hayden, brought grit and experience. While Sal Martinez, a slick and crafty guard, provided depth in the backcourt.

Delano quickly proved himself during the exhibition season, earning a starting position at guard over Sal Martinez. He brought his steady scoring, defensive tenacity, and an innate leadership ability to a team stacked with talent. But no player captured Delano's attention, or that of the entire program, like Art Weathersby.

The Legend of Art Weathersby

Art Weathersby arrived at Phoenix College with an aura of mystique. At 25 years old, he was far removed from the traditional path of a student-athlete. Raised in the turbulent streets of Chicago, Art had spent the last seven years in Joliet State Prison, serving time for a strong-armed robbery. His release marked a second chance, and basketball was his ticket. Despite the obstacles life had thrown his way, Art possessed a magnetic charisma that drew people in, and a ferocious talent on the court that made him unforgettable.

Chapter 3

The Midwest connection between Delano and Art was immediate. Both hailed from industrial hubs with Delano from Gary, Indiana, and Art from Chicago's South Side. Art quickly took on the role of an older brother, calling Delano "Delgado" and introducing him to the realities of life beyond basketball.

Chicago's Influence on Art

Art's upbringing in 1960s Chicago had forged his resistant, unpredictable character. Chicago's inner city was a crucible for young Black men. The city's racial segregation was entrenched, exacerbated by systemic housing discrimination and exploitative practices like contract-buying schemes. Entire neighborhoods were demolished for urban renewal projects, displacing thousands of Black families. Public housing developments, like the infamous Cabrini-Green and Robert Taylor Homes, symbolized both the promise of affordable housing and the stark reality of poverty.

Amid these challenges, Chicago's Black communities built their own institutions. Bronzeville, known as the "Black Metropolis," was a cultural hub of pride, with thriving churches, businesses, and a burgeoning arts scene. Yet, the shadow of inequality loomed large. The Civil Rights Movement had achieved significant legislative victories, but racial tensions remained high. For Art, these tensions shaped a worldview steeped in survival and defiance.

Art's early basketball training mirrored the unforgiving environment of his neighborhood. Coaches in Chicago's all-Black schools demanded excellence through harsh expectations that required sheer grit. Art's extraordinary athleticism earned him respect, but it was his mental toughness, forged in these

Chapter 3

brutal conditions, that set him apart. When he wasn't playing basketball, Art witnessed or participated in the darker side of street life, a reality that ultimately led to his incarceration.

Art's streetwise demeanor initially baffled Delano. Their first trip to the grocery store, "City of Meats," was an education in Art's resourcefulness. Loading a cart with an extravagant assortment of meats, Art instructed Delano to simply push it out the door. Delano hesitated, unsure how they would pay. Art, exuding confidence, dismissed his concerns: "Don't worry about that. Just push that cart straight out the door. I got you covered, Delgado." The duo left with enough food to feed a small army, and back at their apartment, Art turned the stolen goods into a feast, teaching Delano how to make smothered pork chops with gravy.

Art's larger-than-life personality extended beyond his culinary skills. He was a devotee of soul music, often cleaning the apartment while blasting Donny Hathaway's "The Ghetto" and belting out the lyrics with gusto. His unpredictable nature, however, kept the 18-year-old Delano on edge. Passing a bank during a drive, Art once mused, "Boy, if you had any heart, we could go in and rob that bank." Though the comment was likely meant in jest, it underscored Art's tenuous relationship with the straight-and-narrow path he was attempting to follow.

On the court, Art was nothing short of extraordinary. At 6'2 with a sturdy build and powerful legs, he was a force to be reckoned with. His left arm, thinner than the right due to a childhood injury, did little to hinder his athleticism. Art's strength, particularly in his wrists, allowed him to shoot effortlessly from half-court, and his explosive dunks were crowd-pleasers. Delano marveled

Chapter 3

at his teammate's ability to dominate games with a unique blend of finesse and raw power.

During Delano's freshman season, Phoenix College lived up to its reputation as a junior college powerhouse. Art led the team in scoring, averaging an impressive 24 points per game and earning 1st team All-JUCO honors in Arizona. Delano and Charles Flemmings each contributed 16 points per game, solidifying their roles as key players in the team's success.

Art's antics were as memorable as his play. In one particularly tense away game, an opposing player tried to intimidate him during a timeout. Art's response was as chilling as it was direct: "Well, nigga, what you wanna do? Fight? Shoot out after the game?" Delano, standing at the free throw line, missed his shot entirely, rattled by the thought that Art might follow through on the threat. Later that evening, the two laughed about the incident, but the underlying truth was clear: Art was unpredictable, both on and off the court.

During his freshman season at Phoenix Community College, Delano showcased his scoring prowess with multiple 30-point performances. However, the journey wasn't without its challenges. In a game against Cochise College, Delano experienced the first scoreless outing of his basketball career. The disappointment weighed heavily on him, but his resilience shone through in the subsequent games.

In the next matchup against the Arizona State freshmen, Delano rebounded spectacularly, dropping 31 points. He followed this with an electrifying 34-point performance against the perennial national powerhouse Arizona Western College. Arizona Western was known for its roster of Prop 48 athletes, talented players who were ineligible to play at Division I schools due to academic requirements, were effectively stashed at junior colleges. These players often went on to make significant impacts at major universities and professional levels.

One such athlete was Alonzo "Skip" Thomas, a standout two-sport star who excelled in both basketball and football. Thomas, an All-American in both sports, eventually played for USC before embarking on a successful NFL career with the Oakland Raiders. Tasked with guarding Delano during the game, Thomas's stifling defense posed a formidable challenge. Yet, Delano rose to the occasion, displaying his trademark precision and determination. Despite Thomas's aggressive coverage, Delano carved up the defense with his smooth shooting, draining basket after basket on his way to a spectacular 34-point outing.

Delano had opportunities to attend other programs where he could have been the focal point of the offense and potentially scored even more points. However, his decision to play at Phoenix College was rooted in his desire to continue the winning culture he experienced at Tucson High School. While Phoenix College finished the season with a respectable 19-9 record, they fell short of their goal, losing to Arizona Western in the state championship game. Despite the setback, Delano's freshman campaign was proof of his backbone, skill, and ability to rise to the occasion against elite competition.

The End of An Era

As the season ended, Delano and Art's friendship deepened. Art, despite his flaws, saw potential in Delano and encouraged him to stay focused on basketball. "You got a bright future ahead of you, boy," he said. "Keep putting up buckets like you can."

But Art's restless spirit could not be contained. Phoenix, with its slower pace and limited excitement, was stifling for someone accustomed to the chaos of Chicago. At the end of the season, Art announced he was leaving. He didn't specify where he was headed, only that he needed to get back to the fast lane. Delano never saw him again. Rumors swirled over the years. Some claimed Art returned to prison, others said he died in a shootout, but his fate remains a mystery.

Art's Legacy

In 2012, Art Weathersby was recognized by ESPN in an online article titled "Elite 24: America's Playground Legends." Listed among Chicago's basketball icons like Isaiah Thomas, Ronnie Fields, and Ben Wilson, Art's name carried weight in the pantheon of inner-city legends. For Delano, the honor was a bittersweet reminder of a teammate who had shaped his freshman year in both profound and fleeting ways.

Art's departure marked the end of a chapter for Delano, but his lessons, both on and off the court, would stay with him. As Delano prepared for his sophomore year, he carried the memories of their shared season: laughter, the challenges, and the unforgettable experience of playing alongside one of basketball's most enigmatic figures.

Delano's sophomore season at Phoenix College was nothing short of extraordinary. Averaging 22 points per game, he was the undeniable leader of the team, earning MVP honors, making the

All-Conference First Team, and serving as the team captain. It was during this season that Delano fully stepped into the spotlight, cementing his place as one of the most electrifying players in the Arizona Community College Athletic Conference (ACCAC).

In one particularly memorable game, Delano erupted for 47 points, an astonishing performance that left the crowd in awe. Spectators began tossing coins onto the court, a playful nod to his last name, "Price," and his undeniable worth as a player. The clang of coins against the hardwood floor symbolized not just his basketball skill but his rising value in the eyes of the community and college basketball at large. Offers began pouring in from schools like the University of Puget Sound and Kansas University, a testament to the respect he had garnered as a formidable guard with a killer jump shot and unyielding determination.

Yet, while Delano's star continued to ascend, an old friend and rival was making waves of his own. Fate had a way of weaving Delano and Hoegie Simmons back together, even as their paths diverged.

Hoegie Simmons: A Serendipitous Journey to Glendale College

After graduating from Tucson High School, Hoegie was ready to set basketball aside to focus on supporting his family. Tired of watching his mother, Mary, work three grueling jobs to make ends meet, he planned to find work and practice basketball casually on the side. However, destiny had other plans. A friend convinced him to attend a basketball showcase during the summer after high school, and Hoegie reluctantly agreed.

Chapter 3

At the showcase, Hoegie dazzled onlookers with his raw athleticism and breathtaking skills. During a break, as Hoegie stepped away, a coach approached his mother in the stands. When Hoegie returned, Mary intercepted him with a question that would change the trajectory of his life: "Do you love me?" Confused, Hoegie replied, "Of course, Mama. What's going on?"

Mary pointed to the coach and said, "Go to Glendale College with this nice man. He promised he'll take care of you. Don't worry about me. Play ball like I know you want to."

Reluctant at first, Hoegie agreed, and from that moment, his legend began to grow. At Glendale College, he became a one-man highlight reel, tearing up the ACCAC. As a freshman, Hoegie averaged 28.7 points per game, fifth in the nation, and earned All-Conference and Junior College All-American honors. His sophomore season was no different. Although his scoring dipped slightly to 26.5 points per game, he led the league in assists, steals, and even rebounding, showcasing his all-around dominance.

A Clash of Titans: Phoenix College vs. Glendale College

The Phoenix College and Glendale College matchups during their sophomore season became must-see events in the ACCAC. Delano and Hoegie, once the inseparable backcourt duo that led Tucson High School to glory, now found themselves on opposite sides of the court. The anticipation was palpable as fans packed the gym to see the two stars face off.

In their final showdown, both players delivered unforgettable performances. Delano poured in 32 points, his smooth jump shot and precise footwork on full display. Hoegie, ever the showman, countered with 38 points, dazzling the crowd with his lightning-quick drives and impossible fadeaway jumpers. The game was a nail-biter, with Phoenix College narrowly escaping with a 108-103 victory. The bond between Delano and Hoegie remained unshaken, even as they exchanged competitive fire on the court.

The matchups were an authentication to their enduring friendship and their shared roots in the grind-it-out culture of Tucson basketball. More importantly, they demonstrated how two young men could rise above their circumstances, using basketball to chase greatness.

A Turning Point: Family and Responsibility

As the season ended, Delano's life took a pivotal turn. He learned that his high school sweetheart, Jacque Barnes, was expecting their first child. Jacque, who had been the head cheerleader at Tucson High and the first Black cheerleader at the University of Arizona, had grown up alongside Delano in the Sugar Hill neighborhood. Their journey from childhood acquaintances to high school sweethearts was one of destiny and shared courage.

During their senior year of high school, after Tucson High's only loss of the season to Rincoln High, Delano and Jacque crossed paths at a party. Crestfallen and tipsy, Delano found the courage to reveal his softer side. Walking Jacque to her car, he handed her his letterman jacket, a representational gesture that marked the beginning of their romantic relationship.

Now, faced with the responsibilities of impending fatherhood, Delano made a profound decision. He chose to return to Tucson, committed to Jacque, and start a family. On May 1, 1971, they welcomed their daughter, Tanisha Nicole Price, into the world. This decision was emblematic of a larger, deeply rooted belief in the importance of family and the role of a father in strengthening the Black family nucleus, serving as a powerful statement during a time when systemic challenges often undermined the stability of Black households.

Delano's choice to prioritize his family over basketball opportunities spoke volumes about his character. Being present wasn't the only goal as it was about breaking cycles and creating a foundation of love and support for the next generation. Despite being a mediocre student in high school, Delano's focus on academics flourished during this period. He went on to earn a master's degree from the University of Arizona, proving that his dedication to personal growth extended beyond the basketball court.

Delano's decision to stay and build a family not only impacted his life but also set a powerful example for his community. At a time when young Black men often faced societal pressures and systemic obstacles, Delano's commitment to Jacque and Tanisha became a beacon of hope and responsibility. His journey was about basketball as well as using the discipline and determination he honed on the court to build a legacy rooted in family, love, and flexibility.

Chapter 3

Meanwhile, Hoegie's story continued to flourish at Glendale College, and although their paths diverged, their shared experiences and deep bond remained as evidence of their enduring friendship. Together, Delano and Hoegie represented basketball talent and personified the power of perseverance, loyalty, and the strength of community ties.

The chapter of their junior college years closed, but the lessons they carried forward would shape their lives and the lives of those they touched. Delano's family-centered path and Hoegie's rise as a legend in the JUCO circuit were reminders that success takes many forms, and that true greatness comes from staying true to one's values.

Chapter 3

Sharpshooter Delano Price at Phoenix College

CHAPTER 4

THE RISE OF A LEGEND AT TEXAS A&I

In the fall of 1972, Wallace "Hoegie" Simmons arrived in Kingsville, Texas, at Texas A&I University, carrying a reputation that preceded him. Coming off an illustrious JUCO career at Glendale College, Hoegie's transition to the Lone Star State was anything but conventional. What awaited him in Kingsville would not only cement his status as a basketball phenom but also etch his name into the lore of college basketball forever.

The basketball world was rapidly evolving in 1972. Fred Snowden had just made history by becoming the first African American head coach at a major university when he took the helm at the University of Arizona. Snowden was keen on bringing Hoegie to Tucson to join his Wildcats, but a technicality barred the way. Hoegie needed 65 academic credit hours to transfer to a Division I school, and he had only 63.

Chapter 4

This twist of fate set Hoegie on a path toward Texas A&I University. On his way back to Louisiana to play basketball closer to home, Hoegie kept a promise to Snowden to stop by Kingsville, Texas, and meet Snowden's good friend, Coach Donald McDonald. Accompanied by his friend Wayne Jones and Lucy, the mother of his son, Hoegie made a detour that would change his life.

When Hoegie walked into the gym at Texas A&I, the team was engaged in pick-up games under Coach McDonald's watchful eye. The diminutive guard introduced himself, and McDonald, unimpressed by his 5'7" stature, remarked, "I thought you'd be taller."

Without missing a beat, Hoegie replied, "I don't need to be taller."

McDonald decided to give him a chance, blowing his whistle to call Hoegie into the game. Hoegie chose his friend Wayne and a few players from the sidelines to form a team. What followed was pure magic. Hoegie dismantled the competition with an arsenal of moves that left everyone in awe. Then came the moment that sealed McDonald's decision.

During one game, Wayne missed a jump shot, and the ball bounced off the rim. Hoegie, darting through defenders like a phantom, rose above the crowd and slammed the ball back into the hoop with a thunderous dunk. McDonald jumped out of his seat in amazement. Hoegie turned to him and said, "I told you I don't need to be taller."

Chapter 4

A Star Is Born in Kingsville

Coach McDonald wasted no time offering Hoegie a scholarship, even extending one to Wayne as an extra incentive. After some deliberation, Hoegie agreed. Unlike his teammates, who lived in the dorms, McDonald arranged for Hoegie to live in a three-bedroom house, a sign of the coach's belief in his star recruit.

From the outset, Hoegie's impact was undeniable. He brought a no-nonsense attitude to the team, insisting on discipline and focus. "I don't care what you do before or after the season," he told his teammates during summer practices, "but during the season, I'm here to win." His work ethic and leadership were reminiscent of his grueling days in Monroe, Louisiana, where his high school coaches had instilled an unrelenting competitive drive.

The local media doubted whether a 5'7" guard could thrive in a conference dominated by towering players. Hoegie silenced those doubts with performances that bordered on the mythical.

During his two seasons at Texas A&I, Hoegie Simmons became the most electrifying player in the Lone Star Conference. Fans packed the Steinke Center, which seated 5,000 at the time, just to watch him play. Hoegie's warm-up routines became a spectacle in themselves. People arrived early to see him execute jaw-dropping dunks in the layup line, a rare feat for a player of his stature.

When the games began, Hoegie was unstoppable. His range extended far beyond what would later become the three-point line, making him a scoring threat as soon as he crossed half-court. He averaged 29.3 points per game during his senior season, leading the conference in scoring. His athleticism defied logic:

Chapter 4

he averaged two dunks per game, often posterizing players a foot taller than him.

In one memorable game against East Texas State, Hoegie scored 52 points, setting a school record. Another time, he sank 51 points against Howard Payne University. The crowd couldn't get enough of him, and his performances turned the Steinke Center into a carnival of basketball brilliance.

One of Hoegie's most iconic moments came during a game against Southwest Texas State. With the score tied at 68 and just seconds remaining, Hoegie took the ball on the opposing end of the court. Dribbling past mid-court, he launched a jumper from the left corner. Before the ball even reached the basket, Hoegie ran out of the gym and into the hallway, heading for the locker room. The ball swished through the net, securing a 70-68 victory. The crowd erupted, and the legend of Hoegie Simmons grew even larger.

By the time his career at Texas A&I ended, Hoegie had rewritten the record books:

Most points in a game: 52

Most field goals in a game: 22

Most points in a season: 762 (1973-74)

Scoring average in a season: 29.3 (1973-74)

Career scoring average: 27.2 points per game

NAIA All-America honors: Twice, including National Player of the Week for his 52-point performance.

Chapter 4

In just two seasons, Hoegie amassed 1,389 points, a total that still ranks among the highest in school history despite him playing only two years.

Coach McDonald, who was named Coach of the Year during both of Hoegie's seasons, credited much of his success to his star guard. "My wife was happier those two years because I wasn't so stressed at home," McDonald joked. Hoegie's influence extended beyond the court, galvanizing his teammates and bringing out their best performances.

Hoegie Simmons was a phenomenon. His patented 360-degree jump shot, a move he perfected from watching Delano at Tucson High, left defenders helpless. His fearlessness, honed on the streets of Monroe and the courts of Tucson, made him a giant among giants, despite his 5'7" frame.

He was also featured in Sports Illustrated's "Faces in the Crowd" section on the March 11, 1974, edition. To this day, his records stand as a testament to his dominance, and his name is spoken with reverence in Kingsville by the people who saw him play.

Delano returned to Tucson from Phoenix College in 1971 to embark on a transformative chapter of his life, becoming a father, husband, and college graduate while continuing to shine on the basketball court. These were the years that would shape him not only as an athlete but as a man devoted to his family and community.

Delano's academic journey began with his sister Pearl's intervention. When he first brought home his class schedule from Phoenix College, Pearl, a teacher with a keen eye for

Chapter 4

education, quickly dismissed his lineup of remedial courses. She insisted that Delano enrolled in core classes that would transfer to a university, ensuring his long-term academic success. Her guidance bore fruit, as Delano thrived academically and earned his associate's degree. This foundation set the stage for his transition to the University of Arizona.

Returning home was about furthering his education and stepping up for his family. Delano and Jacque, his high school sweetheart, had rekindled their bond during his time away, and with the birth of their daughter, Tanisha Nicole Price, on May 1, 1971, the young couple made the decision to marry and build a life together. The marriage, which required his father's signature as Delano was not yet of legal age, was a poignant moment in his life. His mother, Mattie, had always emphasized the importance of responsibility and manhood, and Delano resolved that no child of his would grow up without a father. Mattie always preached to her sons, "Be a man and not a pair of pants."

Jacque's mother, Freddie E. Kelly Barnes, had long supported the match between her daughter and Delano. Freddie believed in Delano's character and potential, and her endorsement carried immense weight for him. Freddie herself was a remarkable woman whose life and achievements deeply influenced her children. A pioneer in her own right, she attended the University of Arizona but was unable to graduate due to two remaining courses. Before coming to Arizona, Freddie had studied at Paul Quinn College in Waco, Texas, an institution with a rich history of uplifting African Americans.

Freddie moved to Arizona to live near her brother, who worked as a chef on the train. This proximity allowed her to explore various parts of the state and ultimately settle in Tucson. She became the first Black employee for the City of Tucson, working for approximately 25 years at the Recreation Center at Estevan Park on Main Street. The park's name, closely resembling "Esteban," the first Black man recorded in Arizona's history, held a poetic significance in Freddie's life, as she too was breaking barriers in her own right.

Freddie's journey was not without challenges. She faced prejudice and racism both at the University of Arizona and in the broader Tucson community. Yet, she remained steadfast, pressing forward with the mantra that "you never give up." This perseverance wasn't merely personal as it became the linchpin of her parenting. She instilled in her children, Jacque and James "Brother" Barnes, the value of education and pride in their heritage.

Living and working in Tucson's historically Black Dunbar neighborhood, considered the mecca of Black culture in the city, Freddie became an integral part of the community. Her work at "The Center" allowed her to engage with young African Americans, as well as Hispanic youths and young Black men serving in the Air Force. She championed cultural and recreational activities that encouraged pride and unity among the diverse communities she served. Her influence reached far beyond her immediate family, steering generations of young people toward self-improvement and perseverance.

Freddie's steadfast belief in Delano's potential and her unwavering support for Jacque's happiness meant everything to the young couple. Her life of allegiance and enthusiasm for her family and community became an inspiration for them as they began their journey together. For Delano, her approval signified not only love but also an affirmation of his ability to provide and lead as a husband and father, aligning perfectly with Mattie's lifelong teachings. Together, Delano and Jacque set out to build a legacy grounded in love, sacrifice, and the values imparted by the strong women who shaped their lives.

Jacque, a sophomore at the University of Arizona at the time, made the incredible sacrifice of pausing her education to work full-time, supporting Delano in finishing his degree. Her selflessness became a cornerstone of their partnership, allowing Delano to benefit from scholarships, tuition discounts, and the stability of a dual-income household. Jacque's job at the University of Arizona provided critical financial assistance through employee tuition benefits, and Delano's dedication to his studies resulted in a string of academic accomplishments, including earning scholarships like the Ada McCormick and Marvin "Swede" Johnson Scholarships.

Their early years together were challenging. The couple lived in a modest studio apartment, scraping by on Jacque's meager paycheck of $119 a month, while their rent was $121. Delano took odd jobs to fill the gaps, often working weekends or summers as a counselor for the federal "Tucson Manpower" program. Meals were simple many times consisting of oatmeal for breakfast, lunch, and dinner. They clung to each other and found joy in small victories, like receiving a $50 tax refund that helped them buy groceries during a particularly tough stretch.

Despite these struggles, Jacque's resolve was untiring. Her work ethic and fortitude became an inspiration for Delano. She eventually found a more fulfilling role in the athletic department at the University of Arizona, thanks to the kindness of a co-worker named Lilly Grant, who saw her potential. Over time, Jacque continued her own academic pursuits, earning a bachelor's degree in sociology and later a master's in educational leadership all while raising their three children. Her accomplishments, including being the first African American cheerleader at the University of Arizona, were highlighted in a 1998 USA Today article, cementing her status as a torchbearer.

While Jacque worked tirelessly, Delano focused on finishing his undergraduate degree in social studies and secondary education, later earning a master's in secondary administration. His academic journey was marked by consistency and commitment, making the Dean's List several times despite the odds stacked against him. With his degrees in hand and a determination to support his family, Delano secured a teaching position at Apollo Junior High School in Tucson. The school principal, impressed by Delano's demeanor and qualifications, offered him the job before he could even leave the parking lot. Working at a school with a significant portion of students living in poverty, Delano became eligible for a federal program that paid off his student loans, allowing him to graduate debt-free.

While Delano's family life and career were taking shape, basketball remained constant in his life. Though he no longer played collegiately, Delano was a force in local leagues and tournaments. His reputation as a scoring machine followed him, and he often delivered 40- and 50-point performances. One of his most memorable games occurred during a tournament on the Tohono O'odham Indian Reservation at Baboquivari High School. After hitting multiple long-range three-pointers and falling into the crowd while being fouled, tensions flared as a fan from the opposing side began throwing trash at Delano. The situation nearly escalated into a brawl, forcing Delano and his teammates to retreat quickly from the gym.

Delano also played on traveling teams, including one named "Speedway Sport," which took him to Mexico for exhibition games. These experiences kept his competitive spirit alive and allowed him to continue building his basketball legacy. His skill on the court remained so evident that even Fred Snowden, the University of Arizona's legendary coach, took notice. Snowden often joked with Delano about how tremendous a Price-Simmons backcourt would have been at the University of Arizona, had their paths aligned differently after high school.

Through it all, Delano's decision to prioritize his family while continuing to excel in basketball and academics not only honored his parents' teachings but also set an example for his children. By the time Jacque returned to school to finish her degrees and Delano had solidified his career as an educator and basketball icon in Tucson, the Price family had become a testament to buoyancy and strength of character. They had turned their struggles into steppingstones, laying the groundwork for a brighter future for their children and the community they served.

Chapter 4

Hoegie does his thing!

Chapter 4

Harlon Gerhold .... LSC/HM—1960
Leonard Anderson .... LSC/HM—1961
Phil Shirk .... NAIA/1—1962,1964;LSC/1—1962,1964;NAIA/2—1963;
LSC/2—1963;LSC/HM—1961
Jim Koerner .... LSC/1—1963,1965;LSC/2—1964
Jerry Daniel .... LSC/HM—1963,1964
John Lowe .... LSC/HM—1963,1964
Marty Schultz .... LSC/2—1966;LSC/3—1965
Chuck Meyer .... LSC/1—1969;LSC/2—1967,1968
Bob Rainey .... LSC/1—1968;LSC/HM—1967
Gary Wideman .... LSC/HM—1970
Jeff Wildenberg .... LSC/1—1971;LSC/2—1972;LSC/1—1973;
NAIA All-District/1—1973
Algie Neal .... LSC/2—1972
Hoegie Simmons .... LSC/2;AP A-A/HM—1973;
NAIA All-District/1—1973;
AP A-A/HM); NAIA/HM; LSC/1; NAIA All-District/1
Jeff St. Clair LSC/2

LSC Top Ten Leading Scorers

Average	Player and School	Season
31.5	Fred Davis, Howard Payne	1970
29.3	HOEGIE SIMMONS, TEXAS A&I	1974
27.2	Fred Davis, Howard Payne	1969
25.5	Jack Fryman, Sul Ross	1965
25.1	HOEGIE SIMMONS, TEXAS A&I	1973
25.1	Bill Gaines, East Texas	1968
25.0	James Lister, Sam Houston	1971
24.7	Lewis Gilcrease, Southwest Texas	1953
24.4	Jack Fryman, Sul Ross	1966
24.4	PHIL SHIRK, TEXAS A&I	1962

Points	Player and School	Season
883	Fred Davis, Howard Payne	1970
762	HOEGIE SIMMONS, TEXAS A&I	1974
757	Jack Fryman, Sul Ross	1966
734	Fred Davis, Howard Payne	1969
674	James Lister, Sam Houston	1971
646	Bill Mehrens, Sam Houston	1968
639	Jack Fryman, Sul Ross	1965
637	Robert Gords, S.F. Austin	1972
627	HOEGIE SIMMONS, TEXAS A&I	1973
592	Lewis Gilcrease, Southwest Texas	1953

Crowds Set "Record"

One record not on the Texas A&I basketball books, but which would have fallen this season had it been in existence, is the one for best season attendance.

The Javelinas drew an estimated 36,000 fans for 12 home games last season, an average of 3,000 a game. And two of the games that saw the gate dropping below the 3,000 mark were played while the A&I students were on their Christmas holiday break.

The biggest crowds came in the final three home games as the Javelinas broke their record for most consecutive victories (eight).

Over 12,000 fans attended the Howard Payne, Paul Quinn and Abilene Christian games. The season figure also would rate high in the Lone Star Conference. The A&I playing site, the Physical Education Center, has the largest capacity in the LSC.

Before I went to A&I our crowd was about 800 too 900 But they came from all over to see Sweetback the Magician do his magic!

LSC top ten leading scorers

Chapter 4

Physical Education Center Records

INDIVIDUAL—

Field Goals Attempted: 44, Hoegie Simmons, A&I (vs. ACC), 1974
Field Goals Made: 22, Hoegie Simmons, A&I (vs. ACC), 1974.
Field Goal Percentage: (at least five attempts) 1.000 (5-5), Don Hagany, A&I (vs. St. Edward's), 12-1-70.
Free Throws Attempted: 14, Tyler Tull, Tarleton, 12-12-70; Bob Bolden, UCC, 1-21-71; James Parrish, Sul Ross, 2-1-71; Bruce Featherston, SWT, 2-18-72; Jeff Wildenberg, A&I (vs. Tarleton), 1-29-72.
Free Throws Made: 13, Bob Bolden, UCC, 1-21-71.
Free Throw Percentage: 1.000 (12-12) Jeff Wildenberg, A&I (vs. UCC), 12-1-70.
Rebounds: 24, Lawrence Mayberry, UCC, 1-15-72; Robert Gords, SFA, 1-22-72.
Points: 52, Hoegie Simmons, A&I (vs. ETSU), 1974.

TEAM—

Field Goals Attempted: 106, A&I (vs. Texas Lutheran), 11-22-72.
Field Goals Made: 50, A&I (vs. Texas Lutheran), 11-22-71.
Field Goal Percentage: .576 (45-78), A&I (vs. Howard Payne), 2-12-72.
Free Throws Attempted: 47, Angelo, 1-30-71.
Free Throws Made: 32, A&I (vs. Tarleton), 1-29-72.
Free Throw Percentage: 1.000 (10-10) St. Edward's, 11-21-72.
Rebounds: 68, A&I (vs. Texas Lutheran), 11-22-71.
Points: 114, A&I (vs. Paul Quinn), 1974.
Least Field Goals Attempted: 44, Southwest Texas, 2-13-71.
Least Field Goals Made: 17, St. Mary's, 11-25-70.
Least Free Throws Attempted: 9, A&I (vs. McMurry), 1-8-73.
Least Free Throws Made: 4, East Texas, 12-7-72.
Least Rebounds: 29, East Texas, 12-10-70; A&I (vs. Howard Payne), 1-10-73.
Least Points: 48, A&I (vs. St. Mary's), 11-25-70.

A&I Basketball Milestones

Victory	Opponent	Score	Year
1	Alice Firemen	10-07	1925-26
25	Edinburg Junior College	39-16	1928-29
50	St. Edward's	38-32	1932-33
100	Edinburg Junior College	54-21	1937-38
150	St. Edward's	47-39	1949-50
200	Texas Lutheran	73-37	1956-57
250	Corpus Christi	76-59	1961-62
300	Corpus Christi	95-83	1966-67
350	Angelo State	98-92	1971-72
382	Paul Quinn	114-88	1973-74

Simmons Twice Player Of Week

Hoegie Simmons, Texas A&I guard who broke most of the available scoring records last season, was twice named Lone Star Conference Player of the Week. He had received the honor twice the previous season, his first with the Javelinas. After scoring 52 points against East Texas State, Simmons was named NAIA National Player of the Week, and received mention in Sports Illustrated.

— 22 MY NATURAL HIGH MADE ME PERFORM SO GREAT AND AM GLAD THAT MY ONLY ONE I HAVE AND NEED.

Simmons twice player of the week

Chapter 4

Lone Star Conference Records

SINGLE GAME

Individual —
Most Points: 53, Charles Sharp, SWT vs Texas Wesleyan, 1959-60
Most Field Goal Attempts: 44, Hoegie Simmons, A&I (vs ACC), 1973-74
Most Field Goals Made: 20, Bill Gaines, ETSU (vs Austin College), 1967-68
Most Free Throw Attempts: 25, Rudy Davalos, SWT (vs SFA), 1959
Most Free Throws Made: 22, Rudy Davalos, SWT (vs SFA), 1959
Most Rebounds: 31, Pete Harris, SFA (vs A&I), 1972-73

Team —
Most Points, Both Teams: 263, (SFA, 140, HPC 123), 1970-71
Most Points: 150, SFA (vs Paul Quinn), 1972-73
Most Field Goal Attempts: 112, SFA (vs Paul Quinn), 1972-73
Most Field Goals Made: 67, SFA (vs Paul Quinn), 1972-73
Most Free Throw Attempts: 64, ETSU (vs Howard Payne), 1954-55
Most Free Throws Made: 50, Howard Payne (vs Sul Ross), 1965-66
Most Rebounds: 106, Texas A&I (vs Monterrey Tech), 1961-62; SFA (vs Paul Quinn), 1972-73

SEASON

Individual —
Most Points: 833, Fred Davis, Howard Payne, 1969-70
Best Scoring Average: 31.5, Fred Davis, Howard Payne, 1969-70
Most Field Goals Attempted: 685, Hoegie Simmons, A&I, 1973-74
Most Field Goals Made: 279, Hoegie Simmons, A&I, 1972-73
Best Field Goal Percentage: 709 (168-237), Richard Trice, Howard Payne, 1962-63
Most Free Throw Attempts: 321, Lewis Gilcrease, SWT, 1952-53
Most Free Throws Made: 226, Lewis Gilcrease, SWT, 1952-53
Best Free Throw Percentage: 931 (53-58), David Nutt, SFA, 1963-64
Most Rebounds: 422, Joe Cole, SWT, 1956-57; George Johnson, SFA, 1967-68
Best Rebound Average: 17.0, James Lister, Sam Houston, 1970-71

Team —
Most Points: 3183, SFA, 1971-72
Best Scoring Average: 98.7, SFA, 1970-71
Most Field Goal Attempts: 2369, Sul Ross, 1965-66
Most Field Goals Scored: 1134, SFA, 1972-73
Best Field Goal Percentage: .560 (815-1454), Howard Payne, 1965-66
Most Free Throws Attempted: 1030, Sul Ross, 1965-66
Most Free Throws Made: 745, Sul Ross, 1965-66
Best Free Throw Percentage: .805 (449-558), SWT, 1967-68
Most Rebounds: 1448 Sam Houston, 1967-68
Best Rebound Average: 55.2, Sam Houston, 1970-71; SFA, 1971-72

Team Defense —
Least Points by Opponents: 1153, SFA, 1958-59
Least Points Per Game by Opponents: 50.1, SFA, 1957-58

CAREER

Individual —
Most Points: 2304, James Lister, Sam Houston, 1969-73
Most Points Three Seasons: 2026, Fred Davis, Howard Payne, 1967-68
Most Points Two Seasons: 1389, Hoegie Simmons, A&I 1972-74
Best Scoring Average: 28.5, Fred Davis, Howard Payne, 1967-70
Most Field Goal Attempts: 1829, Jack Fryman, Sul Ross, 1962-66
Most Field Goals Made: 906, James Lister, Sam Houston, 1969-73

Most Field Goals Made Two Seasons: 592, Hoegie Simmons, A&I, 1972-74
Best Field Goal Percentage: .681, Richard Trice, Howard Payne, 1960-63
Most Free Throw Attempts: 883, Jack Fryman, Sul Ross, 1962-66
Most Free Throws Made: 6-6, Jack Fryman, Sul Ross, 1962-66
Best Free Throw Percentage: .871, Dennis Leach, Texas A&I, 1966-70
Most Rebounds: 1682, James Lister, Sam Houston

— 21 —

Lone Star Conference records

Chapter 4

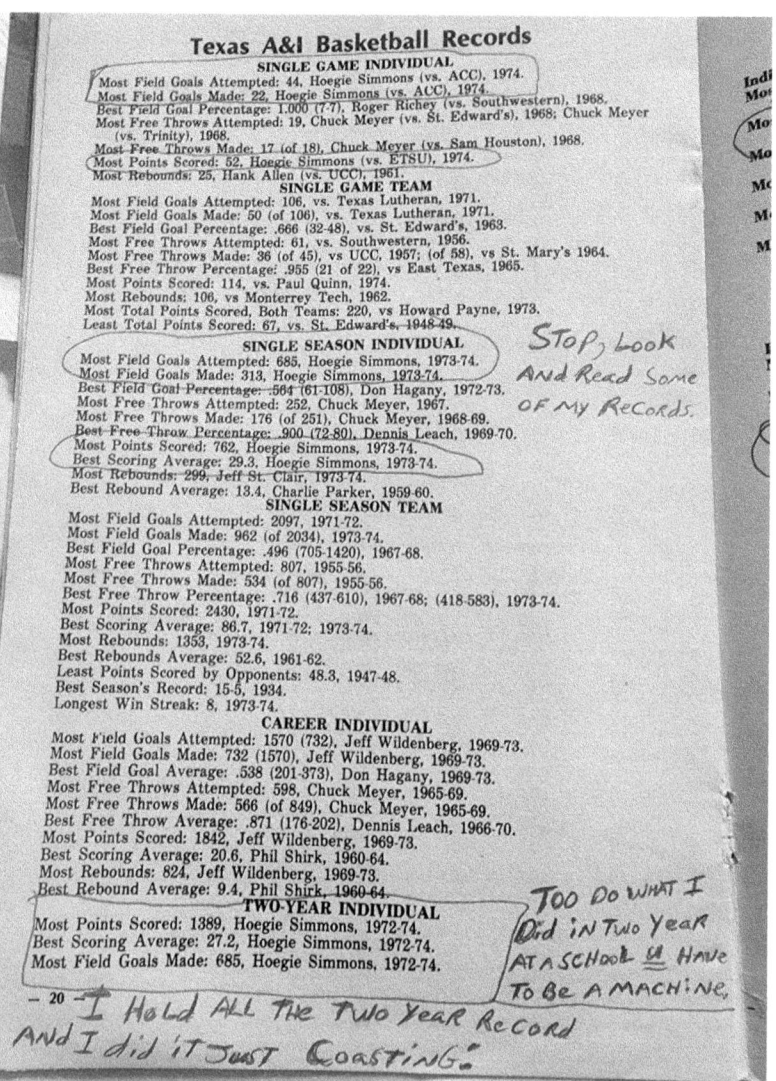

Texas A & I basketball records

Chapter 4

1974-75 Texas A&I University Javelina Basketball Roster

Numbers B	W	Player	P	Ht.	Wt.	Class	Exp.	Hometown
35	34	Bobby Batey	G	6-0	160	So.	Tr.	Laredo (Nixon)
31	30	Rick Calhoun	F	6-6	190	So.	1VL	Chicago (Fenger)
24	24	Rufus Green	G	6-3	185	Fr.	0	Refugio
15	15	Eric Harper	P	6-4	180	Fr.	0	Kingsville
21	20	James Johnson	G	5-11	170	Fr.	0	Tucson, Ariz.
13	10	Kenny Kasper	G	5-11	155	Fr.	0	Corpus Christi (Carroll)
25	25	Ken Kimes	F	6-5	195	Fr.	0	Grand Ridge, Ill.
14	14	Mike Masiello	G	6-2	180	Jr.	Sq.	Buffalo, N.Y.
45	44	Mike Mosenson	F	6-5	180	Jr.	Sq.	Broomall, Pa.
11	11	Ronnie Norrell	G	5-10	140	Fr.	0	Corpus Christi (King)
23	22	Sid Roy	F	6-6	220	Fr.	0	Wilmington, Del.
43	50	Jeff St. Clair	F	6-6	220	Fr.	0	Westminster, Calif.
51	51	Jimmy Thompson	G	5-10	145	Sr.	0	San Antonio (Roosevelt)
33	32	James Williams	F	6-6	180	Jr.	1VL	Syracuse, N.Y.
41	40	Mike Wilson	F	6-6	180	Fr.	0	Alexandria, La.

1973-74 Final Texas A&I Basketball Statistics

Player	G	FGM-FGA	Pct.	FTM-FTA	Pct.	Reb.	Avg.	Pts.	Avg.
Hoegie Simmons	26	313-685	.456	136-171	.795	79	3.0	762	29.3
Jeff St. Clair	27	168-316	.531	87-128	.679	299	11.0	423	15.6
Steve Weems	27	118-222	.531	41-61	.672	268	9.8	275	10.2
Larry Mabry	26	93-180	.516	34-43	.790	124	4.7	220	8.4
Danny Kasper	27	76-183	.415	37-43	.860	55	2.0	189	7.0
George Shivers	25	87-131	.511	31-56	.553	193	7.7	164	6.5
Rick Calhoun	26	59-155	.380	23-42	.547	113	4.3	141	5.4
Mike Masiello	14	22-42	.523	4-5	.800	16	1.1	48	3.4
Arthur Shipp	15	17-39	.436	6-14	.428	29	1.9	42	2.8
Mike Bourg	3	3-5	.600	1-2	.500	3	1.0	7	2.3
Gary Snowden	21	15-42	.357	7-13	.538	25	1.2	37	1.7
David Hobson	18	7-21	.333	5-7	.714	38	2.1	19	1.0
Ken Kimes	3	0-0	.000	2-2	1.000	2	0.6	2	0.6
A&I TOTALS	27	962-2034	.472	418-583	.716	1347	49.8	2342	86.7
OPP. TOTALS	27	944-2083	.453	387-586	.660	1229	45.5	2275	84.2

1974-74 Texas A & I basketball statistics

Chapter 4

Javelinas In NAIA District IV

The Texas A&I basketball team competes in NAIA District 4 along with the other members of the Lone Star Conference and the teams in the Big State Conference.

This season, 17 teams will makeup the district.

The winners of the two conference titles meet annually in a best two of three series to determine the district's representative in the NAIA national tournament in Kansas City. Making up the district this year will be:

LONE STAR CONFERENCE: Abilene Christian College, Angelo State University, East Texas State University, Howard Payne College, Sam Houston State University, Southwest Texas State University, Stephen F. Austin State University, Sul Ross State University, Tarleton State University and Texas A&I University.

BIG STATE CONFERENCE: East Texas Baptist College, Huston-Tillotson College, LeTourneau Tech, St. Edward's University, St. Mary's University, Southwestern University and Texas Lutheran College.

1973-74 All-District Team

Texas A&I guard Hoegie Simmons was named to the NAIA All-District IV basketball team for the second consecutive season last winter, and Javelina coach Don McDonald shared the coach of the year honors.

The team, which includes players from the Lone Star and Big State conferences, included Simmons, Gary Tomaszewski of St. Mary's, Travis Cornett of Southwest Texas, O'Neal Tarrant of East Texas, Andrew Prince of Abilene Christian, Bob Kershaw of Howard Payne, Archie Myers of S.F. Austin, Zembra Everett of St. Edward's, Floyd Allen of Sam Houston and Harry Miller of Texas Lutheran.

Tying for coach of the year honors were McDonald, Jim Gudger of East Texas, Ken Henson of Howard Payne, Bob Rachal of Southwestern, Jim Shuler of Texas Lutheran and Jerry Stone of Tarleton.

— 17 —

1974-74 All-District Team

Chapter 4

Javelina '350' Club

Players who have scored 350 or more points in a single season.

Points	Player	Season
762	Hoegie Simmons	1974
627	Hoegie Simmons	1973
561	Phil Shirk	1962
546	Chuck Meyer	1969
536	Jeff Wildenberg	1973
527	Algie Neal	1972
526	Jeff Wildenberg	1971
521	Jeff Wildenberg	1972
521	Chuck Meyer	1967
456	Gary Wideman	1970
444	Bob Rainey	1968
441	Phil Shirk	1964
428	Chuck Meyer	1968
423	Jeff St. Clair	1974
421	Don McDonald	1957
421	Jim Koerner	1963
403	Bob Rainey	1966
399	Jim Koerner	1965
396	Phil Shirk	1963
389	Phil Shirk	1961
386	Marty Schultz	1966
380	Dennis Leach	1970
380	Fred Clayton	1969
374	Bob Rainey	1968
367	Wayne Johnson	1972
359	Jay Hawley	1958
352	Hank Allen	1961

Texas A&I '35' Club

Players who have scored 35 or more points in a single game.

Points	Player Game	Season
52	Hoegie Simmons vs East Texas State	1974
51	Hoegie Simmons vs Howard Payne	1974
50	Algie Neal vs East Texas State	1972
41	Algie Neal vs McMurry	1972
41	Phil Shirk vs St. Mary's	1962
41	Phil Shirk vs Southwestern	1963
40	Hoegie Simmons vs Texas Lutheran	1972
40	Chuck Meyer vs St. Thomas	1967
38	Hoegie Simmons vs Southwestern	1974
38	Hoegie Simmons vs McMurry	1973
37	Hoegie Simmons vs Texas Lutheran	1974
37	Hoegie Simmons vs Abilene Christian	1974
37	Chuck Meyer vs Trinity	1967
36	Hoegie Simmons vs Southwest Texas	1973
36	Hoegie Simmons vs S.F. Austin	1973
36	Gary Wideman vs Sul Ross	1970
36	Phil Shirk vs St. Edward's	1963
35	Hoegie Simmons vs S.F. Austin	1974
35	Jim Koerner vs Sul Ross	1963
35	Phil Shirk vs Texas Lutheran	1962

— 15 —

Javelina '350' club/Texas A & I '35' club

Chapter 4

1973-74 Lone Star Conference Statistics

INDIVIDUAL SCORING

Player	School	G	FGM	FTM	Pts.	Avg.
HOEGIE SIMMONS	TEXAS A&I	26	313	136	762	29.3
O'Neal Tarrant	East Texas	26	215	172	602	23.2
Archie Myers	S.F. Austin	29	270	105	645	22.2
Andrew Prince	Abilene Christian	29	323	178	642	22.1
Nate Granger	East Texas	26	214	91	519	20.0
Travis Cornett	Southwest Texas	31	251	115	617	19.9
Isaac Atkinson	Tarleton	33	242	130	614	18.6
Floyd Allen	Sam Houston	27	196	37	428	15.9
JEFF ST. CLAIR	TEXAS A&I	27	168	87	423	15.6
Bruce Featherston	Southwest Texas	31	194	81	469	15.1

INDIVIDUAL REBOUNDING

Player	School	G	REB.	AVG.
Bob Kershaw	Howard Payne	28	430	15.4
Andrew Prince	Abilene Christian	29	445	15.3
Floyd Allen	Sam Houston	27	324	12.0
Isaac Atkinson	Tarleton	33	364	11.0
JEFF ST. CLAIR	TEXAS A&I	27	299	11.0
Nate Granger	East Texas	26	286	11.0
Andria Brown	S.F. Austin	29	294	10.1
JEFF ST. CLAIR	TEXAS A&I	27	268	9.8
Bruce Featherston	Southwest Texas	31	288	9.3
Gary Barnes	Sul Ross	28	258	9.2

INDIVIDUAL FIELD GOAL SHOOTING

Player	School	G	FGM	FGA	Pct.
Travis Cornett	Southwest Texas	31	251	409	.614
Bruce Featherston	Southwest Texas	31	194	350	.554
Oscar Lott	Angelo State	26	153	276	.554
Isaac Atkinson	Tarleton	33	242	438	.553
Andres Prince	Abilene Christian	29	232	425	.546
Bob Kershaw	Howard Payne	28	172	315	.546
JEFF ST. CLAIR	TEXAS A&I	27	168	316	.531
STEVE WEEMS	TEXAS A&I	27	118	222	.531
Gary Barnes	Sul Ross	28	130	248	.524
Darrell Hearne	Abilene Christian	29	79	151	.523

INDIVIDUAL FREE THROW SHOOTING

Player	School	G	FTM	FTA	Pct.
Garland Bullock	Howard Payne	28	56	63	.889
O'Neal Tarrant	East Texas	26	172	201	.856
Oscar Lott	Angelo State	26	76	90	.844
Mike Fitzhugh	Southwest Texas	31	89	111	.802
Steve Foster	Angelo State	23	47	59	.797
HOEGIE SIMMONS	TEXAS A&I	26	136	171	.795
John Fortenberry	Sul Ross	27	81	102	.794
Bill Shead	Sul Ross	28	77	98	.786
Ken Lawrence	Sul Ross	23	36	46	.783
David Sisson	Angelo State	15	25	33	.758

— 12 —

Individual scoring

LSC Leading Scorers

Net
1974	Hoegie Simmons, A&I, 762
1973	Hoegie Simmons, A&I, 627
1972	Robert Gords, SFA, 637
1971	James Lister, Sam Houston, 674
1970	Fred Davis, HPC, 883
1969	Fred Davis, HPC, 734
1968	Bill Mehrens, Sam Houston, 646
1967	Jeff Fitch, ETSU, 531
1966	Jack Fryman, Sul Ross, 757
1965	Jack Fryman, Sul Ross, 639
1964	Jack Fryman, Sul Ross, 442
1963	Richard Trice, HPC, 440
1962	Phil Shirk, A&I, 561
1961	Johnny Johnston, Lamar, 558
1960	Noel Fain, ETSU, 554
1959	Charles Sharp, SWT, 483
1958	Al Schomber, Sul Ross, 455
1957	Glen Jochec, Sam Houston, 470
1956	C.L. Nox, SFA, 538
1955	Walter Lee, Sam Houston, 542
1954	Tom Sewell, Sam Houston, 521
1953	Lewis Gilcrease, SWT, 592
1952	J.C. Maze, SWT, 588
1951	James Johnston, SFA, 369
1950	James Johnston, SFA, 368
1949	James Littleton, SWT, 343
1948	James Littleton, SWT, 407
1947	Murray Mitchell, Sam Houston, 285
1946	Guy Lewis, Houston, 210
1941	Van Samford, SFA, 138
1940	Robert Carpenter, ETSU, 129
1939	Marshall Matteson, SFA, 129
1938	J.P. Vinson, ETSU, 92
1935	C.C. Williams, SFA, 98
1933	Sowers, Sam Houston, 121

Average
1974	Hoegie Simmons, A&I, 29.3
1973	Hoegie Simmons, A&I, 25.1
1972	Robert Gords, SFA, 23.6
1971	James Lister, Sam Houston, 25.0
1970	Fred Davis, HPC, 31.5
1969	Fred Davis, HPC, 27.2
1968	Bill Gaines, ETSU, 25.1
1967	Chuck Meyer, A&I, 22.6
1966	Jack Fryman, Sul Ross, 24.4
1965	Jack Fryman, Sul Ross, 25.5
1964	Phil Shirk, A&I, 18.4
1963	Phil Shirk, A&I, 23.3
1962	Phil Shirk, A&I, 24.4
1961	Johnny Johnston, Lamar, 20.7
1960	Charles Sharp, SWT, 22.1
1959	Charles Sharp, SWT, 20.1
1958	Al Schomber, Sul Ross, 20.7
1957	Glen Jochec, Sam Houston, 18.0
1956	Don Pearson, Sul Ross, 20.9
1955	C.L. Nix, SFA, 22.0
1954	Tom Sewell, Sam Houston, 21.7
1953	Lewis Gilcrease, SWT, 24.7
1952	J.C. Maze, SWT, 18.9
1951	Charles Whitten, ETSU, 16.7

LSC Leading Rebounders

Net
1974	Andrew Prince, ACC, 445
1973	Pete Harris, SFA, 472
1972	Pete Harris, SFA, 522
1971	James Lister, Sam Houston, 459
1970	James Lister, Sam Houston, 374
1969	George Johnson, SFA, 368
1968	George Johnson, SFA, 422
1967	George Johnson, SFA, 322
1966	Mike Cook, SFA, 298
1965	Jack Fryman, Sul Ross, 295
1964	Whitney Miller, East Texas, 276
1963	Whitney Miller, ETSU, 325
1962	Frank Miller, SWT, 304
1961	Johnny Johnston, Lamar, 421
1960	Bob Shepard, Lamar, 317
1959	Don Forester, SWC, 252
1958	Al Schomber, Sul Ross, 278
1957	Joe Cole, SWT, 422
1956	Joe Cole, SWT, 300

Average
1974	Bob Kershaw, HPC, 15.4
1973	Pete Harris, SFA, 16.9
1972	Pete Harris, SFA, 19.3
1971	James Lister, Sam Houston, 17.0
1970	James Lister, Sam Houston, 13.9
1969	George Johnson, SFA, 15.3
1968	George Johnson, SFA, 15.9
1967	George Johnson, SFA, 12.9
1966	Mike Cook, SFA, 12.9
1965	Jack Fryman, Sul Ross, 11.8
1964	Whitney Miller, ETSU, 12.0
1963	Richard Trice, HPC, 12.4
1962	Rance Smith, Sul Ross, 13.1
1961	Johnny Johnston, Lamar, 15.6
1960	Bob Shepard, Lamar, 12.7
1959	Don Forester, SWT, 14.7
1958	Al Schomber, Sul Ross, 12.6
1957	Joe Cole, SWT, 16.9
1956	Joe Cole, SWT, 15.7

LSC leading scorers

Chapter 4

Handwritten annotation: I earn all of my records on my own and that what make all of it worthwhile. I am the God Father on the courts and can back it up.

The 1973-74 Record Setters

The Texas A&I basketball team broke four Lone Star Conference records, set 15 school records and tied two others, and broke four Physical Education Center standards during the 1973-74 season.

The total represents one of the Javelinas' all-time biggest assaults on the record book in a season.

Senior guard Hoegie Simmons broke the four conference marks, had 10 of the school records and three of the PEC records.

The Javelinas' all-time-leading-scorer and one of the top players to ever perform in the Lone Star Conference set conference single-game, season and career records.

He scored 1,389 points with the Javelinas to set the LSC two-season record and he had 685 field goals to easily break that mark.

His 685 field goals attempted this season, and his 44 field goals attempted against Abilene Christian also broke records.

Simmons had 52 points against East Texas and missed the conference record by one. In the game against ACC in which he attempted 44 field goals, he made 22, one short of the conference record.

Simmons' school records were for most points scored and field goals made in a two-year career; a 27.2 scoring average in two seasons; his 52 points against East Texas; 22 field goals made and 44 attempted against ACC; 762 points scored in the season; his 29.3 scoring average this year; and his 313 field goals made and 685 field goal attempts this season.

Jeff St. Clair, junior forward, had 299 rebounds to break the season record in that category.

The Javelinas set team records with 114 points against Paul Quinn, with 1,353 rebounds during the season and with an eight-game winning streak.

Team records were tied with a season scoring average of 86.7 and with a .716 field goal percentage.

The PEC records were by Simmons with his 52 points and his 22 of 44 from the field.

The 114 points scored against Paul Quinn broke the PEC record as well as the school mark.

The eight-game winning streak came near the end of the season, and was the best ever recorded by the Javelinas. On seven previous occasions teams had won seven in a row.

Hoegie Simmons   **Jeff St. Clair**

The 1973-74 record setters

134

Chapter 4

The Texas A&I basketball team... was Center this winter.

The $2 million complex, located adjacent to the ...basketball facilities in the state. opened last year and is considered one of the best basketball facilities in the state.

The gymnasium, a part of the large complex, has 5,000 seats for basketball, a Tartan floor and is well-lighted.

The Tartan floor has been used by several universities and has been called one of the best playing surfaces available today. Its durability is useful in that physical education classes also can use the floor for basketball, tennis, badminton and other activities.

Collapsible, rollaway bleachers surround the playing court at all levels on the court level, and two sections are located on the balcony level on the east and west sides of the gym.

The Physical Education Center also includes a T-shaped, Olympic-sized swimming pool, located in the east wing of the building. The pool is 50 meters long and has seven lanes. The diving area, which extends northward at the center of the pool, has one and three-meter diving boards. The slanted roof and pool depth will permit the addition of a 10-meter board at a later date.

The pool is heated and can be used year-round.

The west wing of the building includes eight handball courts, a training room, locker rooms and a large multi-purpose activity room.

Other features are 16 offices, three large classrooms, a large trophy case in the lobby and the Athletic Ticket Office.

The main entrance into the building is through the lobby which faces south. The new parking lots flank the complex on the east and west, and near-by parking facilities give fans attending the games easy access to the building.

Texas A&I Physical Education Center

—8— THis was A Super Super Gym! I Loved too PerForm in iT.

Texas A & I Physical Education Center

CHAPTER 4

1973-74 TEXAS A&I UNIVERSITY JAVELINA BASKETBALL ROSTER

Player	Post.	Ht.	Wt.	Class	Exp.	Hometown
Ricky Calhoun	F	6-6	190	Fr.	0	Chicago (Fenger)
David Hobson	C	6-8	198	Fr.	0	Eldred, Ill. (Carrollton)
Danny Joe Kaspar	G	6-3	180	Fr.	0	Corpus Christi (Carroll)
Ken Kimes	F	6-5	185	So.	Sq.	Grand Ridge, Ill. (Ottawa)
Larry J. Mabry	F	6-5	175	Sr.	2VL	Canton, Miss. (Rogers)
Michael A. Masiello	G	6-2	180	So.	RS	Buffalo, N.Y. (Dougherty)
Greg Padgitt	F	6-7	220	Jr.	Tr.	Dallas (Pinkston)
Chuck Perteete	G	6-2	170	Fr.	0	Rockford, Ill. (Auburn)
Stan Profut	C	6-8	200	So.	Sq.	Andalusia, Ill. (Darnall)
Jeff St. Clair	F	6-5	220	Jr.	Tr.	Westminster, Calif. (LaQuinta)
Hector Serna	F	6-3	185	Fr.	0	Robstown
Arthur Shipp	F	6-3	179	Fr.	0	Freeport, Ill. (Freeport)
George Shivers	F	6-6	187	Fr.	0	Rockford, Ill. (Auburn)
Hoegie Simmons	G	5-7	170	Sr.	1VL	Tucson, Ariz. (Tucson)
Gary Snowden	G	6-3	168	Fr.	0	San Antonio (Roosevelt)
Steve Weems	C	6-9	215	Sr.	2VL	San Antonio (McCollum)

1972-73 FINAL TEXAS A&I BASKETBALL STATISTICS

Player	G	FGM-FGA	Pct.	FTM-FTA	Pct.	Reb.	Avg.	Pts.	Avg.
Hoegie Simmons	25	279-562	.496	74-98	.755	47	1.8	627	25.1
Jeff Wildenberg	27	211-431	.489	114-156	.730	239	8.8	536	19.8
Larry Mabry	24	101-271	.372	26-42	.619	181	7.5	230	9.5
Al Nickerson	27	99-242	.409	35-60	.583	202	7.4	233	8.6
Steve Weems	27	86-189	.455	29-43	.675	164	6.0	201	7.4
Don Hagany	27	61-108	.564	51-76	.671	84	3.1	173	6.4
Mike Chiaventone	11	9-29	.310	4-7	.571	6	0.5	22	2.0
Art Green	14	10-35	.285	3-12	.250	16	1.1	23	1.6
Bill Chilcoat	14	7-16	.437	6-12	.500	29	2.1	20	1.4
Ken Kimes	3	0-0	.000	0-0	.000	1	0.3	0	0.0
A&I TOTALS	27	884-1950	.453	347-522	.664	1105	40.9	2115	78.3
OPP. TOTALS	27	993-1902	.522	413-653	.632	1280	47.4	2279	84.4

1972-73 basketball statistics

CHAPTER 4

LSC LEADING SCORERS

Net

1973	Hoegie Simmons, A&I, 627
1972	Robert Gords, SFA, 637
1971	James Lister, Sam Houston, 674
1970	Fred Davis, HPC, 883
1969	Fred Davis, HPC, 734
1968	Bill Mehrens, Sam Houston, 646
1967	Jeff Fitch, ETSU, 531
1966	Jack Fryman, Sul Ross, 757
1965	Jack Fryman, Sul Ross, 639
1964	Jack Fryman, Sul Ross, 442
1963	Richard Trice, HPC, 440
1962	Phil Shirk, A&I, 561
1961	Johnny Johnston, Lamar, 558
1960	Noel Fain, ETSU, 554
1959	Charles Sharp, SWT, 483
1958	Al Schomber, Sul Ross, 455
1957	Glen Jochec, Sam Houston, 470
1956	C.L. Nix, SFA, 538
1955	Walter Lee, Sam Houston, 542
1954	Tom Sewell, Sam Houston, 521
1953	Lewis Gilcrease, SWT, 592
1952	J.C. Maze, SWT, 588
1951	James Johnston, SFA, 369
1950	James Johnston, SFA, 368
1949	James Littleton, SWT, 343
1948	James Littleton, SWT, 407
1947	Murray Mitchell, Sam Houston, 285
1946	Guy Lewis, Houston, 210
1941	Van Samford, SFA, 138
1940	Robert Carpenter, ETSU, 129
1939	Marshall Matteson, SFA, 129
1938	J.P. Vinson, ETSU, 92
1935	C.C. Williams, SFA, 98
1933	Sowers, Sam Houston, 121

Average

1973	Hoegie Simmons, A&I, 25.1
1972	Robert Gords, SFA, 23.6
1971	James Lister, Sam Houston, 25.0
1970	Fred Davis, HPC, 31.5
1969	Fred Davis, HPC, 27.2
1968	Bill Gaines, ETSU, 25.1
1967	Chuck Meyer, A&I, 22.6
1966	Jack Fryman, Sul Ross, 24.4
1965	Jack Fryman, Sul Ross, 25.5
1964	Phil Shirk, A&I, 18.4
1963	Phil Shirk, A&I, 23.3
1962	Phil Shirk, A&I, 24.4
1961	Johnny Johnston, Lamar, 20.7
1960	Charles Sharp, SWT, 22.1
1959	Charles Sharp, SWT, 20.1
1958	Al Schomber, Sul Ross, 20.7
1957	Glen Jochec, Sam Houston, 18.0
1956	Don Pearson, Sul Ross, 20.9
1955	C.L. Nix, SFA, 22.0
1954	Tom Sewell, Sam Houston, 21.7
1953	Lewis Gilcrease, SWT, 24.7
1952	J.C. Maze, SWT, 18.9
1951	Charles Whitten, ETSU, 16.7

LSC LEADING REBOUNDERS

Net

1973	Pete Harris, SFA, 472
1972	Pete Harris, SFA, 522
1971	James Lister, Sam Houston, 459
1970	James Lister, Sam Houston, 374
1969	George Johnson, SFA, 368
1968	George Johnson, SFA, 422
1967	George Johnson, SFA, 322
1966	Mike Cook, SFA, 298
1965	Jack Fryman, Sul Ross, 295
1964	Whitney Miller, East Texas, 276
1963	Whitney Miller, ETSU, 325
1962	Frank Miller, SWT, 304
1961	Johnny Johnston, Lamar, 421
1960	Bob Shepard, Lamar, 317
1959	Don Forester, SWC, 252
1958	Al Schomber, Sul Ross, 278
1957	Joe Cole, SWT, 422
1956	Joe Cole, SWT, 300

Average

1973	Pete Harris, SFA, 16.9
1972	Pete Harris, SFA, 19.3
1971	James Lister, Sam Houston, 17.0
1970	James Lister, Sam Houston, 13.9
1969	George Johnson, SFA, 15.3
1968	George Johnson, SFA, 15.9
1967	George Johnson, SFA, 12.9
1966	Mike Cook, SFA, 12.9
1965	Jack Fryman, Sul Ross, 11.8
1964	Whitney Miller, ETSU, 12.0
1963	Richard Trice, HPC, 12.4
1962	Rance Smith, Sul Ross, 13.1
1961	Johnny Johnston, Lamar, 15.6
1960	Bob Shepard, Lamar, 12.7
1959	Don Forester, SWT, 14.7
1958	Al Schomber, Sul Ross, 12.6

LSC leading scorers

Chapter 4

GEORGE SHIVERS, Forward, 6-6, 187, Freshman, Rockford, Ill., Auburn ... all-state, all-conference junior and senior seasons ... received All-American mention ... had 22.0 scoring and 14.0 rebound averages last year ... coached in high school by Howard Long ... industrial arts major.

★★★★★

ON. C. H.S. S.S. Simmons Born To Win

WALLACE (HOEGIE) SIMMONS, Guard, 5-7, 170, Senior, Tucson, Ariz. ... in first year with Javelinas last season, led the Lone Star Conference in scoring with 25.1 average ... broke A&I school record with 627 points despite missing several games with an injury ... also set numerous other school marks, including best scoring average ... was NAIA All-District 4 ... received All-American mention ... scored over 35 points in six games ... season's high was 40, against Texas Lutheran in opener ... transferred to A&I from Glendale Community College where he had 28.7 scoring average freshman year and 26.5 sophomore season ... all-state and leading scorer in Arizona Junior College Conference two years ... all-conference and all-regional ... fifth in national junior college scoring and seventh in total points ... led conference two years in assists ... coached in junior college by Ken Weiss ... all-city, all-state, all-conference and All-American mention at Tucson High School ... had 19.5 scoring average in high school ... coached by Tony Morales at Tucson ... married to former Gwen Joyce Jones ... history and health and physical education major.

GARY SNOWDEN, Guard, 6-3, 168, Freshman, San Antonio Roosevelt ... was all-district and all-city at Roosevelt High School ... had 14.5 scoring average last season ... was National Honor Society and honor graduate ... coached by Jerry Tyson in high school.

★★★★★

STEVE WEEMS, Center, 6-9, 215, Senior, San Antonio McCollum ... has lettered two years with Javelinas ... had 7.4 scoring average and 6.0 rebound average last season ... all-district two years in high school, all-city ... had 22.0 scoring average and 16.0 rebound average at McCollum ... coached in high school by Dennis R. Smith ... history major.

Wallace "Hoegie" Simmons

Chapter 4

My Personal Records

THE RECORD SETTERS

Daddy Rigthous Street Back Junior

One Lone Star Conference record and 11 school marks were broken by the Texas A&I basketball team during the 1972-73 season.

Five of the records were broken by Hoegie Simmons. He erased the LSC mark for most field goals made in a season, ending with 279. The record had been 275, set by Jack Fryman of Sul Ross in 1965-66.

In addition to the school and conference records in that category, Simmons also broke the A&I season scoring record, ending with 627 points. He also had the best scoring average for a season (25.1) and most field goals attempted (562).

Jeff Wildenberg, senior forward, had four career records. He became the team's top scorer with 1,842 points over his four-year span. He also broke the rebound record, ending with 824.

Wildenberg's other records came with his field goal shooting, where he hit 732 of 1,570 attempts.

The remaining individual records were set by Don Hagany, senior guard. He broke the career record for best field goal percentage, hitting 201 of 373 shots for a .538 percentage during his four seasons. He also topped the A&I season record for best field goal percentage, hitting 61 of 108 for .564.

A team record fell when the Javelinas and Howard Payne scored a combined 220 points, breaking the A&I record for most points scored in a game by both teams.

"The Main Man"

The Record Setters

Chapter 4

70's couple Delano and Jacque

Chapter 4

1975-75 Texas A & I Javelina basketball brochure

Chapter 4

SPORTS CORNER
DICK MESSBARGER

JUST HOW GOOD is Hoegie Simmons? The 5-7 guard for the A&I Javelinas has led the Hogs to five wins in their first six starts and is carrying a healthy 28.5 scoring average.

When coach Don McDonald excitedly announced the signing of the former Glendale Community Junior College star, he listed his height as 6-1. There is no doubt that the Tucson, Arizona native is capable of jumping as well as any six-footer, but even with elevated shoes and four pair of socks he'd be hard pressed to reach 5-9 in height.

Simmons was the fifth leading scorer in the junior college ranks last year. He posted a 28.7 norm his first year and carried a 26.5 average his sophomore season.

THE PLAYER HE IS MOST often compared with is Algie Neal, last year's hot-shooting guard who scored an A&I individual high of 50-points in one game. Neal and Simmons are similar in some areas but vastly different in the more important sphere — contributions to the team.

Neal was the classic exponent of the philosophy that, "when you're hot, you're hot." And conversely, "when you're not, unfortunately, you're not."

Coach McDonald and members of this year's squad dislike the comparison of the two players. "Hoegie's a team player," sophomore squadman Mike Chiavetone said after the first game. "He gives you leadership in more ways than just scoring."

Simmons received, in the words of Northern Michigan University SID (Sports Information Director) Gil Heard, "the closest thing to a standing ovation I've ever seen at this school for a visiting player."

The junior college transfer led the Hogs with e i g h t straight points early in the second half, putting the visitors back into the game. He fouled out of the Northern Michigan game with two minutes remaining, providing the Michigan fans an opportunity to demonstrate their appreciation for his performance.

IT STILL MAY BE TOO EARLY to judge whether Simmons can compete with the powerhouses in the Lone Star Conference. It's almost unthinkable to picture a 5-7 guard as one of the top performers in the most respected small college conference in the nation.

But, on the other hand, his achievements against Northern Michigan (who lost only one home game last year) and Eau Claire (the nation's fourth ranked small college) indicate that he can handle the pressure against tough competition.

Thursday night the Javelinas meet their first Lone Star Conference opponent of the season, East Texas State. The Hogs will have a week to rest up for the Lions after their four game, week-long northern tour.

Hoegie is carrying a 34-point scoring average at home. He and the remainder of the Javelina starting lineup, which includes four starters from last year, will be primed to open the LSC race with a big win.

Drop by the Physical Education Center on the A&I campus and see for yourself just how good Hoegie Simmons really is. If you like college basketball, you won't be disappointed.

LSC'S TOP SCORER — Hoegie Simmons, 5-7 junior guard for the Texas A&I basketball team, is leading the Lone Star Conference in scoring. He has averaged 29.6 points in nine games, and his hitting .548 (124-226) of his field goal attempts. Simmons has twice been named LSC Player of the Week.

HOEGIE EXPRESS — Texas A&I's Hoegie Simmons attempts to drive past Rick Penny of the McMurry Indians. Simmons collected twelve points in the Monday night contest, well below his 29.3 average. The 5-7 sharpshooter sprained an ankle just before the first half. Penny was high man for the

Sports Corner

Chapter 4

Crowd pleaser

CHAPTER 4

Texas A & I team photo/action shots

Chapter 4

McDonald Excited Over '72 Season

The Texas A&I basketball team is in the final stages of its pre-season workouts and Javelina coach Don McDonald is pleased with the progress the squad has shown thus far.

"I think we'll be able to score," McDonald says. "Our defense hasn't been overly impressive in some areas but I think this will improve as we play together more and have more game-like situations."

McDonald sent his team through a game-like scrimmage last weekend. Wallace (Hoegie) Simmons, a junior guard who transferred to A&I this season, led the Gold team to a 102-71 victory over a Blue squad. Simmons hit 17 of 34 field goals and ended with 39 points.

Larry Mabry, junior letterman at forward, had 26 points for the winners and had 17 rebounds. Jeff Wildenberg, senior forward, had 20 rebounds and Steve Weems, junior center, had 17.

For the Blue team, Bill Chilcoat, senior center, had 27 points and all rebounds while Larry Britton, sophomore forward, had 20 points and seven rebounds.

"I was pleased with the board work of several of our men," McDonald said. "And we feel Simmons will be a scoring threat anytime from anywhere on the court."

HIGH POINT MAN — Hoegie Simmons gets ready to put up another of his long, arching jumpshots that have made him one of the most popular basketball players in A&I history. The 5-7 junior closed out his first season with the blue and gold with a 36 point performance against Stephen F. Austin Monday night. Simmons, owner of the A&I single season scoring record, totaled 627 on the year.

Simmons Selected

EAUCLAIRE, Wis. — Hoegie Simmons has added another honor to his long list of post-season accolades. The 5-7 junior guard for the Texas A&I Javelina basketball team has been named to the UW-Eau Claire All-Opponent first team.

Simmons joins Gary Tyson, 6-11 junior from Eastern Michigan, at the guard positions on the team. The pair of small guards had the distinction of scoring the most points against the Blugolds this past season. Tyson scored 35 points in Eastern Michigan's 72-67 loss to the Blugolds while Simmons poured in 30 points in A&I's 82-69 loss to the Blugolds.

The other three members of the first team all played in victories over the Blugolds. They include Capital's Scott Weakley, the MVP in the Eau Claire Holiday Classic; Stout's Doug Eha; and Green Bay's Tom Jones.

One-third of the way
Hoegie Closes On Mark

(Special to the Record-News)

Hoegie Simmons is only a third of the way through his first season with the Texas A&I basketball team, and he's already over halfway to the team's record season point total.

The 5-7 junior guard from Tucson, Ariz., has scored 267 points in the Javelinas' first nine games of the season. Still remaining on the schedule are 19 games.

Phil Shirk, All-American for the Javelinas in the early 1960s, holds the season scoring mark with 591 points. These came in the 1961-62 season.

Simmons also is on track for the season scoring average record. He is averaging 29.6 points a game, and Shirk had an average of 24.4 in the 1961-62 campaign.

The Javelina standout also is expected to wipe out the season field goal records: Goals attempted and made, and shooting percentage. Several of these marks could fall even before the Javelinas reach the halfway point in the 1972-73 season.

Simmons has been the top scorer in the Lone Star Conference since hitting 40 points in his debut against Texas Lutheran. He has twice been named LSC Player of the Week.

The Javelinas, now on their holiday break, will return to play Jan. 3 when they meet Angelo State in San Angelo in a conference game.

Hoegie on the mark

Chapter 4

Simmons stays hot

Chapter 4

Small Hoegie Simmons helps Javelinas

Chapter 4

Hoegie with family/girlfriend Denise/sister/ sister and mother Mary Simmons

Chapter 4

Hoegie backwards dunk at A & I

CHAPTER 4

Hoegie one handed leaning dunk (signaling 2 points with the other hand) at A & I

Chapter 4

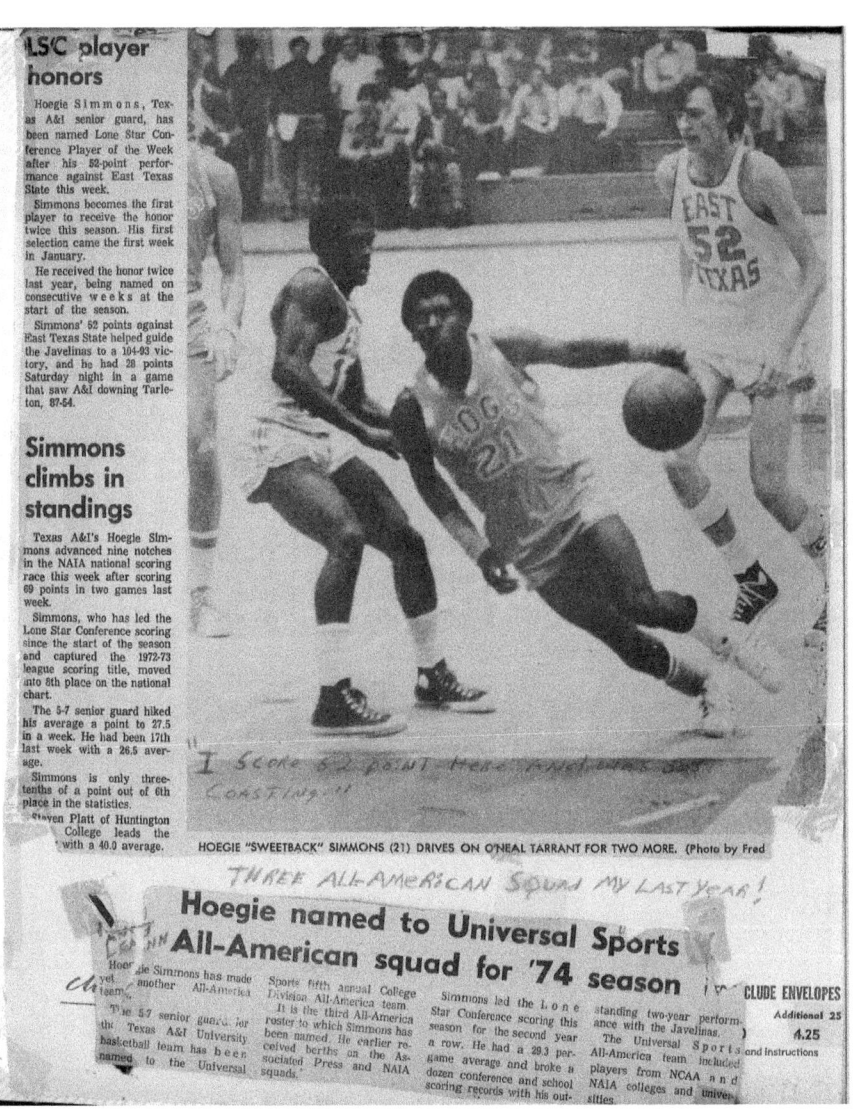

Hoegie named to universal sports All-American squad

Chapter 4

Hoegie one handed dunk at A & I

Chapter 4

Hoegie two handed dunk at A & I

Chapter 4

Hoegie reverse dunk at A & I

Chapter 4

Back to back 50 point games at A & I

CHAPTER 5

THE DOUBLE-EDGED LEGEND OF HOEGIE SIMMONS

Hoegie Simmons' journey after Texas A&I seemed destined for the professional basketball stage. Known for his jaw-dropping talent, he had become a household name in the Lone Star Conference, shattering records and leaving spectators in awe. Yet, life's trajectory often holds unanticipated detours, and for Hoegie, those detours became pivotal chapters in his life marked by both ability and turbulence.

"Hoegie," the name was given to him by an opponent during his freshman year at Pueblo High School in Tucson. The player remarked that Hoegie's stooped-over walk reminded him of Hokey Wolf, the Hanna-Barbera cartoon character. The nickname stuck, accompanying Hoegie throughout his career as he developed into one of the most exciting players to emerge from Tucson's basketball scene.

Despite his rousing performances on the court, including record-breaking scoring feats, the professional leagues bypassed Hoegie during the draft after the 1972-1973 season. At the time, both the NBA and ABA had room for undersized guards who could dazzle, but scouts were divided on Hoegie. While his talent was undeniable, his ultra-confident demeanor and blunt self-assessments came across as arrogant and difficult to manage. It didn't help that Hoegie, ever self-assured, made bold comparisons to established stars like Calvin Murphy.

At Texas A&I, scouts from the Houston Rockets regularly attended Hoegie's games, captivated by his ability to shoot from anywhere and dominate opponents with indefensible moves. However, when they approached him with the offer of a non-guaranteed contract, Hoegie scoffed, saying, "Bring Calvin Murphy here. If I beat him one-on-one, give me his guaranteed contract."

This wasn't simple bravado; it reflected Hoegie's belief in his own game. At 5'9", Calvin Murphy was a similarly undersized guard who had proven himself in the NBA with astonishing athleticism and scoring prowess. Murphy's collegiate career at Niagara University was legendary, boasting a 33.1 points-per-game average over three seasons. Some of his college and professional accolades included:

NBA All-Star (1979)

NBA All-Rookie First Team (1971)

Houston Rockets' No. 23 jersey retired

Consensus first-team All-American (1969, 1970)

Career-high 25.6 points per game during the 1977-78 NBA season.

Murphy was an established force, known for his high-flying ability and scoring precision. Comparing himself to such a star was bold, but Hoegie truly believed he was as good, or better. The Rockets, unwilling to take the gamble without proof, let the offer dissolve.

Not only was Hoegie not drafted, but he was also unable to draw interest from any pro team willing to give him a decent tryout after rejecting the non-guaranteed contract. Unlike today, where summer pro leagues and social media provide players with avenues to showcase their talents, Hoegie's highlights were confined to word of mouth. Without a platform to continue proving himself, his professional dreams slipped away. Frustrated but undeterred, Hoegie returned to Tucson, where his life would take an unpredictable turn.

Back in Tucson: Art Imitates Life

Returning to his hometown, Hoegie found himself pulled between two worlds. By day, he was still the basketball phenom, gracing courts around Tucson with his unmatched skills. By night, he embraced a darker lifestyle, one steeped in street culture. Gambling, fleeting romances, and brushes with the law began to define his existence. He adopted the persona of Sweet Sweetback, the anti-hero from Melvin Van Peebles' revolutionary film Sweet Sweetback's Baadasssss Song. The character's defiance and gritty survivalism mirrored Hoegie's own journey, blurring the lines between his real life and the cinematic rebellion he admired.

Chapter 5

The streets in Tucson became Hoegie's stage. Known as much for his swagger as his basketball acumen, he earned respect and notoriety in equal measure. His exploits, whether dunking on opponents at pick-up games or dominating dice games in shadowy corners, fueled his mystique. However, as his basketball dream dimmed, the allure of quick money and fast living tightened its grip.

Trouble found Hoegie in 1974 when a seemingly minor decision changed the course of his life. While giving acquaintances a ride to a hotel, Hoegie unknowingly became an accomplice in their armed robbery. Witnesses later testified they saw him driving the getaway car, and despite his protests of innocence, Hoegie was convicted and sentenced to 32 months in Florence Prison.

The robbery yielded a mere $57, money that Hoegie didn't even need, as he already had $300 in his pocket. The arrest shook his family, particularly his mother, Mary. On the day of his arrest, Mary was returning from church as the police escorted her son away. Desperate, she followed their car, pleading for his release, only to be silenced by the booming command of the officers' bullhorn. It was a crushing moment for the family, who had seen Hoegie's potential shine so brightly just a few years prior.

In prison, Hoegie turned to the one constant in his life: basketball. On a bent rim with a lopsided ball, he quickly established himself as the best player in the facility. His one-on-one battles with 6-foot-9 Wil Smiley, a fellow inmate and former Scottsdale Junior College player, became legendary. Despite Smiley's height and skill, Hoegie defeated him every time, solidifying his reputation as the court's reigning monarch.

CHAPTER 5

Florence Prison became an unlikely stage for Hoegie's talent. Visiting teams, including those from Eastern Arizona Junior College, came to play against the inmates. Lafayette "Fat" Lever, a future NBA star from Tucson, recalled hearing about these games through his brother Anthony, who played for Eastern Arizona. Anthony would return home, raving about Hoegie's performances, where he routinely dropped 50, 60, and even 70 points in games against Eastern Arizona.

Throughout his incarceration, Hoegie's surrogate family stood by him. Delano, his brother Michael, their father "Daddy" regularly visited him, bringing home-cooked meals Mattie made and encouragement. On one visit, they brought Hoegie a new pair of basketball shoes, a small but meaningful gesture that underscored their unwavering support for him. For Delano, seeing his backcourt mate behind bars was a sobering reminder of how quickly life could veer off course.

Hoegie's time in prison was marked by reflections. While he downplayed the pain of the experience, it was clear that it had left an indelible mark on him. "Hey, I gave these dudes a ride," he would later say, shrugging off the incident with a mix of resignation and defiance. "I knew 'em, but I didn't know what they were gonna do."

Yet even in the bleakness of prison life, basketball remained a source of light. Hoegie's unmatched skill drew admiration from fellow inmates and guards alike, reminding everyone, himself included, of the talent that still burned within him.

By the time of his release, Hoegie's basketball career was a distant memory for many. The professional opportunities that once seemed inevitable were now long gone, replaced by the harsh

Chapter 5

realities of a criminal record and a tarnished reputation. Still, his legend lived on in whispers and anecdotes, from the courts of Tucson to the halls of Florence Prison.

Lafayette "Fat" Lever, who would go on to become one of the NBA's premier point guards, never forgot the stories he'd heard about Hoegie. For Lever and others, Hoegie Simmons was a player and a symbol of untapped potential, a cautionary tale of talent lost to circumstance and choices.

As Hoegie emerged from prison, his path forward remained uncertain. Would he find redemption and rebuild his life, or would the streets reclaim him once more? For now, his story stood as a testament to the heights of greatness he had achieved, and the depths to which he had fallen.

Before life took Hoegie to Florence prison, the Simmons-Price backcourt reassembled for one final hurrah during the early to mid-1970s. Though they now played on different stages, one on the streets and the other as a teacher and family man, their chemistry on the court remained as electric as ever.

When Delano wasn't teaching social studies at Apollo Junior High School, he and Hoegie hit the courts together twice during the week and every weekend. Summers, when Delano had breaks from school, meant daily basketball marathons. It was a rekindling of the synergy they had shared during their Tucson High School glory days. Back then, they roamed the courts across town, challenging players to two-on-two games for cash. Undefeated, they amassed a jar full of winnings that symbolized their dominance.

Chapter 5

During one of these legendary pickup sessions, the two made their now-famous wager: a $100 bet on who would play basketball the longest. It was a testament to their competitive spirit and love for the game, a pact that would span decades.

Even as Hoegie's game reached new heights, it was he who marveled at Delano's evolution. Delano had stayed in peak physical condition, extending his shooting range even further while maintaining the flawless form of his jump shot. "Boy," Hoegie would say, "I been all over the world playing, and you still got the purest jump shot I've ever seen."

When they arrived at the gym, assembling a five-man team was effortless. They would pick three players, no matter what their skill levels, and carry the load. Sometimes they would go for days without losing a single game.

Delano's jump shot: A weapon of fear

Delano's jump shot was as multidimensional as it was lethal. He could catch and shoot off screens, drain pull-ups from mid-range or deep, and nail off-balance shots in transition. His quick release and perfect follow-through made defenders panic. Opponents would attempt to deny him the ball or guard him full court, but once Delano squared his shoulders, the result was inevitable.

Hoegie, knowing exactly where Delano liked to get the ball, would flick him a pass and turn away, already jogging back on defense. "I didn't even need to watch it go in," Hoegie said. "Once he shot it, it was good as gold."

Chapter 5

NBA star Lafayette "Fat" Lever, a Tucson native who idolized the duo, weighed in on Delano's game. "Delano shot that jumper with power in his legs and shoulders, releasing it at the apex. He could really fill it up," Lever said. "No better ambassador for Tucson basketball than Delano."

Lever went further, emphasizing the impact of Delano and Hoegie on the history of basketball in Tucson: "That '69 Tucson High School championship with Delano and Hoegie, to me, were the history starters even before the 'Kiddie Corp.'" The "Kiddie Corp" was a celebrated group of recruits brought to the University of Arizona by coach Fred Snowden between 1972 and 1977, featuring standout players like Jim Rappis, Eric Money, Coniel Norman, Al Fleming, Herman Harris, Len Gordy, Gilbert Myles, Larry Demic, and Bob Elliot (right behind the "Kiddie Corp") who all became stars in Tucson.

Lever recalled being taken to Bear down Gymnasium by his junior high coach, Herb Buckner, to watch Delano and Hoegie dominate pickup games. "Hoegie would be outside shooting dice, and then someone would call his name. He'd walk into the gym and put up numbers with Delano waiting for him, ready to light it up also. That '69 championship team; they're the history starters."

A Divergence in Paths

Off the court, however, their lives were moving in starkly different directions. Delano, now a father and husband, was deeply entrenched in building a life for his family. He and Jacque welcomed their second child, Adrian Anitra Price, on June 14, 1976.

Chapter 5

Delano's days were spent teaching 7th and 8th grade social studies at Apollo Junior High School, a job he had started in the fall of 1973. His first career position put him on the path as an educator, where he found fulfillment in shaping young minds. He also coached basketball for three years, leading the school's program and bonding with players who weren't much younger than himself.

Coaching was a learning experience for Delano. Though his teams didn't win many games, he formed lifelong connections with his players and grew as a leader. He would often practice and scrimmage with the students, blending his love for basketball with his natural gift for teaching.

In 1976, Delano and Jacque purchased their first home, a milestone that marked a turning point in their journey. Using savings from working year-round, Delano put aside $11,000, a small fortune in his eyes, to buy a house for his growing family.

The house at 2602 West Calle Genova became a place of profound sentimental value. Delano's father, "Daddy," visited after they moved in, standing in the middle of the home with pride. Gazing at the beehive fireplace, he said, "If I had been more like you with the sense that you have, my life would have been different."

For Delano, his father's approval meant everything. The moment reinforced the value of sacrifice and hard work, lessons he carried forward as he built a better life for his family.

Chapter 5

Hoegie's Shadowed Life

While Delano thrived as a family man and educator, Hoegie remained tethered to the streets. Despite their frequent court reunions, Hoegie never involved Delano in his underworld dealings. Out of respect, he kept that part of his life hidden, maintaining a boundary that shielded Delano from his extracurricular activities.

When Delano arrived to pick him up for morning basketball, Hoegie was often still entangled in the previous night's escapades. Delano would find him with a woman at his mother's house, call out to him from the window, and leave when Hoegie didn't immediately respond. Yet, without fail, Hoegie would show up at the gym just in time to join Delano, ready to run the court as if he'd had a full night's sleep.

Hoegie's late-night exploits and streetwise persona contrasted sharply with Delano's structured, family-centered existence. Yet their bond remained undismayed, embedded in mutual respect and a mutual love for basketball.

In 1976, Delano's hard work and dedication paid off in tangible ways. The purchase of their home on Calle Genova was a testament to his commitment to his family and his determination to rise above the struggles of his upbringing.

At the same time, Delano was balancing multiple roles as a husband, father, teacher, coach, and still an active basketball player. He continued to compete in Tucson's top leagues, where his scoring prowess earned him a reputation as one of the city's most consistent and feared shooters. His love for the game remained undiminished, even as his responsibilities grew.

Chapter 5

Though their paths were diverging, the bet Delano and Hoegie had made years earlier about who would play basketball the longest remained a playful undercurrent in their relationship. Despite their differences, the court was always a place where they could reconnect and relive the magic of their shared past.

The bond between Delano and Hoegie was a brotherhood forged through basketball, a shared history, and an unspoken understanding of their respective struggles and triumphs. For Delano, life was about building a foundation for his family. For Hoegie, it was about navigating the complexities of a life shaped by both extraordinary talent and poor choices.

Together, they represented two sides of the same coin which was a duality that highlighted the power of talent, the weight of choices, and the enduring connection between two friends who had once ruled the courts of Tucson.

As the mid-70s ended, their journeys continued to unfold in vastly different directions. Yet, on the court, they remained a team, their shared history a constant reminder of what they had built together and what could have been.

Chapter 5

Hoegie and girlfriend Lynda

CHAPTER 5

Hoegie styling

Chapter 5

Hoegie and girlfriend Denise

Chapter 5

Hoegie solo in tank top with bell bottoms.

Chapter 5

Hoegie and girlfriend Denise

Chapter 5

Hoegie taking flight in Florence correctional facility league against collegiate athletes.

Chapter 5

Hoegie in Tucson cactus/Young boy Hoegie Simmons/ Sister, Hoegie, mother Mary Simmons

CHAPTER 6

THE RISE OF BEAR DOWN GYM AND THE IMPACT OF BOB ELLIOTT

During the mid-1970s to mid-1980s, Bear Down Gymnasium at the University of Arizona transformed into a basketball mecca, drawing some of the most skilled and competitive players in Tucson and beyond. Known for its gritty pickup games, Bear Down became a proving ground for anyone serious about their game. The gym's reputation mirrored legendary basketball haunts like St. Cecilia in Detroit and Rucker Park in New York, places where talent, toughness, and reputation were forged through grueling competition.

Bob Elliott, a standout player at the University of Arizona during this era, described the gym as "the place where you went if you wanted to play against the best." The intensity of the games often rivaled organized college matches, with players of all sizes and skills embracing a positionless style of basketball reminiscent of St. Cecilia. "You learned to play against size and skill. Bear Down had both," Bob said, reflecting on the diverse talent pool that graced the court.

Bear Down's open-door policy encouraged a mix of university athletes, local legends like Delano Price and Wallace "Hoegie" Simmons and aspiring high school stars eager to test their mettle. Players and spectators alike were captivated by the sheer athleticism and skill on display. Pickup games featured powerhouse pairs like Delano and Hoegie, who dominated the court with their interchangeable guard play.

Bob Elliott admired their versatility, saying, "Delano and Hoegie were always a matchup problem for other teams because they could switch seamlessly between point guard and shooting guard." Their competitive fire and knack for scoring made them favorites among the gym's regulars, inspiring the next generation of Tucson players.

Bob Elliott's Arrival in Tucson

Bob Elliott's own journey to Tucson began in Ann Arbor, Michigan, where he grew up playing basketball. Ann Arbor, a college town, provided Bob with early exposure to high-level basketball, but it was the competitive pickup games in nearby Detroit that shaped his approach to the sport. "The games in Detroit weren't just about winning; they were about earning respect," he recalled.

CHAPTER 6

When it came to be time to choose a college, Bob and his father approached the outcome with precision. They created a decision tree that considered both academic and athletic priorities. A standout student-athlete, Bob knew he wanted to major in accounting, which narrowed his options significantly. Although heavily recruited by over 300 schools, including UCLA, Bob chose the University of Arizona because it met his academic and athletic goals.

Arriving in Tucson in 1973, Bob quickly became a cornerstone of the University of Arizona basketball program under coach Fred Snowden. Snowden, the first African American head coach at a major university, brought a transformative energy to the Wildcats. His arrival coincided with a shift in the university's basketball culture, moving from the intimate confines of Bear Down Gymnasium to the newly constructed McKale Center, which seated 14,000 fans. The transition was symbolic of the program's growing prominence under Snowden's leadership.

Bob thrived both on and off the court, becoming a three-time Academic and Athletic All-American and earning a Bachelor of Science in Accounting and an MBA. On the court, he was a force, averaging 18.6 points per game during his collegiate career. He left an indelible mark on the program, ranking second in all-time scoring at the University of Arizona, a record surpassed only by Sean Elliott.

Reflecting on his time in Tucson, Bob recalled the cultural adjustment some of his teammates faced. "For some of the guys coming from inner cities, Tucson was a culture shock. It was different. For me, coming from Ann Arbor, it felt like home," he said. Bob became a bridge between Snowden and his players, helping teammates navigate the challenges of college life while maintaining a strong connection to the coach who had recruited him.

Bear Down's Legacy and Impact

Bear Down Gym was a sanctuary for basketball and a cultural hub that reflected Tucson's evolving sports landscape. Before Snowden's arrival, the Wildcats struggled to draw crowds. Bear Down, with its 3,000-seat capacity, rarely sold out. But Snowden's inaugural season brought new energy, and the gym became a hotbed of excitement.

Without air conditioning, Bear Down relied on swamp coolers and open windows, which allowed fans outside to listen to games. By midseason, the Wildcats' games moved to McKale Center, but Bear Down retained its reputation as the ultimate proving ground for pickup basketball.

Elliott likened Bear Down's intensity to that of St. Cecilia, where future NBA stars like Magic Johnson and George Gervin honed their skills. "Bear Down reminded me of St. Cecilia in Detroit. The competition was fierce, and the environment pushed you to be better," Bob said.

Bob Elliott's Reflections on Delano and Hoegie

"Delano and Hoegie were two different people in a major way," Bob noted. "Delano went on to be a well-regarded educator, administrator, and community leader in town, whereas I lost track of Hoegie after a while." Still, Bob marveled at their synergy on the court, describing their backcourt partnership as one of the best he had seen. Both players left a lasting impression on Tucson basketball. Delano's pure jump shot, and disciplined play contrasted with Hoegie's explosive athleticism and flair, but together, they were unstoppable.

Bob Elliott's Post-Basketball Legacy

After a stellar collegiate career, Bob briefly played professionally, splitting a season between the Philadelphia 76ers and a team in Italy before joining the New Jersey Nets for three seasons. Post-retirement, he focused on his passion for education and community building. In 2023, Bob and his wife, Beverely, co-founded the African American Museum of Southern Arizona, inspired by their grandson's curiosity about African American history in the state.

The museum, located in Tucson, aims to preserve and share the rich history and culture of African Americans in the region. "Our biggest hope for the museum is that people will walk away saying, 'I didn't know that'" Beverely said. The couple hopes the museum will inspire continued learning and community engagement, much like Bear Down Gym inspired generations of basketball players.

The Visionary: Coach Fred Snowden

Fred Snowden's journey from humble beginnings in Brewton, Alabama, to becoming the first African American head coach at a major university is a testament to perseverance, vision, and groundbreaking achievements. Born to a sharecropping family, Snowden moved with his mother and two brothers to Detroit, Michigan, at the age of six, while his father remained in Alabama. Detroit became a new starting point, offering opportunities and challenges that would shape Snowden into a leader both on and off the court.

Snowden attended Detroit's Northwestern High School, where he excelled in academics and sports. Following high school, he pursued higher education at Wayne State University, where he met his wife, Maya. The couple married in 1962 and raised two children: Charles Anthony and Stacey Shannon.

After college, Snowden returned to his alma mater as a coach, marking the beginning of his remarkable basketball journey. His five-year tenure at Northwestern High was nothing short of historic. The junior varsity team compiled a perfect 90-0 record, while the varsity team achieved an 87-7 record, showcasing Snowden's ability to inspire excellence in young players.

His success caught the attention of the basketball world, leading him to a brief stint as a sportscaster before joining the University of Michigan as an assistant coach. At Michigan, Snowden worked under coaches Dave Strack and Johnny Orr, honing his skills and strategies while preparing for a groundbreaking opportunity that would change the trajectory of his career and the sport.

Breaking Barriers at Arizona

In 1972, Fred Snowden shattered a significant racial barrier by becoming the first African American head coach at a major university and the second Black head coach at a Division I school. His hiring at the University of Arizona in Tucson marked a historic moment, symbolizing progress during a time of social and cultural transformation in America. Snowden inherited a struggling Wildcats program, which had finished the previous season with a 6-20 record and an average attendance of about 1,000 fans per game at Bear Down Gymnasium.

Snowden's impact was immediate. In his inaugural season, the Wildcats improved to a 16-12 record (.571), a significant turnaround that energized the campus and the Tucson community. Attendance surged, with an average of 3,000 fans per game, as Snowden's leadership and charisma drew attention and support. His success on the court was matched by his ability to connect with people, earning him the title of Western Athletic Conference (WAC) Coach of the Year, Tucson's Man of the Year, and two television hosting opportunities.

By the time McKale Center opened midseason, the Wildcats were selling out games in the new 14,000-seat arena. Snowden's ability to revive the program and energize the fan base not only cemented his status as a transformative figure in Tucson but also set the stage for the program's future successes.

The Wildcats made two NCAA tournament appearances during Snowden's tenure, reaching the Elite Eight in 1976, a crowning achievement that solidified his legacy. His fast-paced, high-energy style of play captivated fans and opponents alike, turning Arizona into a must-watch team. The Wildcats' success under Snowden also brought national attention to Tucson, elevating the city's basketball culture and paving the way for future stars to emerge from the region.

Chapter 6

Fred Snowden's contributions went far beyond wins and losses. His presence as a Black head coach during a period of racial tension and societal change carried profound significance. Snowden became a role model not only for aspiring athletes but also for young African Americans striving to break barriers in various fields. His success demonstrated the power of perseverance and the importance of representation at the highest levels.

Bob Elliott spoke about Snowden's influence: "Coach Snowden was so much more than a coach. He was a vanguard, a mentor, and a father figure to many of us. He showed us what was possible, not just in basketball but in life."

Elliott credited Snowden with nurturing a sense of community among the players, helping them navigate the challenges of college life, and instilling values that extended beyond the court. "He understood the importance of education and preparing us for life after basketball," Elliott said. "That's why so many of his players went on to succeed in various fields."

Building a Basketball Community in Tucson

Snowden's arrival in Tucson coincided with the rise of Bear Down Gymnasium as a hub for pickup basketball, a phenomenon that complemented the Wildcats' resurgence under his leadership. The gym became a proving ground for players from all walks of life, a place where stars like Delano Price, Hoegie Simmons, and others showcased their skills alongside university athletes and professional players.

Chapter 6

Snowden's influence extended into these spaces, inspiring players to embrace competition and camaraderie. The sense of community he encouraged at the University of Arizona reverberated throughout Tucson, leaving a lasting impact on the city's basketball culture.

Despite his many achievements, Snowden faced significant challenges during his tenure. As a Black head coach, he circumnavigated the pressures of being a catalyst in a predominantly white field while dealing with the expectations of leading a major university program. His ability to rise above these challenges and excel spoke to his intestinal fortitude.

Snowden's tenure in Arizona eventually came to an end, but his legacy endured. He laid the foundation for the program's future success and left an indelible mark on the sport. His influence continues to be felt in Tucson and beyond, serving as a reminder of the power of leadership and vision.

Bear Down Gymnasium, built in 1926 and named after the legendary rallying cry of John "Button" Salmon, became much more than just a building on the University of Arizona campus. It emerged as a sacred space for sports, community, and culture, hosting decades of athletic and social events that captured the spirit of Tucson. For basketball players, however, Bear Down was a proving ground, a sanctuary for both legends and hopefuls to test their mettle in an environment as intense and unpredictable as the game itself.

Tom Danehy, a longstanding columnist for The Tucson Weekly and avid participant in Bear Down's pickup games, painted a vivid picture of the gym's allure. In his own words, "Bear Down was Baller Central, and these were righteous ballers. No Has-Beens,

Chapter 6

no Never-Were's. Just a couple of Used-To-Be's and a bunch of Still-Are's, ready to take on all comers."

Bear Down Gym was far from luxurious. Danehy described the environment as "always too-something." Too cold in the winter, unbearably hot in the summer, and always a cacophony of sounds and smells that signaled its vibrant life. The massive fan mounted on the wall made more noise than it provided relief, merely circulating the thick, warm air inside. Yet, none of this mattered to the players. It was about the competition, the camaraderie, and the unyielding drive to improve.

On any given Saturday, the gym was packed with a blend of University of Arizona students, local legends, and streetball royalty, each vying for dominance on the hardwood. Those lucky enough to get on a team with someone like Wallace "Hoegie" Simmons or other legends knew they had a chance to play all day.

Among the most notable players was Larry Demic, a University of Arizona standout who would later be drafted fourth overall in the NBA Draft. Despite being a rising star, Demic respected the unique culture of Bear Down, famously telling coach Fred Snowden, "McKale is where we work. This is where we play. This is Bear Down." This sentiment captured the gym's role as an egalitarian battleground, where NBA hopefuls and weekend warriors clashed with equal fervor.

Pickup games at Bear Down were intense and brazenly competitive. University players like Demic, Bob Elliott, and others sharpened their skills alongside and against Tucson legends like Delano Price and Hoegie Simmons. The games were about accolades and scholarships; but they were also about pride, respect, and survival in a gladiatorial arena.

CHAPTER 6

A Venerable History

Bear Down Gym's rich history extended far beyond basketball. During World War II, it was converted into a naval training center, humorously nicknamed the U.S.S. Bear Down despite its desert location. In the 1940s, it housed cots for temporary student housing at the start of the school year, a scene immortalized in the film Revenge of the Nerds, filmed on the University of Arizona campus.

In 1970, Bear Down Gym became the backdrop for a historic protest against the University of Arizona's affiliation with BYU, whose policies toward Black and minority members had drawn national criticism. The gym, already a hub for athletic and social gatherings, was transformed into a stage for activism, demonstrating its place at the intersection of sports and cultural movements.

A Snowy Saturday and the Height of Pickup Basketball

Danehy's recollection of May 6, 1978, encapsulates the magic of Bear Down. Despite freakish weather, including snow on the Catalina Mountains, Bear Down was filled with players eager to compete. By mid-morning, a crowd of talented ball players had gathered, including members of the University of Arizona basketball team. Though NCAA rules prohibited dunking in games at the time, Bear Down pickup games offered players a chance to unleash their aerial artistry.

Chapter 6

When coach Fred Snowden suggested moving the game to the more modern McKale Center, Demic's retort, "This is Bear Down," underscored the gym's cultural significance. Bear Down was a facility that served as a crucible where legends were engineered, a venue where raw talent met uncompromising grit.

The Decision to Transform Bear Down

As the years passed, Bear Down Gym's role as a basketball mecca waned, eventually succumbing to the pressures of university expansion and modernization. In a controversial decision, the University of Arizona repurposed the historic gym into office space. Today, Bear Down Office Space stands as a stark reminder of what once was, its transformation lamented by those who experienced its glory firsthand. "Anyone who has ever done anything even remotely athletic in that venerable masterpiece of a building will have a visceral reaction when stepping into what is now a brightly lit, carpeted, air-conditioned thing," Danehy wrote, mourning the loss of the gym's soul.

Bear Down Gym's legacy endures, even as its courts have been replaced by offices. It remains a symbol of Tucson's rich basketball history, a place where players like Larry Demic, Bob Elliott, Delano Price, and Hoegie Simmons left their mark. For those who played, watched, and learned in its hallowed halls, Bear Down represents more than just a gym. It is a commemoration to the enduring spirit of competition, community, and the love of the game.

Today, the name "Bear Down" continues to resonate, reminding Tucsonans of the gym's storied past and the players who made it

Chapter 6

legendary. It serves as a rallying cry not only for the University of Arizona's athletic teams but also for the countless athletes and dreamers who found a home on its courts. While the games may have moved elsewhere, the spirit of Bear Down lives on in the hearts of those who played, coached, and competed there.

Larry Demic and the Legends of Bear Down: From Gary to Tucson

Larry Demic, a towering 6'9" power forward from Gary, Indiana, grew up in the gritty basketball culture of the Midwest. A standout at Westside High School, Demic's natural athleticism and work ethic earned him a scholarship to the University of Arizona in 1975. Over the next four years, he developed into one of the premier players in the Pac-10 Conference, culminating in a First-Team All-Pac 10 selection in 1979. His collegiate success led to him being drafted ninth overall in the first round of the 1979 NBA Draft by the New York Knicks. But before all the accolades, Larry was an impressionable freshman exploring a new world in Tucson. A world where Bear Down Gym would play a pivotal role in shaping his basketball journey.

Discovering Bear Down

Larry wasn't initially aware of Bear Down Gymnasium when he first arrived on campus. It wasn't until a few of his University of Arizona teammates clued him in that he learned about the legendary pickup games. "If you were a good player, you went to Bear Down to play," they told him. The gym was an arena of respect where reputations were made or broken.

The first time Larry stepped into Bear Down, the atmosphere overwhelmed him. The gym was alive with the sounds of squeaking sneakers, bouncing basketballs, and the constant banter of players competing at a high level. It was raw, intense, a cauldron of competition, everything Larry loved about the game.

Meeting Hoegie Simmons

The first player to catch Larry's eye at Bear Down was Hoegie Simmons. Larry noticed him immediately, not just because of his unusual pigeon-toed stride and deep, base voice, but because of the sensational things Hoegie was doing on the court. Standing at just 5'7", Hoegie moved with fluidity and precision that defied his stature.

"He was just blowing by defenders and dunking over people, me included," Larry recalled. What stood out most was Hoegie's unorthodox shooting form. "He'd scratch the back of his shirt before releasing the ball. It looked awkward, but it was deadly." Watching Hoegie control the court was like seeing a maestro conduct an orchestra. It was unorthodox, mesmerizing, and undoubtedly effective.

Meeting Delano Price

It wasn't long before Larry encountered Delano Price, and their introduction was equally memorable. "I first met Delano playing on Saturday mornings," Larry said. "He always had sweatpants on! I had never seen anyone play in sweatpants in a gym that hot."

While Hoegie astonished others with his speed and flash, Delano displayed a noiseless conviction and precision that made him just as formidable. "Delano was one of the purest shooters I've ever seen," Larry recalled. "He shot the ball the same way every time. When he shot the ball, just get ready to fix the nets."

What made Delano and Hoegie a force to reckon with wasn't just their individual brilliance. It was their uncanny chemistry on the court. Larry quickly realized that they were much more than two gifted players; they were an energetic pair who elevated each other's games to another level.

The Sensational Duo of Bear Down

"Delano and Hoegie were quite a pair together," Larry said. "If there was an all-time Bear Down team, Delano and Hoegie would be the starting guards."

Together, the two guards embodied everything Bear Down stood for: relentless competition, unmatched skill, and an unyielding love for the game. They played to dominate. "They didn't back down from anyone," Larry noted. Whether it was a group of college players, former pros, or talented newcomers, Delano and Hoegie took on all challengers with the same intensity.

Their games at Bear Down often set the tone for University of Arizona practices. "Practice at the U of A started with Delano and Hoegie at Bear Down," Larry explained. The competitive edge they homed in on pickup games translated seamlessly to more structured environments, making them a nightmare for opponents and a dream for teammates.

Ahead of Their Time

For Larry, Delano and Hoegie's greatness wasn't limited to their era. "They were both ahead of their time," he said. Their style of play, interchangeable guard roles, deep shooting range, and the ability to create their own shots, would have been perfectly suited to today's modern game.

"In today's game, you wouldn't have enough NIL money to pay them," Larry quipped, referencing the lucrative Name, Image, and Likeness deals now available to college athletes. "They were that good."

Beyond their basketball skills, Delano and Hoegie left an indelible impression on Larry as people. Delano's disciplined approach to life and basketball resonated with Larry, who admired his commitment to family, education, and community. Hoegie, on the other hand, embodied a free-spirited passion for the game that reminded Larry why he fell in love with basketball in the first place.

"They were both incredible in their own ways," Larry said. "Delano was the steady, reliable shooter, and Hoegie was the unpredictable spark plug. Together, they were unstoppable."

Chapter 6

Building bonds at Bear Down – Delano, Eric Money, and Sean Elliott: The connection with Eric Money

Delano Price first met Eric Money at Bear Down Gymnasium, the legendary site of Tucson's fiercest pickup basketball games. Known for his astonishing speed and scoring prowess, Eric was a young player with a lot to prove. The two quickly established a rapport that extended far beyond the court. During the summers, they worked together at Fred Snowden's basketball camp, mentoring up-and-coming players and sharing their basketball wisdom. It was here that they encountered a lanky, headband-wearing boy named Sean Elliott, who would later become one of the greatest basketball players Tucson had ever seen.

Eric and Delano became close friends off the court as well. Eric frequently joined Delano at family gatherings, meeting Jacque, Delano's wife, and their children, Tanisha and Adrian. He even shared holiday meals at Delano's mother Mattie's house, where the Price family's warmth left a lasting impression. Decades later, Eric would reflect on their enduring friendship, noting how they still talked monthly. "Delano was one of the two or three biggest influences on me during my time at Arizona," Eric said, "and I've never forgotten what I learned from him."

Eric Money's Basketball Career

Eric Money was no ordinary player. A 6'0" guard from Detroit, Michigan, he had been a high school phenom at Kettering High School, playing alongside future NBA players like Coniel Norman

Chapter 6

and Lindsay Hairston. His talents translated seamlessly to the collegiate level, where he joined the University of Arizona as part of the first class eligible to play as freshmen. Eric made an immediate impact, averaging nearly 20 points per game during his debut season. His sophomore year saw him continue to dominate with an average of 18.1 points per game, but he declared hardship eligibility and entered the NBA draft early.

Selected by the Detroit Pistons in the second round of the 1974 NBA Draft, Eric quickly established himself as a starting point guard, particularly during the 1975–76 season when he averaged 13 points and 4.2 assists per game. His best season came in 1977–78, when he posted averages of 18.6 points and 4.7 assists per game, cementing his reputation as a top-tier NBA guard. Eric's career saw stops with the New Jersey Nets and the Philadelphia 76ers, but despite his early exit from the NBA in 1980, his legacy as a gifted scorer and playmaker was secure.

Building Sean Elliott's Foundation

It was during their time working at Fred Snowden's basketball camp that Delano and Eric began mentoring a young Sean Elliott. The boy stood out not just for his skinny frame and trademark headband but also for his hunger to learn and love for the game. "Sean loved to shoot and score the ball," Delano recalled. "Even as a kid, you could see his potential."

Sean would go on to become a two-time All-American at the University of Arizona under coach Lute Olson. A versatile small forward, he broke records and redefined what it meant to be a Wildcat. In 1989, Sean won the John R. Wooden Award,

Chapter 6

the Adolph Rupp Trophy, and the NABC Player of the Year Award. His college success led to a stellar NBA career, highlighted by an NBA championship with the San Antonio Spurs in 1999. Reflecting on his early days, Sean credited Delano for his development: "Growing up, I played countless pickup games with and against Delano, and he was always a tough competitor—hardworking, and smart about the game of basketball. He also had a deadly jumper! There's no doubt that playing with Delano made me a better basketball player."

For Delano, Bear Down Gymnasium was a cultural epicenter. "Beardown was the Mecca for us," he said. "During the summertime, you would see the best high school, college, professional, and playground players. There was a code in there that if you went into Beardown to play, you picked the best guys to assemble on your team because if you lost, you might not get back on the court to play again that day."

Delano and Hoegie Simmons were nearly unbeatable in the summer pickup games. They understood each other's game so well that their chemistry overwhelmed opponents. "We seldom lost," Delano said. Meanwhile, his daughters, Tanisha and Adrian, spent long days at Bear Down with their father. While he dominated the hardwood, they entertained themselves outside, drawing on the sidewalk with chalk or roller-skating around campus. Years later, both daughters would graduate from the University of Arizona, further solidifying the Price family's deep connection to the institution.

Chapter 6

Eric Money on Delano and Hoegie

Eric Money's admiration for Delano and Hoegie extended beyond friendship. He saw them as the epitome of Tucson basketball greatness. "Delano and Hoegie were the Curtis Jones caliber playground legends in Tucson," Eric said, drawing a comparison to the Detroit streetball legend who inspired players like George Gervin and Spencer Haywood. Curtis Jones was considered one of the greatest playground players of all time, and for Eric to put Delano and Hoegie in that company spoke volumes.

Delano's mentorship of Eric and Sean went beyond teaching them the game's physical aspects. He instilled in them a sense of discipline, respect, and love for basketball that would carry them through their careers. For Eric, Delano was a steady influence during his time at the University of Arizona. For Sean, Delano was one of the first players to push him to be better. Both men would carry those lessons into their respective careers, becoming stars.

The gatekeeper of Bear Down – Hoegie Simmons' Twofold Life

By the mid-1970s, Hoegie Simmons had firmly established himself as the "gatekeeper of Bear Down Gymnasium." A name earned not just from his sheer dominance on the court, but also from his unwavering presence, day in and day out. While Delano Price balanced basketball with a burgeoning teaching career and a growing family, Hoegie's life revolved around the gym and the game. Bear Down became his domain, where his reputation as the most formidable player in Tucson grew with each passing day.

Chapter 6

Hoegie's skills were historic. His unmatched speed, accurate shooting, and unorthodox style often left opponents floundering. But his dominance wasn't without consequences. The court could be a place of fellowship and rivalry, but for some, it became a battleground of bruised egos. Players who couldn't match Hoegie's talent often resorted to confrontation rather than concede defeat.

Confrontations On the Court

One of the most infamous incidents came on a day when a burly 6'5" player from out of town arrived at Bear Down, determined to challenge the locals. The stranger tried and failed to guard Hoegie, who dashed past him with ease, sinking shot after shot over his head. Frustrated and embarrassed, the man jumped in Hoegie's face, challenging him to settle things outside.

Hoegie, unfazed, walked calmly to his bag, pulled out a gun, and brandished it at the man. "You still want to settle this?" he asked coolly. The challenger didn't hesitate as he turned and ran out of the gym, sprinting down the street. The message was clear: Bear Down was Hoegie's territory.

In another incident, a 6'6" white player who had been thoroughly outplayed by Hoegie decided to threaten him. This time, Hoegie left the court and went to his car, returning with a tire iron in hand. Without delay, he chased the man into the parking lot, darting between cars in pursuit. It was pure chaos.

Delano, running late that day, arrived just in time to witness the spectacle. Pulling up in his car, he saw Hoegie sprinting between vehicles, wielding the tire iron as the man tried to escape.

Chapter 6

"What the hell is going on?" Delano thought as he parked and then hurried over.

The incident was the final straw for Bear Down's administrators, who barred Hoegie from the gym for good. It was a heavy blow to Hoegie, whose life revolved around the court. But for many, his legacy as the ultimate Bear Down competitor was already set in stone.

The Phantom by Night, Phenom by Day

By day, Hoegie's skills made him a basketball phenomenon. But by night, he lived a spectral existence, deeply cemented in Tucson's criminal world. While Delano was busy teaching and raising a family, Hoegie's life followed a much darker path. He moved through Tucson's seediest corners, gambling, hustling, and associating with dangerous individuals. For Hoegie, the adrenaline he chased on the court bled into his nights, where the stakes were far higher, and far deadlier.

He often found himself in Russian roulette-style situations, playing high-stakes games of chance, sometimes literally. Hoegie's life after dark was a world of whispers and shadows, where trust was a liability and survival depended on instincts honed as sharply as his jump shot.

Despite the perils of his nocturnal lifestyle, Hoegie's ability to perform on the basketball court remained undiminished. His game seemed almost impervious to the toll his street life might have taken. Teammates and opponents alike marveled at how he could stay out all night and still dominate on the court the next day.

Chapter 6

Delano often wondered how Hoegie managed it. The two would still play together occasionally, meeting up in the mornings for pickup games at other courts after Hoegie's banishment from Bear Down. Delano would pick him up, and often Hoegie would have a story to tell, though it was never the whole story.

Delano couldn't help but admire how Hoegie's game never faltered, even as he lived his life on the edge. "His game had gone to another level," Delano later said. "But what really amazed me was how he could play like that while living the way he did. He stayed sharp, no matter what."

As the years went on, the pull of the streets grew stronger for Hoegie. The adrenaline that once came from hitting game-winning shots or outplaying bigger opponents was now tied to riskier ventures. His run-ins at Bear Down were just the beginning of a series of escalating incidents that showed how deeply he was being consumed by the life he was leading.

For many, basketball was an escape. A way to find focus and purpose amid life's challenges. But for Hoegie, it seemed to be the opposite. The court became a stage for his frustrations and anger, a place where his brilliance shone but where his volatility often surfaced. As his reputation grew, so did the resentment from others who wanted to knock him off his pedestal.

Even as his street life cast a shadow over his basketball legacy, those who played with and against Hoegie during his Bear Down days continued to speak of him with awe. Players who once challenged him now told stories of his legendary performances. "He was the best player I'd ever seen at Bear Down," said one former opponent. "And I hated him for it but only because I couldn't stop him."

Chapter 6

Hoegie's banishment from Bear Down marked the end of an era. For years, he had been the gym's gatekeeper, the player everyone wanted to beat but few ever could. His absence left a void that couldn't be filled.

Delano and Hoegie's paths couldn't have been more different. While Delano's life was one of steady growth and purpose, Hoegie's was a tale of extreme, unmatched talent on the court, coupled with a dangerous descent into Tucson's underworld. Yet, despite their differences, their bond endured. Delano never judged Hoegie for his choices, and Hoegie respected Delano's commitment to his family and career.

For those who knew them both, Delano and Hoegie represented two sides of the same coin. Together, they were Bear Down's most formidable backcourt, a duo that could dominate any game they played. But off the court, their lives followed trajectories as divergent as they were intertwined.

The Impact of Daddy – A Giant Among Men

In 1979, Delano Price faced a loss that shook him to his core: the passing of his father, "Daddy." At just 28 years old, Delano was still finding his footing as a teacher at Apollo Junior High School, balancing his promising career, family life, and a love for basketball. Yet, the death of the man who had been his rock of strength and wisdom left a void that would forever alter Delano's life.

Daddy passed away at the age of 73 from heart disease, but his legacy lived on in the hearts of his children. His death impacted

Chapter 6

Delano so deeply that, for two months, he barely spoke. After teaching his classes during the day, Delano would return home to the modest house on Genova and sit silently on the little back porch, lost in thought. Grief, guilt, and reverence for the man who had been his father swirled inside him, leaving Delano to reflect on Daddy's life, sacrifices, and enduring influence.

For Delano, Daddy represented a parent, and he was a living endorsement to resilience and survival. Born and raised in the segregated South, Daddy had endured systemic racism, poverty, and unimaginable hardship. The challenges Daddy overcame just to see Delano and his siblings grow up were nothing short of heroic.

Daddy's passing left a profound mark on the family. He had been the balance to Mattie's fiery tenacity, providing calm and strength when emotions ran high. "The family was never the same when Daddy left," Delano later said, underscoring the profound void his father's absence created.

The day before Daddy passed, Delano's wife, Jacque, visited him at his bedside. She returned home that evening to tell Delano that his father didn't look well and urged him to go see him. But Delano, still stewing with frustration after a basketball league championship game in which he had fouled out and been ejected, told her he would visit Daddy in the morning.

That night, Delano struggled with guilt over the game, where his team had been left to play with only four players after his ejection. He had shattered a glass in anger on his way out of the gym, a rare moment of lost composure for someone so typically even-tempered. Exhausted, he promised himself he would visit his father first thing in the morning.

Chapter 6

But by morning, it was too late. Daddy had passed. Delano never got the chance to say goodbye, and that regret stayed with him for years. It was a hard lesson in the fleeting nature of time and the importance of prioritizing what truly matters.

Before he passed, Daddy gathered Delano and his brothers Alex, Randle, Raymond, and Michael by his bedside. His message was simple but profound: "Take care of your mother. Don't let her want for anything." Daddy's words reflected his lifelong commitment to his family, ensuring that even in his absence, Mattie would be supported and loved.

Daddy had lived his life with integrity. Before his death, he had paid off all his debts, including credit cards and gambling dues, ensuring that he left nothing unfinished. To Delano, these final acts of responsibility symbolized Daddy's transformation and the pride he took in his role as the family's pillar.

Delano often reminisced about the special moments he shared with his father. As a child, Daddy would walk Delano to and from Amphi Little League baseball games, cheering him on from the sidelines. Baseball was Delano's first love, and Daddy was his biggest supporter. One game stood out when Delano's pitching was so dominant that an opposing player accused him of tampering with the ball. Daddy marched out to the mound, standing tall against the coaches who questioned his son's skill. "He's just that good," Daddy said, defending Delano with unwavering confidence.

Daddy's pride in Delano extended beyond sports. When Delano was at Phoenix College, struggling to make ends meet, Daddy's social security check became a lifeline. Though modest, the money helped Delano pay his share of the $120 monthly rent he split with teammates. Daddy's support wasn't just financial;

it was representational of his belief in Delano's promise and fortitude to help him succeed.

Throughout his life, Delano only ever described three men as being larger-than-life to him: Wilt Chamberlain, Willie Mays, and Daddy.

As a boy, Delano had the unforgettable experience of sneaking into the San Francisco Giants' locker room at Hi Corbett Field during spring training. There, he saw Willie Mays, his baseball idol, shirtless and preparing to play. To young Delano, Mays was "like seeing God in the flesh." Years later, as a college student, Delano met Wilt Chamberlain at the Phoenix Suns' Veterans Memorial Coliseum. Standing next to the towering basketball legend, Delano asked if he could touch his arm. Wilt laughed and obliged. Delano described the moment as surreal, saying Chamberlain felt like "steel."

Yet, of these three giants, it was Daddy who left the deepest mark. His love, sacrifice, and dedicated presence shaped Delano in ways no sports hero ever could. Daddy's influence was woven into the fabric of Delano's values, work ethic, and commitment to his own family.

Even in moments of lightheartedness, Daddy's pride in his role as a provider shone through. Delano fondly recalled how excited Daddy would get when his social security check arrived each month. Playfully, Delano would act like he was going to take the check, prompting Daddy to laugh and exclaim, "Get away from that check, mane!" The shared laughter in those moments reflected their deep bond, a blend of respect and love that would stay with Delano forever.

Chapter 6

Delano's love for baseball and his early talent on the field were thanks in large part to Daddy's encouragement. As a standout player in the Amphi Little League, Delano's skills as a pitcher and hitter drew attention. But it was Daddy's support, walking him to games, cheering him on, and protecting him from doubters, that made those memories so cherished.

These formative experiences taught Delano the importance of being present, a lesson he carried into his role as a father and educator. Just as Daddy had supported him, Delano strove to be a source of stability and encouragement for his own children.

At Daddy's funeral, Hoegie stood alongside Delano and the Price family, offering his support. For Delano, the moment was a reminder of the connections that bound them all, even amid loss. Daddy's death was a watershed moment, marking the end of an era for the family. Yet, his lessons, values, and spirit lived on in the children he raised.

Delano's silence in the months following Daddy's passing was sheer reverence. In the quiet moments on that back porch, he reflected on the life of a man who had given so much and asked for so little in return.

Chapter 6

Doris, A.D. Price, Mattie C. Price

Chapter 6

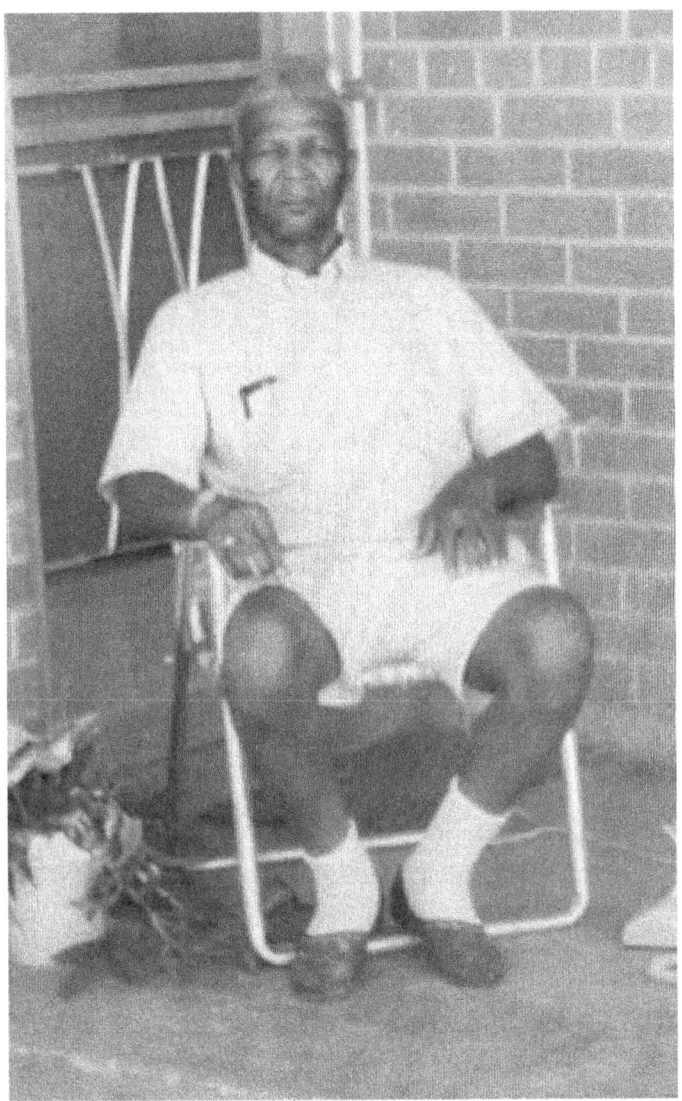

A.D. Price

CHAPTER 7

HOEGIE'S DESCENT – THE GAME SLIPS AWAY

By the late 1980s, Hoegie Simmons found himself at a crossroads. For two decades, basketball had defined him, providing structure, identity, and hope. Yet, the game that had once opened doors for him now seemed determined to shut them. Hoegie's dream of playing professionally had dimmed, and with every missed opportunity, the allure of the streets grew stronger.

Hoegie had long believed that his talent on the court would secure him a place in the professional ranks. His athleticism with a 45-inch vertical, relentless willpower, and unusual skill set were undeniable. Yet, the harsh realities of the basketball world, a mix of politics, timing, and opportunity, had other plans.

The sting of rejection was especially acute in his hometown of Tucson. In 1978, when the newly formed Western Basketball Association (WBA) held tryouts for the Tucson Gunners, Hoegie was there, ready to claim his spot. He was easily the best guard in the camp, hypnotizing onlookers with his ability to fly past defenders and shoot with exactitude. But when the roster was announced, Hoegie's name was nowhere to be found. The team's coach, Herb Brown, opted for other guards, including Gerald Henderson, who would go on to have a solid NBA career.

"Man, I thought for sure somebody would draft me," Hoegie later reflected. "A bunch of guys I used to tear up on the court made it to the NBA. It used to make me sick. Couldn't none of them stop me."

For Hoegie, the rejection was a personal affront. Watching players, he knew he could outplay thrive in the NBA while he struggled to make ends meet was a bitter pill to swallow. "I never got my shot," he said. "I think I would have accepted it back then if I got a shot and blew it, but I never got it."

As the 1980s progressed, Hoegie began to drift further from the game and deeper into street life. He became embroiled in the crack cocaine epidemic that swept through America's inner cities, particularly devastating African American communities. Crack was cheap, addictive, and incredibly profitable, drawing countless individuals into its destructive orbit.

For Hoegie, the transition from basketball to the drug trade was gradual. At first, he justified it to an end, a way to support himself while waiting for another shot at basketball. But as the opportunities in basketball became more evanescent, the lure of fast money grew powerful. The streets became his new arena, one where survival depended not on jump shots and assists but on wits and ruthlessness.

Chapter 7

The Crack Epidemic

By the early 1980s, crack cocaine had infiltrated cities across the United States. Its affordability and immediate euphoric effects made it wildly popular, especially in communities already ravaged by economic decline and systemic neglect. Selling crack required little startup capital and offered massive returns, making it a tempting option for many young men like Hoegie who felt excluded from traditional avenues of success.

The consequences, however, were devastating. The drug left a trail of addiction, violence, and broken families in its wake. In neighborhoods like those where Hoegie operated, the crack epidemic became synonymous with despair. Crime rates soared, and the War on Drugs, spearheaded by President Ronald Reagan's administration, disproportionately targeted African American communities. Harsh sentencing laws and mandatory minimums sent thousands of small-time dealers and users to prison, exacerbating the cycle of poverty and incarceration.

Yet, even as he asserted his dominance in this new arena, the toll of his choices was evident. The camaraderie and joy of basketball were being replaced by the cold, transactional nature of the streets. Hoegie's relationships with others grew strained, and the sense of purpose he once found in the game was slipping away.

A System Stacked Against Him

The War on Drugs, which intensified during the Reagan era, cast a long shadow over individuals like Hoegie. The federal government's focus on punishment over rehabilitation led to skyrocketing incarceration rates, particularly for African American men. While crack dealers were vilified as the root cause of urban decay, little attention was paid to the systemic factors: job loss, underfunded schools, and racial inequality that had created fertile ground for the drug's proliferation.

Hoegie was caught on this web, both a product and a casualty of his circumstances. The same society that had cheered him on the basketball court now viewed him as a criminal. The promise of the American Dream, so tantalizingly close during his basketball career, had become a bitter irony.

By the end of the 1980s, the weight of Hoegie's choices began to catch up with him. The streets, like the basketball court, were unforgiving. Friends and acquaintances fell victim to addiction, violence, and incarceration. The sense of invincibility that had defined Hoegie's early years was giving way to a harsh reality: the streets offered no safety nets, no second chances.

Still, Hoegie clung to the remnants of his basketball identity. On the court, he was "The Gatekeeper," a player who commanded respect and fear. But off the court, he was a man adrift, searching for purpose in a world that seemed determined to deny him one.

For Hoegie, the 1980s marked the slow unraveling of a dream. Basketball, once his salvation, had become a distant memory, replaced by the harsh realities of the crack epidemic. Yet, even as he descended deeper into the streets, a part of him remained tethered to the game. It was the one thing that had ever made sense to him, the one place where he felt truly alive.

But the game, like the streets, had its limits. And for Hoegie, the cost of living on the edge was becoming increasingly steep.

Chapter 7

The man who had once soared above the rim was now grappling with the weight of choices that threatened to pull him under. The crack epidemic had claimed countless lives, and Hoegie's path was growing more perilous with each passing day.

Delano's Decade of the 1980s

The 1980s marked a transformative chapter in Delano Price's life, as he continued to grow professionally, personally, and athletically. After eight impactful years teaching at Apollo Junior High School, Delano transitioned to Sunnyside High School, an institution where many of his former Apollo students advanced. It was a new challenge, a fresh start, and an opportunity to make a difference in a broader arena.

Sunnyside High School: A New Era

Delano began his tenure at Sunnyside as a social studies teacher, bringing with him a reputation for passionate teaching and strong leadership. His impact wasn't confined to the classroom. Shortly after joining Sunnyside, he became Tucson's first black head varsity basketball coach, carving out another chapter in Tucson's basketball history. Although

Delano was an exceptional player in his prime, coaching presented challenges he hadn't anticipated.

"I had high expectations for my players," Delano admitted. "Sometimes I forgot they weren't me, Hoegie Simmons, or Kenny Ball. I had to learn to meet them where they were." Sunnyside, unlike powerhouse programs, didn't have an abundance of natural talent, but Delano poured his heart into the role, emphasizing fundamentals, and teamwork.

Coaching and Scrimmaging with Hoegie

During his five-year stint as head coach, Delano often leaned on his lifelong bond with Hoegie Simmons. Sometimes, when Sunnyside players were scrimmaging, Delano would call Hoegie to come play. Together, they would form a backcourt during practices that left the players in awe.

"He'd walk in like it was nothing, and we'd be out there going to work like any other time on the court," Delano recalled with a laugh. Players who weren't born when Delano and Hoegie won their championship in 1969 would find themselves mesmerized by their chemistry.

"They were unstoppable," said Marc Johnson, one of Delano's standout players who went on to play professionally in France. "Coach Price and Hoegie were playing and teaching us with every move."

While Delano remained rooted in teaching and mentoring, Hoegie brought an edge that challenged the players in unique ways. Deron Johnson, a Sunnyside legend who scored over 2,100 career points and later played for the University of Arizona, summed it up best:

"Delano was like a father figure. He'd hoop with us, but he'd always ask about our grades afterward. Hoegie? He represented the other side of the track. After we played ball, he might shoot dice with us."

Chapter 7

"Together, they were like a backcourt in life, balancing each other out."

The Faculty Game

One of the most memorable moments of Delano's time at Sunnyside came during a faculty-versus-varsity basketball game in 1989. Designed as a fundraiser, the event pitted Delano and a ragtag team of out-of-shape faculty members against a varsity squad led by the formidable Deron Johnson.

The gym was packed with students, eager to see their varsity stars dominate. Delano, however, had other plans. On the first play of the game, he launched a long three-pointer that swished through the net. From there, it was a scoring clinic.

Delano, at 38 years old, finished the game with 38 points, showcasing his trademark jumper, crafty drives, and a sharp wit that left the varsity players shaking their heads. After the game, Delano went back to teaching, but not before leaving two names on his classroom chalkboard: "Payday" and "Bigtime," nicknames he had told the varsity players to call him after his dominant performance.

The players laughed about it for weeks, but the memory stood as tribute to Delano's enduring competitiveness and his ability to connect with his students through basketball.

Chapter 7

The YMCA Incident

While Delano was widely respected for his calm demeanor and professionalism, there were moments when his fiery competitive spirit got the better of him. One such incident occurred during a pickup game at the YMCA, where Delano's team lost to an inferior squad led by an eccentric, goofy-looking player.

As Delano walked off the court, visibly frustrated, the man began taunting him.

"Aren't you Delano Price? The hotshot superstar? Well, today you got your ass kicked!"

Delano tried to brush him off, but the taunts continued. Finally, in a fit of fury, Delano pushed the man away by his face. The man retaliated with threats, mimicking a gun with his hand and warning Delano to "look over his shoulder."

Infuriated, Delano ran back and punched the man, splitting his face open. Blood splattered across the gym, and the man called the police. When they arrived, the man gloated, claiming he would ruin Delano's career. Though the incident resulted in a civil compromise and a $400 medical bill, Delano carried the weight of the event for a few months.

"I let my temper get the better of me," he reflected. "But sometimes people forget that even teachers and coaches are human."

Chapter 7

The Full-Court Battles with Pat Frink

Another memorable connection Delano made during the 1980s was with Pat Frink, a former NBA player who had a brief career with the Cincinnati Royals. Delano first encountered Pat during a pickup game at the YMCA, where Pat's sharpshooting and relentless play immediately caught Delano's attention.

"He was like the White Shadow," Delano joked. "He could score from anywhere, and he didn't back down from anyone."

The two developed a mutual respect and became colleagues when Pat joined the faculty at Sunnyside High School. Their shared love for basketball led to regular full-court, one-on-one games during their free periods. Despite their age and responsibilities, the games were fiercely competitive, with each man pushing the other to his limits.

One day, during a particularly heated matchup, the two wrestled for a rebound, ending up on the gym floor grappling for the ball. Just as the scuffle reached its peak, the school principal, Carl Brunenkant, walked in. The two men quickly assured him that everything was fine, though their passion for the game was evident.

Pat and Delano's friendship extended beyond the court. Pat even introduced Delano to Oscar Robertson, his former teammate with the Cincinnati Royals. Their bond, however, was tested when Pat was arrested for growing marijuana in his backyard, an incident that ultimately led to his departure from Sunnyside.

Amid his professional and athletic endeavors, Delano's family remained his anchor. The early 1980s marked another significant milestone for the Price household with the birth of their third child, Márquez Delano Price. Welcoming Márquez into the family brought joy and a renewed sense of purpose to Delano and Jacque, who were already raising their daughters, Tanisha and Adrian.

Delano instinctively knew that the 1980s would be a particularly pivotal decade, especially as a father to a Black son. The era's challenges were impossible to ignore with rising racial disparities, economic inequality, and the devastating grip of the crack epidemic on communities across the nation. He watched these forces wreak havoc on neighborhoods, tearing apart families and, most heartbreakingly, ensnaring Hoegie, his closest friend and longtime basketball partner.

Seeing Hoegie, a man of immense talent and potential, struggle under the weight of the volatile street life underscored the urgency for Delano to provide his son Márquez with the foundation and guidance necessary to navigate a world fraught with pitfalls. To Delano, fatherhood was a generational mission to break cycles of disenfranchisement and create opportunities for his children to thrive.

Delano often reflected on the lessons imparted by his own father, "Daddy," whose strength and stamina had shaped Delano into the man he was. He was determined to be a pillar of support for Márquez, teaching him discipline, integrity, and the value of education. Delano understood the critical role a father played, especially in the Black community, where systemic challenges had robbed many children of paternal guidance. He resolved that Márquez would never experience the absence of a father figure and would always know the security of having a role model close at hand.

Jacque, after graduating from the University of Arizona with a degree in sociology, played an equally crucial role in creating a nurturing environment for their children. Together, Delano and Jacque were partners in parenting, determined to raise strong, compassionate, and thoughtful children. Jacque's ability to balance work, family, and personal growth inspired her children and reinforced the values the couple held dear.

Delano's experiences on the basketball court, in the classroom, and as a community leader further reinforced his understanding of what it meant to be a father during such a tumultuous time. He had seen firsthand how the absence of strong parental figures could leave young men vulnerable to the allure of the streets. Watching Hoegie struggle was both a source of heartache and a reminder of the stakes at play. Delano saw his role as a father to combat the destructive forces gripping his community, one child at a time.

Márquez's arrival added a new layer of responsibility to Delano's life. He approached fatherhood with the same dedication and intensity he brought to the basketball court and classroom, often drawing strength from the example set by "Daddy." While he continued to mentor students and coach basketball, his greatest joy and most important role was at home, raising a family that would thrive despite the challenges of the era.

Fatherhood was about being present for Delano as well as intentional and proactive. Whether playing ball in the driveway with Márquez, encouraging Tanisha and Adrian in their academic pursuits, or simply being a steadfast presence in their lives, Delano ensured his children had the tools to succeed. He wanted Márquez

CHAPTER 7

to understand his worth, to rise above societal expectations, and to know that his father would always be there to guide him.

Delano's commitment to his family became the cornerstone of his legacy. As he balanced work, community leadership, and parenting, he found his greatest pride in watching his children grow and thrive. The lessons he taught, the love he gave, and the example he set were all part of a broader mission to uplift not only his family but the community. Through the highs and lows of his career, Delano always found his greatest joy at home, surrounded by the love and laughter of Jacque, Tanisha, Adrian, and Márquez. This family-centered approach not only defined his 1980s but laid the groundwork for the values and accomplishments his children would carry forward into their own lives.

As the decade ended, Delano transitioned from coaching to administration, becoming the first Black administrator as assistant principal at Sunnyside. Though he stepped away from the sidelines, his influence on the school and its students remained profound. He continued to mentor young athletes, offering guidance on and off the court.

In 1989, fate brought one of Tucson's brightest basketball stars, Deron Johnson, to Sunnyside. Though Delano was no longer the coach, he played an integral role in shaping Deron's journey, proving once again that his reach extended far beyond the classroom and the court.

Deron summed up Delano's legacy best: "Delano is a town father figure. He's been like a surrogate to kids growing up in Tucson for decades. He was a hell of a hooper too."

Chapter 7

The Rise of Paula Dotson: A Star Shaped by Mentorship

Paula Dotson's basketball prowess emerged from humble beginnings in Tucson's Santa Rosa Projects, where she spent her childhood perfecting her skills on the court at the Santa Rosa Recreation Center. She was a forerunner for women's basketball in Tucson during the 1980s, defying gender norms and setting records that still stand today. With a natural flair for the game and a work ethic shaped by relentless practice, Paula became one of Tucson High School's most iconic athletes. Her journey, deeply intertwined with the mentorship of Delano Price and Hoegie Simmons, elevated her from a local prodigy to a legend whose influence continues to resonate.

The Foundation of a Basketball Phenom

Paula's basketball journey began in unconventional fashion. She learned to play street ball by going one-on-one against boys, developing an edge and toughness that would define her game. At just seven years old, she joined the boys' basketball team in the Police Athletic League and later played Tucson Youth Football and Little League baseball with boys.

Her first real chance to play on an organized girls' basketball team came during the summer before her freshman year at Tucson High School, when she joined the Salvation Army League. Her talent was undeniable. Coach Will Kreamer recalled, "We knew she was tough when she started school." Breaking barriers, Paula secured a starting position on Tucson High's varsity team before she even played her first game.

In her varsity debut, Paula scored 17 points against Buena High School, the top team in the AAA-South division. From there, she never looked back, averaging 24 points per game over her first five matches. As a sophomore, Paula led the AAA-South in scoring, averaging 19.6 points per game. She topped the division in scoring every year of her high school career, culminating in a staggering 26.6 points per game as a senior. Her astounding play caught the attention of 50 college recruiters, solidifying her reputation as one of Arizona's brightest stars.

Meeting Hoegie Simmons: The Santa Rosa Connection

Paula's life changed when she crossed paths with Hoegie Simmons at the Santa Rosa Recreation Center. One day, while Paula and a group of children were playing basketball, Hoegie arrived. The kids, captivated by his reputation, challenged him to a game, all of them against him. What followed was a masterclass in basketball brilliance. Hoegie, with his uncanny ability to hit every shot, left an indelible impression on the young Paula.

"I swear Hoegie didn't miss a shot that day, against us or the grown men who played after us," Paula recalled. "I had never seen anything like that on the court."

Hoegie's regular appearances in Santa Rosa became a source of inspiration for Paula. Watching him dismantle opponents with his extraordinary skill and unmatched precision fueled her own basketball dreams. "He was just incredible," Paula said. "He made me believe that anything was possible on the court if you worked hard enough."

Paula Meets Delano Price: A Lifelong Mentor

While honing her skills at the YMCA, Paula encountered another Tucson legend: Delano Price. Delano immediately recognized Paula's talent and began mentoring her. Paula admired Delano not just for his pure jump shot and impeccable fundamentals, but also for his character. "I really looked up to Delano as a father figure," she said. "I wanted to shoot just like him, and I even played in sweatpants because he did."

Delano and Paula quickly formed a bond, both on and off the court. During pickup games at the YMCA, Delano always picked Paula first for his team, recognizing her ability to compete with the best. Their harmony on the court was unified, with Paula learning the intricacies of the game by playing alongside one of Tucson's finest.

The mentorship extended beyond the court. Delano's focus on education and discipline had a deep influence on Paula, who credited him with helping her pilot with the pressures of being a high-profile athlete. "Delano taught me so much about basketball and about life," Paula said. "I still look up to and love that man today."

CHAPTER 7

The Legacy of "Popcorn"

Paula's game was a spectacle. Her quick drives, hanging double-pumps, and between-the-legs dribbles captivated audiences. She was equally adept at scoring and distributing the ball, making her a dual threat. Opponents labeled her a "showboater" due to her flashy style, but Paula shrugged off the criticism. "I wasn't showing off," she said. "That was just me. It was my style of play, my talent. I was out there to play the best game I could, and I liked to show them what I could do."

Her prolific scoring earned her the nickname "Popcorn" from her teammates, who marveled at her ability to light up the scoreboard with ease. She routinely scored 30 and 40 points in games, often while being double or triple teamed. Her combination of strength, quickness, and versatility set her apart from her peers.

By the time she graduated, Paula had made history. She was named to every All-Metro team since its inception in 1980, led the AAA-South in scoring during consecutive high school seasons, and was crowned Tucson High's most celebrated girls' basketball player. Paula's coach, Jerry Curtis, summed up her legacy: "She was a natural talent. She not only shot the ball well, she was an assist person and could rebound. She could do it all."

Paula's stellar high school career earned her a scholarship to the University of Missouri, where she continued to excel on the court. Her achievements at Tucson High, including state scoring records that still stand, cemented her status as one of the most talented players to emerge from Arizona.

Even as her basketball journey took her beyond Tucson, Paula remained deeply connected to her roots. She credited her time playing with Delano and Hoegie as instrumental in her development, both as a player and as a person. "I got to learn greatness firsthand with Delano and Hoegie," Paula said. "They showed me what it meant to be a competitor and a leader."

Paula Dotson's journey from the Santa Rosa Recreation Center to becoming an all-state high school star and collegiate athlete is an illustration of her talent, work ethic, and the mentorship she received from legends like Delano and Hoegie. Her story is a reminder of the transformative power of sports and the importance of community in nurturing talent.

Today, Paula's legacy lives on in the records she set, the players she inspired, and the lessons she imparted to others. Her name is etched in Tucson's basketball history alongside Delano and Hoegie, who remain her lifelong mentors and friends. "Paula is in the pantheon of exceptional athletes," Delano said.

Chapter 7

Hoegie outside

Chapter 7

Hoegie with family

Chapter 7

Jacque Price, Adrian Price, Marquez Price, Tanisha Price/Delano Price, Adrian Price, Marquez Price, Tanisha Price at Disneyland/Delano and Marquez mowing the lawn/Delano, baby Marquez, Tanisha, Adrian at house on Genova.

Chapter 7

Tanisha, Delano, Jacque, Márquez, Adrian/Delano, Jacque, Tanisha, Adrian, Márquez at Tanisha's 8th grade graduation/Adrian, Jacque, Marquez, Tanisha at Disneyland/Jacque, Delano, Mattie C. Price, Adrian, Tanisha, baby Márquez at house on Linden

CHAPTER 7

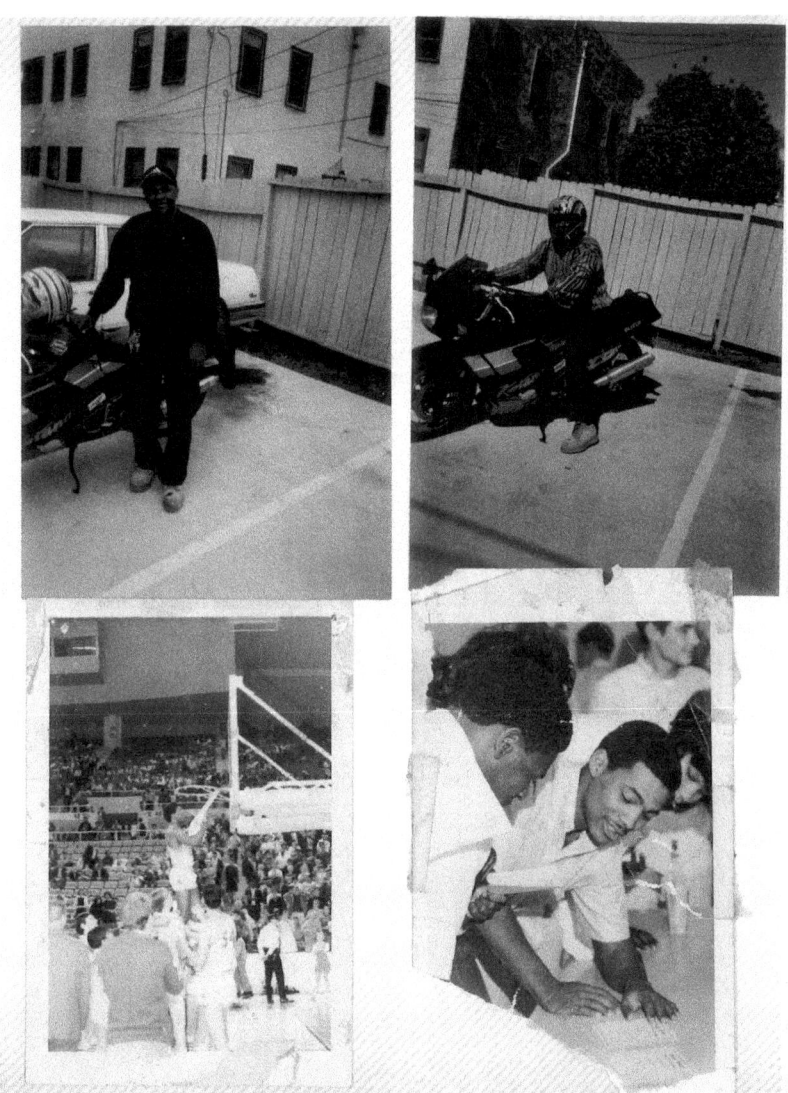

Hoegie with his "Cycles"/Hoegie cutting down '69 state title nets/Delano in class at Tucson High School

Chapter 7

Hoegie's mother Mary Simmons, Delano's mother Mattie C. Price, and Chuco Miranda's mother Alice Miranda

Chapter 7

Delano and Sean Elliott in the Tucson Weekly

CHAPTER 7

*Delano Price with Sunnyside High
School team (team picture)*

Chapter 7

Delano coaching at Sunnyside

Chapter 7

Coach Price, Sunnyside team picture.

CHAPTER 7

Sunnyside coach gets first victory

Chapter 7

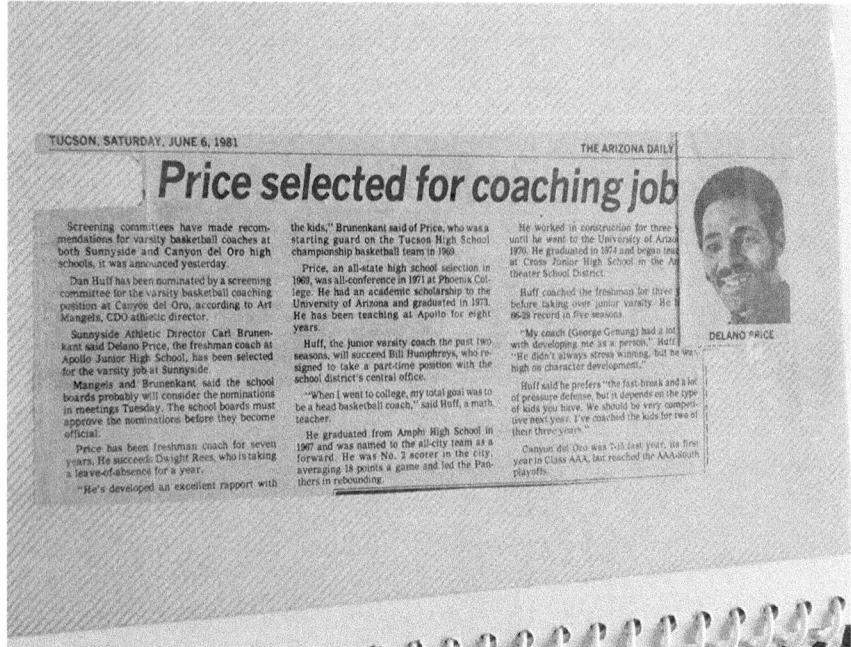

Price selected for coaching job at Sunnyside (first Black boys basketball coach in Tucson, Arizona)

Chapter 7

Sunnyside team picture with coach Price

Chapter 7

Apollo has the ball.

Coach Price

Coach Price shows his style.

Basketball
By Margaret Cardenas

The basketball season for the last 9th-grade team at Apollo has come to an end. This team had pride in their school and played each game with enthusiasm. They practiced for many hours and showed the schools around Tucson that they had spirit and pride. Losing wouldn't get them down and make them quit. Instead they showed their great sportsmanship and kept on trying. That's why we all here at Apollo should thank this team for representing our school with Eagle Pride.

Team members are: Jerry Cruz, Mike Page, Jerry Davis, James Valdez, Eddie Godoy, Ken Harper, Kevin Pollard, Rene Valencia, Richard Encinas, Greg Gastellum and Victor Meranzio. Manager was Oscar Valenzuela.

Thanks to Mr. Price for coaching a great team!

Basketball cheers
By Lupe Herrera

The 1980-81 basketball cheers are Letty [?]ido—captain, Alexis Lim—co-captain, [K]im Tang, Mercy Robles, Veronica [J]uarez and Susana Ng. They've been [p]racticing hard and working on new [ch]eers and stunts for their games. For the [g]ames they've got to be on their best [be]havior and well-mannered, since they [re]present our school, Apollo Jr. High. In order to be a cheerleader you don't [on]ly have to be good but you also need [go]od grades and must know how to behave right during schooltime. Our cheerleaders have a lot of spirit and pride in their school!

Basketball interview with Mr. Price
By Ansonia Pace

Sonia: "How many years have you been teaching?"

Price: "I have taught school for eigh[t] years, all at Apollo."

Sonia: "How many years have yo[u] been coaching basketball?"

Price: "I have coached basketball f[or] seven years."

Sonia: "What university did you atten[d] and what type of degree did yo[u] receive?"

Price: "I graduated from the Univ[er]sity of Arizona in 1973 with a BA degr[ee] I received a master's degree in 1977."

Sonia: "Did you play any sports [in] college? What were they?"

Price: "I played basketball in colleg[e]

Sonia: "Tell me a little bit about y[our] life."

Price: "I was born in Gary, Indiana [in] 1951. I came to Tucson when I wa[s] years old. I attended elementary, ju[nior] high and high school here in Tucson. [I'm] married to my high school sweethe[art]. We have two daughters.

"I love it here at Apollo."

Sunnyside school write up of coach Price

Chapter 7

Coach Price team picture with Apollo Junior High

Chapter 7

Coach Price coaching at Apollo

Chapter 7

Coach Price coaching at Sunnyside

Chapter 7

Delano Price teaching at Sunnyside High School

CHAPTER 8

THE LEAN ON ME ERA AT CATALINA HIGH SCHOOL

When Delano Price arrived at Catalina High School in the early 1990s as an administrator, he walked into a situation as volatile as Eastside High School from the movie "Lean on Me" that was based on a true story. Catalina was a school in disarray, plagued by gangs, drugs, and violence. For Delano, it was an opportunity to make a difference. Much like Joe Clark, the protagonist of "Lean on Me," had done.

As gang culture from Los Angeles spread across the country, fueled by the crack epidemic and glorification of gang life in media, schools like Catalina became battlegrounds. The Crips and Bloods, originally rooted in South Central Los Angeles, began to influence Tucson's youth through gang propaganda, entertainment, and street-level recruitment. Catalina High School

Chapter 8

reflected this cultural and social unrest. Students and staff alike were intimidated by the escalating gang presence, and a culture of apathy had settled over the campus.

Delano's journey to Catalina High itself displayed his flexibility and character. Having served as an administrator at Sunnyside High School, Delano had already established himself as a community leader. Despite being overlooked for a higher-ranking position in Sunnyside School District due to political favoritism, Delano's reputation and qualifications spoke for themselves. His departure from Sunnyside was met with a rare and powerful demonstration of support: 300 faculty members, parents, and students marched on the central administration building to protest the loss of such a dedicated and gifted educator.

This groundswell of community support didn't go unnoticed. The Tucson Unified School District (TUSD) assistant superintendent, Jerry Minjarez, recruited Delano to join TUSD as an administrator. Delano accepted, becoming an administrator at Catalina High School, ready to tackle the challenges ahead.

Catalina High School in Crisis

Catalina High had become a hotbed of gang activity, where Crips and Bloods influences were intense. Fueled by media portrayals and the spread of gang culture across the United States, gang members flaunted their affiliation through colors, hand signs, and intimidation tactics. As in Lean on Me, the environment in Catalina called for radical change and strong leadership. Delano, with his unrelenting work ethic, charismatic leadership, and no-nonsense attitude, was the right man for the job.

Chapter 8

Delano wasted no time asserting his authority. On his first day at Catalina, he encountered what would be his initiation into the chaos of the school. He walked into the weight room, a place notorious for being a gathering spot for the roughest students and disengaged campus monitors. When a monitor casually referred to the space as the "initiation hall," Delano immediately asked what that meant.

One of the students explained that anyone entering the weight room needed to "prove" themselves by bench-pressing a certain weight. Delano, already in peak physical condition from his weightlifting regimen, decided to play along. He shed his suit jacket and flipped his tie over his shoulder, feigning a novice demeanor. When the students loaded 250 pounds onto the bench, Delano pumped it ten times.

The stunned silence that followed was broken by murmurs of admiration. Delano had earned the respect of the weight room's toughest circle, and that moment set the tone for his tenure at Catalina. "I wasn't just here to talk about change," Delano later said. "I wanted them to know I could meet them on their level and lead them to a better one."

The Joe Clark Persona

Delano's leadership style bore striking similarities to Joe Clark's in "Lean on Me." Like Clark, Delano believed in accountability, respect, and creating a sense of pride among students. He walked the hallways in a suit and tie every day, exuding professionalism and commanding respect. His sharp attire and confident demeanor

CHAPTER 8

earned him the title of "the most dapper dresser in TUSD," an accolade even mentioned in his performance appraisals.

However, the challenges of Catalina weighed heavily on Delano. He faced resistance from faculty, skepticism from parents, and outright defiance from some students. The socioeconomic issues impacting the school, such as poverty, broken homes, and exposure to gang violence, added layers of complexity to his role.

The Rise of Gang Culture

The early 1990s were a pivotal time for the proliferation of gang lifestyle throughout America. The Bloods and Crips, originally formed in South Central Los Angeles, began to expand their reach into smaller cities like Tucson. Fueled by the crack cocaine epidemic and glorified in music and films such as "Colors" and "Boyz n the Hood," gang life became a disturbing aspiration for many young people.

At Catalina, gang affiliations were evident in the colors students wore, the graffiti tagging the school's walls, and the increasing presence of drugs on campus. Delano, deeply attuned to the cultural influences at play, recognized that gang life appealed to students who felt alienated and powerless. He knew he needed to offer an alternative, a sense of belonging that wasn't mired in violence and self-destruction.

Delano's approach to turning Catalina around involved a combination of discipline, mentorship, and community engagement. He walked the campus daily, speaking with students, breaking up fights, and building relationships. He made a point

Chapter 8

to learn students' names and their stories, establishing a personal connection that was often missing in their lives.

Like Joe Clark, Delano believed in holding students to high standards. He introduced programs to improve school spirit, organized community events, and worked tirelessly to stimulate a sense of pride in being a Catalina student. He also implemented stricter policies to address truancy, drug use, and gang activity.

One of Delano's most impactful initiatives was organizing Saturday workshops for at-risk students, focusing on academic tutoring and life skills. These sessions became a space where students could see a path beyond the streets. Delano also extended his mentorship to parents, encouraging them to engage in their children's education and emphasizing the importance of family stability.

Despite his success, the pressures of Catalina's environment took a toll on Delano. The school's transformation wasn't immediate, and the daily battles against gangs, drugs, and systemic inequities were exhausting. Delano often worked long hours, sometimes staying on campus well into the evening to ensure the safety and well-being of his students.

The broader context of the crack epidemic and the War on Drugs only heightened the challenges. The U.S. prison population was skyrocketing, disproportionately affecting Black and Latino communities. Many of Catalina's students had family members caught up in the criminal justice system, creating a cycle of despair that Delano sought to break.

By the mid-1990s, Catalina High School was no longer the chaotic institution it had been when Delano arrived. While challenges remained, the school had made significant strides in improving safety, academics, and community engagement. Delano's leadership left an enduring mark, not just on the school but on the lives of countless students.

One of the students Delano mentored during his time at Catalina later said, "Mr. Price was someone who cared about us when no one else did. He gave us hope."

For Delano, Catalina was a chapter in a lifelong mission to uplift and empower young people. As he reflected on his time there, he often said, "Catalina was a calling."

Elder Kings of the Court

By the early 1990s, Delano and Hoegie had cemented their status as Tucson's "elder kings of the court." In their early 40s, they continued to dominate on basketball courts across the city, refusing to pass the torch just yet. Their favorite haunts were the downtown YMCA and the Randolph Recreation Center, which had become a mecca for pickup basketball, rivaling Bear Down Gymnasium's heyday. Randolph attracted elite talent, including University of Arizona stars like Chris Mills, Sean Rooks, Khalid Reeves, Deron Johnson, and Corey Williams. Despite their ages, Delano and Hoegie were still regarded as top-tier competitors, their skills honed by decades of dedication to the game.

The duo's enduring bond was anchored by their friendly wager: Who would outlast the other in basketball? "Me and Delano made a vow that we were going to play until we can't play anymore," Hoegie said in an interview at the time. "It's in my blood. I'll play

Chapter 8

until I can't walk. I play six days a week. The only time I don't play is Sundays, and that's because the gym is closed."

The respect they commanded was unmistakable. Former Pima College coach Mike Lopez described them as "living legends," and their exploits on the court backed up the claim.

Delano's jump shot was as lethal as ever. His reputation as a consistent and efficient scorer kept him on the radar of younger players who knew better than to leave him unguarded. "Delano was a guy that when he shoots, he's deadly. You've got to always be on him," said Gerald Jeffery, a former standout player and longtime friend.

Though Delano's game was less flashy than Hoegie's, it was no less effective. His precise footwork, calm demeanor, and ability to create space for his jumper made him a nightmare for defenders. At an age when many players had retired their sneakers, Delano continued to school players half his age with a jumper that seemed to defy the passage of time.

If Delano's game was a symphony, Hoegie's was a rock concert. Known for his gravity-defying athleticism and audacious moves, Hoegie continued to awe audiences with plays that seemed impossible for someone his size. At just 5'7", his ability to challenge and often humiliate players nearly two feet taller became the stuff of legend.

One such moment was recounted by Jeffery, who remembered a time at Bear Down Gym when 6'10" University of Arizona center Tom Lee came barreling down the court for a dunk. "He went down to dunk on Hoegie, and Hoegie was under the basket," Jeffery said. "Hoegie took one step and blocked the shot. But he didn't just block it, he threw it. This guy was 6-10, and Hoegie was 5-7. That was the most incredible thing I saw Hoegie do."

Offensively, Hoegie's arsenal was unmatched. He could perform standing 360-degree dunks, spin jumpers, and acrobatic shots that left defenders flat-footed. His feats included dunking on 6'9" University of Arizona Hall of Famer Larry Demic and pulling off trick shots that turned skeptics into believers. Hoegie was quick to back up his braggadocio with bets. "Most people would say I couldn't do this or that. Ooohhh, I loved that," he said.

Hoegie's Hustles

Hoegie turned basketball into a lucrative hustle. Known for his penchant for gambling, he often challenged players to one-on-one games with high stakes. Using make-it-take-it rules, where the player who scores retains possession, and playing to 21 points, Hoegie would routinely spot opponents a 16-point lead and still win without letting them take a single possession.

"One-on-one, that was my world," Hoegie said. "There's no bragging. I just would prove my point and collect the money. Everyone wanted to challenge me for money, and I took on all challengers."

Coach Mike Lopez shared a memorable story about Hoegie's confidence. A trash-talking opponent challenged him to a $50 game at Bear Down. Unfazed, Hoegie retrieved a large wad of cash from his bag and raised the stakes to $500. They eventually settled on $100. The result? Hoegie won 15-2, leaving no doubt about his prowess.

Chapter 8

The Final Matchup

In 1993, Delano and Hoegie teamed up at the downtown YMCA, running pickup games as they had countless times before. Their chemistry and skills remained intact, and they won eight of nine games that day. Afterward, the two faced off in a game of H-O-R-S-E, a tradition they had kept alive for years.

Despite their many battles, Delano had never beaten Hoegie in H-O-R-S-E or one-on-one. But on this day, fate intervened. Delano sunk an impossible shot standing behind the backboard, 20 feet out on the baseline. The ball arced perfectly, swishing through the net. Hoegie and Delano burst into laughter, their guffaw reverberating across the gym.

"That big head boy never beat me before today," Hoegie joked to Delano's son, Márquez, who had witnessed the spectacle. "He got me today!"

It was a moment of levity, but it would also prove to be a harbinger of change. Just a week later, the DEA raided Hoegie's apartment, looking to arrest him on charges of drug distribution and trafficking. Tipped off by an anonymous source, Hoegie fled Tucson before law enforcement arrived, leaving behind the courts where he had reigned supreme.

For decades, Delano and Hoegie had been pillars of Tucson basketball, inspiring generations with their talent, tenacity, and larger-than-life personalities. Their exploits at Bear Down, the YMCA, and Randolph Rec Center became legendary, etched into the fabric of Tucson's basketball history.

Chapter 8

The Rise of Márquez Price

By the late 1980s and into the 1990s, Delano's attention shifted toward raising his son, Márquez, who was rapidly emerging as a basketball boy wonder. From the moment Márquez could hold the ball, Delano nurtured his son's talent. Márquez spent countless hours in the gym, soaking up lessons from both his father and "Uncle Hoegie."

Márquez's exposure to basketball legends from such a young age became foundational to his development. Whether watching Delano's perfect jump shots or witnessing Hoegie's flabbergasting athleticism, Márquez was surrounded by excellence. As Hoegie once remarked to Delano during a drive to the gym, "That boy got it. He's gonna be big-time."

By high school, Márquez had blossomed into a star at Delano's alma mater, Tucson High School. His performances captivated the city, with Márquez earning All-Region and All-City honors all four years of high school. By his sophomore season, he was already averaging 20 points per game and ranked as one of the top 20 Point Guards on the West Coast. His standout performances at the Adidas West Coast All-Star Camp, alongside future NBA players Richard Jefferson and Carlos Boozer, further solidified his reputation as a rising star.

Despite his success, Márquez's journey wasn't without adversity. After breaking his foot during the summer before his senior year, Márquez fought to return to form. Though he faced challenges with his team's coaching changes, his leadership and talent helped lead the Badgers to the state tournament in his senior year.

Chapter 8

Márquez received interest from several Division I programs, including DePaul, Tulane, Washington State, and UNLV. However, he ultimately decided to play JUCO basketball at Mesa Community College before returning to Tucson to complete a double major in Philosophy and Psychology at the University of Arizona. His graduation marked a proud moment for the Price family, as every member of Delano's immediate family had now earned degrees from the University of Arizona.

Delano and Márquez: A Father-Son Duo on the Court

As Márquez's skills developed, Delano remained an integral part of his basketball journey. By eighth grade, Márquez was regularly playing in pickup games with grown men, holding his own and often excelling. During those games, the chemistry between father and son was apparent. Márquez would dart through transition and throw no-look passes to Delano, who, even in his 40s, would drain long-range jumpers with ease.

Their bond on the court extended into life. Delano's influence as a father ensured Márquez understood the importance of discipline, education, and drive. For Delano, the opportunity to share the game he loved with his son was a fulfillment of the promise he made to himself when Márquez was born: to stay good enough to play alongside his son until he came into his own.

Chapter 8

The Changing of the Guard

By the late 1990s, the torch was passing. Delano, though still one of the most respected players in Tucson, began stepping back from competitive play as Márquez emerged as the next generation of Price basketball excellence. Márquez carried the family legacy forward, with his high school achievements a source of immense pride for Delano, Jacque, and the extended Price family.

For Delano and Márquez, basketball was a shared language, a bridge between generations, and a demonstration of spirit. As Márquez prepared to forge his own path, the Price legacy remained firmly cemented in the lessons of the court and the bonds of the family.

Meanwhile, Hoegie's fate stood as a cautionary tale. His unparalleled genius on the court was overshadowed by the charm of the streets, where the seductive pull of the ghetto glitterati fueled his insatiable appetite.

Delano's Legacy as a Transformative Administrator

By the mid-1990s, Delano Price had solidified himself as a transformative force in Tucson's educational system. When an opportunity arose to become the assistant principal of instruction at Sahuaro High School, Delano eagerly accepted. The move to Sahuaro became one of the most rewarding chapters of his career, as he thrived in the supportive environment and upheld meaningful relationships with students and staff.

Chapter 8

During this period, Delano's nephew, Wesley Price, was a varsity basketball player and a well-loved figure on campus. "It probably sounds biased because he's my nephew," Delano would later say, "but Wesley was one of my favorite students during my entire career. He was very intelligent, gifted, and the kids at school gravitated towards his cool. Seeing him and his boys like Trevon, made me think of me and my brother Randle growing up."

The presence of his nephew and the comradeship among students created an inspiring atmosphere for Delano. He relished the opportunity to mentor students, using his vast experience to guide them not only academically but also in their personal growth. Sahuaro High School became a beacon of positivity under his watch, and his ability to connect with students from diverse backgrounds began to shine even brighter.

Navigating Tension at Sabino High School

Despite his success at Sahuaro, Delano's leadership was called upon in a much more challenging environment. At Sabino High School, a predominantly white institution on Tucson's east side, racial tensions were simmering. The alienation of Black students escalated when a white student placed a hangman's noose on a Black student's locker, an event that sent shockwaves through the community. Unbeknownst to Delano, a group of Black parents demanded the school administration bring in a leader who could represent their children and address the rising tensions.

Recognizing Delano's unique ability to route complex social dynamics, Sabino's principal, Carl Roberts, requested Delano's immediate transfer to the school. Delano was blindsided by the announcement and deeply upset. He had found a home at Sahuaro and wasn't eager to leave. Moreover, Sabino's reputation for alienating Black students only compounded his reluctance. Nevertheless, Delano accepted the challenge, embodying his lifelong philosophy of serving wherever he was most needed.

At Sabino, Delano's charisma, diplomacy, and steadfast commitment to equity became invaluable. Despite initial skepticism, he quickly won over the student body, parents, and faculty. Delano met the tensions head-on, creating an inclusive environment where all students felt seen and valued. By promoting dialogue and addressing systemic issues, he helped Sabino find balance and move forward as a community. His ability to cultivate trust and unity was a hallmark of his leadership, and Sabino became yet another testament to his transformative influence.

After his impactful tenure at Sabino, Delano was finally able to return to Sahuaro High School in the early 2000s. The school welcomed him back with open arms, and he resumed his role with renewed passion. It was at Sahuaro that Delano would remain until his retirement, completing a storied career that spanned over three decades.

Delano often described his work as akin to that of Michelangelo, seeing each student as a block of granites with immense potential waiting to be freed. His role, as he saw it, was to sculpt, guide, and release that potential into the world. This philosophy drove him to impact hundreds of thousands of students, helping them proceed through their own unique paths, whether they were on the verge of greatness or struggling to find their way.

Chapter 8

Delano's influence extended far beyond the classrooms and administrative offices of Tucson's schools. His adaptability allowed him to thrive in any setting, whether he was mentoring athletes, mediating tense situations, or encouraging students to believe in themselves. He left a permanent mark on schools like Catalina, Sabino, and Sahuaro, shaping them into environments where students and faculty alike could flourish.

His legacy is carried forward in the countless lives he touched. From hardened criminals who later turned their lives around, to highly accomplished professionals, many point to Delano as the pivotal figure who changed their trajectory. The stories of his impact echo through time, inspiring new generations and cementing his place as a legendary figure in Tucson's educational history.

As Delano transitioned into retirement, his contributions were celebrated across the community. Yet, for those who knew him, the real measure of his success wasn't in accolades or awards but in the profound and lasting difference he made in the lives of those he served. Delano Price was an administrator, teacher, a mentor, and a sculptor of futures.

Chapter 8

Márquez at Adidas Double Pump West Coast basketball Camp at California State University, Dominguez Hills/Delano and baby Marquez

Chapter 8

Price siblings– Maxine, Raymond, Michael, Pearl, Delano, Doris, Bertha, Randle, Alex

Chapter 8

Delano's brother Leslie "Micky" Sims

Chapter 8

Pickup artists

CHAPTER 8

Delano plays against professional women's team while teaching at Sunnyside High School

CHAPTER 9

HONORING LEGACY

As the 2000s unfolded, Delano and Jacque's lives became enriched by the arrival of their grandchildren. Jernei C. Johnson was born on November 5, 2003, followed by Jaiden O. Bullock on March 29, 2007, and Savion A. Bullock on May 13, 2008. These children represented a continuation of the Price family legacy, filling their home with laughter, joy, and the promise of a bright future.

Delano and Jacque took immense pride in their grandchildren, watching them grow and guiding them with the same principles of resilience and dedication that have defined their lives. Jacque, as always, provided the nurturing foundation for their family, ensuring that their grandchildren knew the value of love and education.

This commitment to education was further exemplified by Jacque and Tanisha's academic achievements. In May of 1998, mother and daughter graduated together with their master's degrees, an extraordinary milestone that demonstrated their

Chapter 9

shared dedication to learning and personal growth. Their joint accomplishment was a source of immense pride for the entire family, symbolizing the strength of their bond and their drive to excel.

In 2013, Tanisha reached another pinnacle of academic success by earning her PhD, a crowning achievement that cemented her place as a role model for future generations. This moment reflected Tanisha's endurance and the family's continuing heritage of educational excellence and aspiration.

A Bittersweet Reunion

In 2006, tragedy brought an unexpected reunion. Mary Simmons, Hoegie's mother and a maternal figure to Delano during his youth, passed away. Delano and Jacque attended the funeral to pay their respects. Unbeknownst to them, Hoegie had also slipped into town under the alias "Charles Freeman." Still a fugitive, Hoegie had evaded law enforcement for years.

During the funeral, Delano stood at the podium, sharing heartfelt words about Mary's kindness and the motherly role she had played in his life. As he scanned the congregation, his eyes locked on a familiar figure in the front row, Hoegie. Overcome with emotion, Delano said, "I'm so happy to see my old friend Hoegie Simmons here." Hoegie, attempting to remain inconspicuous, slouched in his seat and glanced nervously over his shoulder.

After the service, as Delano escorted Jacque to their Mercedes Benz, he heard a booming, unmistakable voice: "Delano, I like that car! You and Jacque still got a marriage made in heaven!" Delano turned to see Hoegie peeking from around the church. A mix of joy and caution washed over him as he realized Hoegie was still on the run. It was a fleeting but poignant moment. Thirteen years had passed since they had last seen each other at the YMCA. Before Delano could say much more, Hoegie disappeared into the shadows once again.

Recognitions and Inductions

Delano's achievements continued to be recognized and celebrated in the years that followed. In the spring of 2007, he was inducted into the Tucson High Athletic "T" Club Hall of Fame and later appointed as a board member. The ceremony was a heartfelt affair attended by dozens of family members and friends who witnessed Delano's impact both on and off the court.

Delano took his role on the board seriously, lobbying for the inclusion of many of his heroes from Tucson High School, as well as athletes who had made an impact after his time. The "T" Club, established in 1993, served as a gathering place for former athletes who shared a deep love for their alma mater and its rich sports history. Over the years, the organization provided over $180,000 in scholarships and support to student-athletes, ensuring that the legacy of excellence at Tucson High endured.

A legacy Honored: Delano Price and Ernie McCray's connection

In 2010, Delano Price received one of the most profound honors of his life: induction into the Pima County Sports Hall of Fame.

CHAPTER 9

The event was momentous, with over 100 family members, friends, and colleagues gathering to celebrate his achievements. Among the crowd of admirers stood a figure who elevated the occasion to a once-in-a-lifetime moment, Ernie McCray. For Delano, having McCray, a hero and legendary figure in Tucson sports history, attend the ceremony was an indescribable honor that underscored the evening's significance. Their shared history and mutual admiration represented not only a connection between two great athletes but a celebration of the enduring legacy of sports and community.

The Legacy of Ernie McCray

Ernie McCray's legacy looms large in Tucson and beyond. A former Tucson High School and University of Arizona basketball standout, McCray was an architect and role model for generations of athletes. He was the first African American basketball player to graduate from the University of Arizona, and his record-breaking 46-point game against Cal State-Los Angeles on February 6, 1960, still stands as authentication to his unique talent and fortitude. McCray's name is immortalized in the University of Arizona's Ring of Honor at McKale Center, as well as in numerous halls of fame, including:

- The Alumni "T" Club Tucson High Athlete Hall of Fame
- The Pima County Sports Hall of Fame
- The Tucson High Badger Foundation Hall of Fame
- The University of Arizona Ring of Honor at McKale Center
- The University of Arizona Hall of Fame

These awards reflect not only McCray's athletic prowess but also his impact as a mentor, educator, and activist. For Delano, McCray was the originator, someone who set the bar high for what could be achieved both on and off the court.

Invited to Greatness

In 2023, McCray was honored at the University of Arizona with his induction into the Ring of Honor at McKale Center. Recognizing the importance of this milestone, McCray extended a personal invitation to Delano and Jacque Price to attend the ceremony. As McCray stood center court at McKale, surrounded by fans and luminaries, Delano and Jacque watched beside him with pride and admiration. For Delano, witnessing McCray's well-deserved recognition reinforced his admiration for the man who had inspired him since his youth. It was a moment of shared achievement, celebrating not only McCray's accomplishments but also the unbroken thread of excellence that connected their lives.

A Full-Circle Moment

When it was Delano's turn to be inducted into the Pima County Sports Hall of Fame, McCray returned the gesture by attending the ceremony. Delano was deeply moved, calling it one of the highlights of his life. Having McCray there felt like a validation of the values they both held dear: hard work, perseverance, and giving back to the community.

McCray shared his thoughts on Delano's basketball talent and character:

Chapter 9

"I remember seeing Delano playing a couple of times when I was visiting Tucson from San Diego. And what I remember most from so long ago was how comfortable, if you will, he and his teammates were with a basketball. They could flat-out play with Delano displaying an amazing array of shots, flying by a defender for a layup, breaking somebody's ankle with a sudden pull-up jumper, with some pure textbook shooting also in his repertoire. Kind of undefendable as far as I could see."

These words, coming from someone Delano had long considered a mentor, carried an immense weight of gratitude and pride.

What made McCray and Delano's bond unique was their shared commitment to using their platforms to uplift others. Both men were deeply grounded in their love for Tucson and the communities that shaped them. McCray reflected on this connection:

"My bond with Delano is special because we love Tucson and how it's become a nice city. And we both have a ton of respect for the old hoods. I'd like to think that the Old Pueblo is proud of what we've done and what we've given since our heydays as star athletes."

This mutual respect was evident in the way they supported one another, whether attending each other's ceremonies or collaborating to mentor young athletes. For both men, basketball was a tool for building relationships, encouraging community, and inspiring future generations.

Chapter 9

The Influence of McCray's Story

McCray's story as a pioneer in Arizona sports was a source of inspiration for Delano. As the first African American basketball player to graduate from the University of Arizona, McCray faced challenges that few could fully comprehend. His self-subsistence and success in the face of adversity demonstrated the sovereignty of determination and the importance of breaking barriers. For Delano, McCray's journey was a blueprint for navigating his own path as an athlete, educator, and leader.

McCray spoke candidly about his love for basketball and the values it instilled in him:

"Basketball gave me an opportunity to entertain, to show off legitimately. A way to give to my community and, since my playing came under the heading of 'Be the Best,' which was the motto of the school where I learned to play, and later 'Bear Down' at the University level, I developed a work ethic from the game and learned how to work with others to achieve a goal."

These principles echoed deeply with Delano, who carried them forward in his own life and work. Whether coaching students, mentoring young players, or serving as an administrator, Delano embodied the ethos of excellence and teamwork that McCray championed.

One of the most striking similarities between McCray and Delano was their untiring commitment to giving back to their communities. McCray, a longtime educator, actor, and activist, used his platform to advocate for social justice and community empowerment. Delano, through his roles as a coach, administrator, and mentor, dedicated his life to nurturing the potential of others.

Their bond is a demonstration of the enduring impact of mentorship and the power of representation. By standing on stage together, whether at McKale Center or the Pima County Sports Hall of Fame, they symbolized the progress that could be achieved through integrity and a commitment to uplifting others.

As the Pima County Sports Hall of Fame ceremony concluded, Delano stood among family, friends, and peers, his heart full of gratitude. Having Ernie McCray in attendance was not just an honor; it was a reminder of the legacy they both carried forward. Together, they represented the best of Tucson, a city that had shaped them, inspired them, and celebrated their contributions.

For Delano, the moment was a validation of the values he had dedicated his life to upholding. And for McCray, it was an opportunity to honor the ripple effect of his own journey, seeing how his influence had inspired others like Delano to reach new heights.

In that shared celebration, the legacy of Ernie McCray and Delano Price stood as an exemplification of hope and vision, a reminder that excellence is a journey that is best traveled together.

Delano's impact extended beyond the ceremony. He was asked to join the Hall of Fame board and later served as Vice President for 14 years. His leadership and charisma made him a natural fit as the master of ceremonies for the annual induction event, where he continues to eloquently celebrate the accomplishments of others while reflecting on the rich history of sports in Pima County.

CHAPTER 9

A Visit with Coach Morales

Among Delano's most cherished memories was a reunion with his high school basketball coach, Coach Morales, who had retired to Hemet, California. Delano arranged a visit, bringing along Jacque, Kenny Ball, and Chuco Miranda. When they arrived, Delano couldn't resist teasing Coach Morales. "Hey Coach, these guys are lost," Delano said, gesturing toward Kenny and Chuco.

Not recognizing them at first, Coach Morales asked, "Where are you guys trying to go?"

Delano grinned. "Coach, do you know who these guys are? That's Kenny Ball and Chuco Miranda."

The realization dawned on Coach Morales, and he exclaimed, "Son of a gun!" He embraced his former players, tears streaming down his face. The visit was filled with nostalgia and laughter, as Coach Morales, true to form, started coaching his old players again, asking if they were still running drills and staying in shape.

Inside Coach Morales's home, the only memorabilia on display were a picture of the 1969 state championship team and an award he had received for Coach of the Year. As they reminisced, Coach Morales inquired about Hoegie, unaware of how extraordinary his basketball journey had become after high school.

When Coach Morales passed away in 2014, Delano led the memorial service held at Tucson High School. The event drew dozens of former players, all united by the profound impact Coach Morales had on their lives.

CHAPTER 9

The Ultimate Honor

In 2017, Delano was inducted into the Tucson High Badger Foundation Hall of Fame. This honor carried special significance for Delano, as it celebrated not only his athletic achievements but also his lifelong dedication to education, mentorship, and community service. His picture and plaque now grace the halls of Tucson High School, serving as a tribute to his lasting influence.

"The award means more to me than anything because it encompasses my whole life," Delano said, reflecting on the honor.

The Tucson High Badger Foundation Hall of Fame recognizes individuals who have distinguished themselves in fields such as arts, athletics, business, education, and public service. Delano's induction solidified his status as a community icon, a role model for generations of students, and a badge of excellence for his beloved Tucson High School.

Hoegie Returns

By 2013, Hoegie had started to reappear in Tucson, believing, due to faulty information from an old girlfriend's friend at the courthouse, that the statute of limitations on his past crimes had expired. His return was initially tentative, but it soon became frequent as he tested the waters of his newfound sense of freedom.

One of Hoegie's first reunions was a dinner with his former teammates Delano, Kenny Ball, and Chuco Miranda. The gathering, attended by Delano's wife Jacque and son Márquez, was a deeply sentimental occasion. For Márquez, the reunion was particularly emotional as he hadn't seen Hoegie since 1993,

Chapter 9

when Hoegie went on the run. As a teenager, Márquez had deeply felt Hoegie's absence, mourning the void left by someone he had admired as an additional uncle among his many celebrated uncles. Seeing Hoegie again stirred a flood of memories and emotions, reigniting their cherished bond.

At dinner, laughter flowed freely as the group reminisced about their glory days such as state championships, Bear Down dominance, and countless pickup games that became the stuff of local legend. Hoegie shared stories of his life on the run, carefully omitting the more precarious details. He had traveled far and wide, playing basketball in cities like Chicago and Los Angeles, carving out a reputation as a playground legend even in his 40s and 50s. Hoegie was still Hoegie, telling tales of hustling younger players on courts across the country and proving skeptics wrong with his matchless talents and athleticism.

In one of his more surreal accounts, Hoegie described playing basketball in Chicago during the mid-90s against none other than Michael Jordan. At a local racquetball club, Hoegie recalled how Michael Jordan would regularly pick him for pickup games. "He looks old, but he plays young," Jordan would say, acknowledging Hoegie's agility and court savvy. Still dunking in his 40s, Hoegie continued to astonish opponents, often hustling those who questioned his abilities. His tales enthralled Márquez, who saw the fabled man behind the myths of his childhood.

The reunion also included attending a few local high school basketball games as a group, bringing back the camaraderie and shared love for the sport that had bonded them all in the first place. Everything seemed to be falling into place until 2014, when Hoegie was arrested in California. He was living there at the time

Chapter 9

and was picked up by law enforcement on the old charges that had forced him into hiding years earlier.

Hoegie's arrest was a jarring reminder of his risky life. He was sentenced to six years in prison. Though he was offered the possibility of early parole, Hoegie chose to serve his sentence in full, determined to put his time behind bars completely in the past and emerge with full freedom.

During those six years, Márquez and Hoegie maintained a consistent correspondence through letters. The letters became a lifeline for Hoegie's who found solace in Márquez's staunch support. They shared stories, exchanged philosophies, and built a connection that transcended the confines of time and distance. Márquez became the keeper of Hoegie's many untold tales, concealing the more sensitive ones in confidence while vowing to honor the parts Hoegie entrusted to the public.

When Hoegie was released in 2020, amid the COVID-19 pandemic, the first person he called was Márquez. The two spoke for hours, catching up and discussing the life that awaited Hoegie outside of confinement. Hoegie returned to California, but by 2022, he reunited with the Price family, marking a moment of closure and renewal.

Hoegie's stories of his time on the run were larger than life. Hoegie spoke of playing in housing projects across the country, hustling younger players with his one-on-one mastery. In Chicago, he would dominate courts until an older spectator, someone who recognized him from decades earlier, would blow his cover. Once word got out about who Hoegie was, the games would dry up as younger players realized they stood no chance against the legendary figure.

Chapter 9

The stories shared here, chronicling Hoegie's prodigious journey, are the ones he permitted to be told. They represent not just the life of a man who lived by his own rules but also the lasting impact he left on those who know him.

The system and the individual: Hoegie Simmons in the context of the Prison Industrial Complex

The story of Hoegie Simmons is of a gifted basketball player who made choices that led him down a tumultuous path. It is also a lens through which we can examine the systemic forces that shaped his environment, dictated the rules of engagement, and ultimately consumed him. Hoegie's life was influenced as much by the broader prison industrial complex as by the personal decisions he made within it.

The Systemic Trap

The 13th Amendment, with its critical exception allowing slavery "as a punishment for crime," laid the groundwork for a system that has disproportionately targeted Black Americans since its inception. After the Civil War, when the country faced the economic challenge of compensating newly freed Black workers, vagrancy laws and mass incarceration emerged as tools to recapture lost labor. Black men were criminalized for mere existence in public spaces such as being unemployed, loitering, or even walking without a clear purpose.

This systemic oppression paved the way for generations of Black Americans to navigate life in a society designed to exclude them from economic opportunity and social equity. By the 20th century, cultural reinforcements like the film "Birth of a Nation" perpetuated the stereotype of Black men as threats to societal order, justifying their mass incarceration under the guise of public safety. This stigmatization not only robbed individuals like Hoegie of dignity but also placed them in a cycle of systemic criminalization.

A Society Shaped by Fear and Profit

The war on drugs, launched in the Nixon era and amplified during Reagan's presidency, became a crucial chapter in this systemic oppression. While framed as a battle against addiction and crime, it was a tool to disrupt communities and dismantle movements for Black liberation. Nixon's advisor John Ehrlichman's admission that drug criminalization was a deliberate strategy to target Black Americans highlights the insidiousness of this policy. Reagan's subsequent escalation transformed the figurative war into a literal one, with militarized police forces patrolling urban neighborhoods and mandatory minimum sentencing laws devastating families.

By the 1980s, the crack epidemic ravaged Black communities, and the sensationalized narrative of the "crack dealer" as a predatory figure became a convenient scapegoat for society's ills. Meanwhile, the systemic roots of poverty, disinvestment, and unequal access to education remain unaddressed. The public perception of figures like Hoegie was shaped by this narrative, reducing them to caricatures of criminality without considering the structural forces that left them with limited choices.

Chapter 9

The Choices within the System

For Hoegie, the allure of the streets and the promise of quick money represented a path to survival and self-determination in an environment with few legitimate opportunities. He was not alone in this choice as thousands of young Black men were drawn into the drug trade, a byproduct of economic neglect and systemic exclusion. While it is easy to attribute Hoegie's trajectory to personal failings, such a narrative ignores the broader context in which his life unfolded.

Hoegie's sparkle on the basketball court, where he flashed unrivaled extraordinary skill, was never fully leveraged into a professional career. The political nature of sports, the lack of support structures, and the limited opportunities for someone from his background meant that his dreams were never within his full control. This harsh reality mirrored the systemic inequalities he faced off the court. The streets, with their promise of autonomy and financial gain, offered an escape but at an incalculable cost.

A Complex Interplay

The question of whether Hoegie's downfall was a result of systemic oppression or personal choices does not have a simple answer. It is a combination of both. Systemic forces created the environment in which Hoegie lived, dictating the limited opportunities available to him and shaping the societal perceptions that influenced his interactions with the world. Within that environment, he made choices that further entrenched him in a destructive cycle.

Chapter 9

It is crucial to recognize that systemic oppression does not absolve individuals of accountability but instead highlights the need for a deeper understanding of the forces at play. Hoegie's story is evidence of the ingenuity required to navigate a system designed to marginalize and exploit. Yet it also serves as a cautionary tale about the consequences of succumbing to the very forces one seeks to escape.

A Call for Change

The prison industrial complex, with its roots in slavery and its perpetuation through mass incarceration, remains a blight on American society. The exploitation of incarcerated individuals, the criminalization of poverty, and the demonization of Black men are all symptoms of a system in dire need of reform. Addressing these issues requires incremental changes as well as demanding a fundamental reimagining of justice, accountability, and community investment.

For individuals like Hoegie, the path to redemption and reintegration must be paved with opportunities for education, employment, and community support. Breaking the cycle of incarceration and recidivism requires addressing the root causes of poverty and systemic inequality. Only by dismantling the structures that perpetuate exploitation can society begin to repair the harm done to generations of Black Americans.

Hoegie's story is not only a personal narrative as it reflects the broader struggles faced by Black men in America. While the choices he made cannot be ignored, they must be understood within the context of a society that offered him few alternatives.

CHAPTER 9

By acknowledging the interplay between individual agency and structural oppression, we can begin to chart a path toward a more just and equitable society.

Chapter 9

Delano and Fat Lever

Chapter 9

Top 10 high school players of all time from Tucson, Arizona

CHAPTER 9

football, gave the Rebels a tremendous bench.

If it wasn't for East High's buzzsaw defense, which upset South 63-61 in the state finals, this Rebel five would be rated higher. Petroff's best ever club beat East twice, 56-52 and 61-55, before falling in three games. During a spectacular regular season game, South edged Phoenix Union 80-76 in three overtimes. The game featured seven future major college players and two soon-to-be NBA starters.

8) TUCSON PUEBLO, 1977-78 (28-0)

The Warriors great quickness and devastating press enabled Roland LaVetter to win back-to-back crowns, the first such accomplishment by a Tucson school since 1948-49. Not one starter was taller than 6-3, yet the Warriors averaged 51.3 rebounds per game. The premier player was 6-2 senior Lafayette "Fat" Lever, who went on to star at Arizona State and continued a surprising 12 year career in the NBA. Ironically, Lever was not highly touted by the national media as a schoolboy, and was not a member of any of the nation's premier high school All-America selections.

Ken Martin, 6-2 and super quick, played forward or guard. Lever, Jeff Moore, playmaking guard Tony Mosley and Pat Adams were returning starters from the Warriors' 1977 championship club, which finished 25-5.

Pueblo blewout city rival Rincon 70-54 in the finals. But the big test came in the semifinals, when the Warriors edged Phoenix East 29-28 in a slowdown game at ASU's Activity Center.

9) PHOENIX EAST, 1974-75 (28-0)

When the victory net was cut down

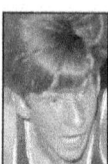
Steve Malovic, Alhambra

Roland Campbell, Phoenix East

at the Activity Center in Tempe, head coach Royce Youree told *The Phoenix Gazette*, "I'd have to say this was the best team, overall, that I've had at East." It was the Purple Gang's first unbeaten slate and the school's third state crown in five years. Tucson Rincon, coached by Bill Mehle, was the victim, 67-61, played before 8,722 fans at ASU.

Between 1974-76, East lost only two games and both were in four overtimes. In between they won 54 games in a row - 28 by these guys. John Hawkins, Dennison Dawson, Huey Lowery, Hap Smith, Mike Hiralez and Marion "Bud" Bellamy led the charge. Bellamy, a transfer from Phoenix St. Mary's who later played at Oklahoma City, was the catalyst in the finals, where East enjoyed a 39-27 rebound edge. The Rangers' lineup included Dave Henson, Chuck Goslin and Steve King. Later, the *National Sports News Service* in Minneapolis ranked East No. 20 in the U.S.A., the highest basketball ranking for an Arizona school since 1969.

10) TUCSON HIGH, 1968-69 (23-1)

A very athletic team, led by first team all-state guard Delano Price (5-10) and all-state forward Kenny Ball (6-3). The Badgers stomped their first 11 opponents by 22 points per game. Ball led the team in scoring. Price poured in 26 points during a state tournament win over Phoenix Union. Elizaro "Chuco" Miranda (6-10) excelled in rebounding and shot blocking. Senior Bruce Klewer (6-8) started at forward. Point guard Hogie Simmons was a good scorer, too. John Redmond, a promising 6-4 junior, helped mold one of the biggest state championship teams in Arizona history.

In their only 100-point outing of the season, Tucson nearly doubled Sunnyside's score with a Class 5A record 128 point game. To this day, no 5A school has scored that high. In 24 games the Badgers averaged a record 83.3 points. Joe Petroshus, a 6-2 forward and a *Scholastic Coach* All-American halfback in football, was a member of this Tony Morales-coached team.

Tucson won a great state title game.

Brian Fair, South Mountain

David Haskin, Tucson Sahuaro

In the finals in Phoenix, a *great* team beat a *good* team, as the Badgers edged Tempe 80-76. The 6-10 Miranda made the difference as the big guy bombed the Buffs for 21 points and 13 boards. "You don't see many 15-foot hook shots like that, even in the pros," said Tempe head coach Sam Duane afterwards. Miranda made two of them during one stretch when Tucson built a 68-56 lead.

11) PHOENIX ALHAMBRA, 1973-74 (26-3)

Steve Malovic has to be considered one of the best centers to play high school basketball in Phoenix, and it showed in the Lions surprising run for the 1973-74 title. Malovic played for three NBA teams after a stint at USC and San Diego State. But his promising career started with the Lions, who finally got to No. 1 East in the finals of the region playoffs, 62-53. One week later they beat East again, this time in four overtimes, 68-66 in the Class 5A finals. "Big Steve" scored 36 points and controlled the boards.

On the season Malovic averaged 28.5 points and scored a city record 835. He averaged 16.4 rebounds per game. Coached by the late Phil Kemp, Malovic had a good supporting cast, including Kansas transplant Chuck Fabion, a tough, competitive 6-5 forward, 6-3 forward Terry Daly and 5-8 point guard Chester Soto. Junior Ken Troutt also contributed.

All three of Alhambra's losses were to East, which featured a tall, physical front line and a sensational point guard in Roland Campbell.

12) PHOENIX EAST, 1973-74 (27-2)

This is the highly regarded East five that lost to Alhambra in four overtimes

---

Tucson High 1969 state title team ranked top 10 in Arizona state history.

Chapter 9

THE 2010 INDUCTEE WE HONOR TONIGHT

E. DELANO PRICE
ATHLETE/COACH

A 1969 graduate of Tucson High, Delano started in basketball for three years, and captained the 1969 team that won the 5A state championship and was an all-city selection, averaging 21.5 points per game. The team set a state single-game scoring record of 128 points, a mark that still stands. Price started for two years at Phoenix Community College and was all-conference in 1971. He was the team's leading scorer (20.0). From 1978 to 1982, Price coached basketball at the middle school (Apollo) and freshman (Sunnyside) level. In 1982, he became the first African-American to be appointed head boys' basketball coach in Tucson when he was hired by Sunnyside. His 1983 team reached the Southern Region semi-finals. He became assistant principal at Sabino High and worked with baseball coach Mike Bejarno to install dugouts, one of the first high schools in the city to do so. In 1990, he became the first African-American administrator (assistant principal) at Sunnyside High, with responsibilities of activities/athletics, operations, and discipline. In 2001, he was an honorary lifetime pass recipient from the Arizona Interscholastic Association in recognition of exemplary service to the interscholastic programs for the youth of Arizona. In 2007, he was inducted into the Tucson High Badger "T" Club Hall of Fame.

-14-

Delano's 2010 inductee of the Pima County Sports Hall of Fame.

Chapter 9

Delano and Jacque's grandchildren- Jaiden, Savion, Jernei.

Chapter 9

Tanisha, baby Jernei, Delano, Adrian, Márquez, Jacque at Adrian's graduation from the University of Arizona

Chapter 9

Delano and Jacque at Pima County Sports Hall of Fame ceremony

CHAPTER 9

*The Tucson High Badger Foundation Hall of Fame
at Tucson High School in Tucson, Arizona.*

Chapter 9

Delano Price in the Tucson High Badger Foundation Hall of Fame at Tucson High School.

Chapter 9

Tucson High Alumni "T" Club Hall of Fame

CHAPTER 9

Bob Elliott, Ernie McCray (with wife, Jacque and Delano Price at Ring of Fame honor for Ernie McCray at Mckale Center- University of Arizona, Tucson, Arizona.

Chapter 9

Tucson High 1969 state championship team from left to right– Norvell Watson, Chuco Miranda, Delano Price, Bruce Klewer, Kenny Ball, Donny Gin, Joe Petroshus, Frank Postillion. Hoegie Simmons (not pictured)

CHAPTER 10

CONNECTIONS TO GREATNESS

Tucson's basketball history is rich, layered, and filled with extraordinary talent, and few have been closer to its evolution than Delano and Hoegie. As players, coaches, and mentors, their lives intersected with some of the greatest players emerging from the city. The court was not just a place for competition; it was a stage where bonds were formed, lessons were taught, and traditions were born.

Sean Elliott: The Pinnacle of Tucson Basketball

Sean Elliott, one of Tucson's most iconic athletes, embodied greatness at every level of basketball. At Cholla High School, Elliott's senior-year scoring average of 31.3 points per game set a standard that had not been seen in Arizona since 1960. His dominance earned him the rare distinction of being Tucson's only McDonald's All-American. Delano had the privilege of coaching Sean during his formative years, alongside Eric Money, another future NBA player.

Elliott's stellar career continued at the University of Arizona, where he was a two-time All-American and the recipient of every major national award in 1989, including the John R. Wooden Award, Adolph Rupp Trophy, NABC Player of the Year, and AP Player of the Year. Delano remained a mentor and friend throughout Elliott's journey, playing pickup games with him during high school and college and even in the off seasons during Sean's NBA career with the San Antonio Spurs.

Elliott's professional accolades include being the third overall pick in the 1989 NBA Draft, a two-time NBA All-Star, and a member of the 1999 NBA Championship team. His No. 32 jersey is retired by both the University of Arizona and the San Antonio Spurs.

When Elliott returned to Tucson, he frequently partnered with Delano at the Boys and Girls Club, playing two-on-two games with his brother Noel, former Tucson High superstars like Val Hill, Sean's close friend Monday Rios, and Delano's son Márquez after they finished competitive play. Márquez, still a young boy, marveled at sharing the court with someone of Elliott's caliber, solidifying the bond between the Elliott and Price families.

Chapter 10

Fat Lever: A triple-double King

Fat Lever's legacy began at Pueblo High School, where he led his team to an undefeated 28-0 state championship season in 1978 while averaging a triple-double with 20.5 points, 12.8 rebounds, and 9.6 assists per game. Lever would go on to make two NBA All-Star teams, earn an All-NBA Second Team selection, and become one of the league's all-time leaders in triple-doubles, finishing his career with 43 which is more than Michael Jordan or Kareem Abdul-Jabbar.

Lever's junior high coach Herb Buckner introduced him to the backcourt tandem extraordinaire of Delano and Hoegie, taking him to watch the pickup games at Bear Down Gym. Those experiences inspired Lever to hone his skills and pursue excellence. Delano and Hoegie, in turn, watched Lever's rise with admiration, witnessing him become a household name at Pueblo, the University of Arizona State, and the NBA. The bond between Lever and Delano was one of mutual respect, rooted in their shared love of the game.

Terrell Stoglin: A Scoring Machine

Terrell Stoglin rewrote the record books during his career at Santa Rita High School, finishing as the city's all-time leading scorer with 2,911 points and leading his team to 96 victories as a four-year starter. He later became the Atlantic Coast Conference scoring leader at Maryland and set scoring records in international leagues, including a 74-point game in the Lebanese Basketball

League and multiple 40-point games in the Basketball Africa League (BAL).

Stoglin's basketball lineage runs deep, as Delano had coached against his father Joe and uncle James when they starred at Pueblo High School in the 1980s. The Prices and Stoglins shared a strong familial bond, with both families attending each other's games over the years. Delano and Márquez were in awe of Terrell's exploits, recognizing him as a continuation of Tucson's storied basketball tradition.

Chuck Overton and Robert Johnson: The Cholla Duo

Chuck Overton dominated the court at Cholla High School, scoring 2,530 points during his career and leading his team to a state championship. His teammate, point guard Robert Johnson, brought a Brooklyn flair to Tucson with his flamboyant dribbling and passing. Delano's daughters, Adrian and Tanisha, attended Cholla and became friends with Overton and Johnson, adding a personal connection to their athletic success.

Delano frequently brought Márquez to watch Cholla's games, particularly during their championship run in 1992. The father and son duo loved to watch Overton's scoring ability and Johnson's court vision, buttressing their admiration for the Cholla program.

Chapter 10

Sean Flannery: The Lancer Star

Sean Flannery's career at Salpointe Catholic High School was nothing short of spectacular. As a four-year starter, Flannery scored 2,332 points, earning first-team All-City honors each year. He later added to his legacy at the University of San Diego, where he surpassed the 1,000-point milestone as a college forward.

Delano and Márquez attended numerous Salpointe games, particularly when Flannery faced off against rivals like Tucson High's Eric Langford, an all-around blend of fundamentals and flamboyancy who averaged 25 points per game alongside Val Hill and Cholla's Chuck Overton. The intensity of those matchups was incomparable, and Delano often shared lessons about competition with Márquez after watching those rivalries between Flannery, Langford, Hill, Overton, and Johnson.

Deron Johnson: Sunnyside's Southpaw Sensation

Deron Johnson's impact at Sunnyside High School was legendary. Leading a 23-4 team in 1989, Johnson set a city record with 2,169 points, earning Arizona Gatorade Player of the Year honors. He went on to play at the University of Arizona and later at Clarke University in Atlanta where he set scoring records. Delano served as a mentor to Johnson during his Sunnyside days, frequently playing pickup games with him and offering guidance.

Márquez idolized Johnson, captivated by his effortless left-handed shooting and ability to dominate games. The wiry Johnson possessed NBA-level talent, overpowering the interior with his

CHAPTER 10

length while seamlessly transitioning to the perimeter, where he was equally impactful. He could shoot over smaller defenders with range extending to the three-point line, and his explosive first step allowed him to blow by defenders for crowd-pleasing dunks once they closed out on his shooting threat. The Prices attended many of his high school games, witnessing firsthand the rise of a talent destined to secure his place in Tucson's basketball history.

Jermaine Watts: Sunnyside's Unstoppable Force

Jermaine Watts was the epitome of dominance during his time at Sunnyside High School, leading the team to a perfect 29-0 season and a state championship. He earned Arizona State Player of the Year honors and went on to shine at DePaul University, averaging 16.2 points, 5.3 assists, and 2.6 steals per game as a sophomore. Watts was known for his lightning-quick first step and his ability to dunk over taller defenders despite standing at just 5-11.

Delano played pickup games with Watts at Randolph Recreation Center, where Márquez often tagged along, mesmerized by Watts' explosiveness and flair. Jermaine's journey from Sunnyside to collegiate stardom was another attestation to Tucson's deep basketball roots and the enduring mentorship of figures like Delano.

Chapter 10

Anthony Lever Pedroza: The Swiss Army Knife of Tucson Basketball

At 6'3, Anthony played international basketball in France, Croatia, Bosnia, the NBA, and the professional league in Mexico with Soles de Mexicali in the Liga Nacional de Baloncesto Profesional. On the court, he was cat-quick, with long, praying mantis arms, impressive leaping ability, and a multi-skilled game akin to a Swiss Army knife. He is also a member of the Mexico national basketball team.

Pedroza was a long-time member of the Mexico national basketball team and son of Fat Lever. He competed for the team at the FIBA Americas Championship in 2003, 2005, 2007, and 2009. In 2009, Pedroza scored a team-leading 17 points against the Virgin Islands in Mexico's preliminary round victory.

In high school, Anthony was a 1997 All-State guard at Canyon del Oro high school, netting 57 points in a game, and later playing in the rotation for the University of Oregon's 2002 Pac-10 championship squad.

Still in junior high, Márquez came across a newspaper clipping of the all-city team from 1995. Anthony, a sophomore at the time, had already made the first team. Two years later, Márquez found himself starting for the Tucson High varsity team as a freshman, facing off against Anthony, now a senior. Anthony lived up to the hype, averaging 27 points per game. Competing against him was the ultimate experience, giving Márquez a firsthand look at what it was like to face a college-level player while still in high school.

Chapter 10

Anthony Lever Pedroza's remarkable journey from Tucson to international stardom was an embodiment of his talent and the rich basketball tradition of the city.

The Threads that Bind

Delano and Hoegie's connections to these basketball standouts accentuate the rare role they played in shaping Tucson's basketball identity. Whether mentoring future stars, playing alongside them in pickup games, or simply cheering from the sidelines, their presence was constant. They bridged generations of talent, from the heyday of Fat Lever to the rise of Jermaine Watts, offering guidance, inspiration, and friendship.

For Delano, the court was always a place to compete and a space to nurture potential and celebrate the artistry of the game. His relationships with Tucson's greatest players reflect a legacy not just of athletic excellence but of kinship, mentorship, and an affinity for the game that united them all.

The Pride of Sugar Hill – Bryce Cotton

Growing up in Tucson's Sugar Hill neighborhood, Bryce Cotton developed as the brightest basketball star to come out of the same streets where Delano Price and Hoegie Simmons once honed their skills. Sugar Hill, known for its united community and historic ties to African American culture in Tucson, became the fertile ground for Cotton's extraordinary rise. From battling on outdoor courts to dominating international basketball, Cotton's journey had become one of the crowned jewels of community pride.

CHAPTER 10

The Early Days of Basketball

Bryce's introduction to basketball was shaped by the outdoor courts of Sugar Hill, where he competed in pickup games against older and taller players. Though he initially played multiple sports, including football and baseball, his love for basketball became his sole focus. Recognizing his height as a potential disadvantage, Bryce worked tirelessly with his uncle to develop the skills necessary to compete against bigger opponents, later developing into a world class athlete with a mid-40-inch vertical.

His efforts paid off in high school. Bryce attended Palo Verde High School after spending his junior year in Las Vegas. As a senior, he averaged 23.6 points, 7.5 rebounds, 4.0 assists, and 3.7 steals per game, leading Palo Verde to a 24–7 record and a berth in the state 4A semifinals. He set school records, including a 37-point, 11-rebound, 11-assist triple-double and a career-high 40 points in a playoff game. Despite his accomplishments, Bryce was overlooked by many college recruiters, a pattern all too familiar for underdog athletes from underserved communities.

Providence College: The Breakthrough

Providence College extended Bryce a last-minute scholarship offer just days before freshman orientation. This opportunity became a turning point in his life. After a modest freshman season, he emerged as a standout player, earning first-team All-Big East honors in his junior and senior years.

In his senior year, Cotton led Providence to its first Big East Tournament title since 1994 and an NCAA Tournament appearance. Known for his stamina, he averaged 40.1 minutes per game, the highest in the nation. In the NCAA Tournament, Cotton scored a career-high 36 points against North Carolina, solidifying his reputation as one of the most reliable and prolific players in college basketball. He graduated with a degree in sociology, a feat that is underlined by his dedication both on and off the court.

The Professional Journey

After going undrafted in the 2014 NBA Draft, Bryce faced a challenging path to professional basketball. He played short stints with the Utah Jazz, Phoenix Suns, and Memphis Grizzlies in the NBA while spending time in the NBA Development League and overseas leagues in China, Turkey, and Italy. Despite his undeniable talent, Bryce struggled to find a permanent home in the NBA, a common story for undersized guards.

His life and career changed when he joined the Perth Wildcats in the Australian National Basketball League (NBL) during the 2016–17 season. Bryce immediately made an impact, leading Perth to the NBL Championship and earning Grand Final MVP honors. Over the next several years, he became the face of the league, winning four MVP awards, seven scoring titles, and leading the Wildcats to three championships.

The Sugar Hill Connection

For Delano and Hoegie, watching Bryce's rise was deeply personal. Bryce grew up walking the same streets and shooting on the same hoops they had decades earlier. He embodied the spirit of Sugar Hill, a tenacity to rise above circumstances and excel against all odds. Delano, a mentor to many young athletes, took pride in seeing someone from his neighborhood achieve greatness on a global scale.

Bryce's story resonated with the young athletes in Tucson, particularly those from Sugar Hill, who saw in him a path to success. His relentless work ethic on the court, and his humility of it have made him a role model for the next generation.

Achievements and Legacy

Bryce's accolades are staggering. In the NBL, he is a four-time MVP, a three-time champion, and a two-time Grand Final MVP. His scoring titles and consistent All-NBL First Team selections cement his status as one of the greatest players in league history. Despite his professional success, Bryce remains grounded, often returning to Tucson to give back to his community.

A Model for Future Generations

As Bryce continues his career, his legacy grows not just in Tucson but around the world. For Delano and Hoegie, his journey is a reminder of the enduring power of basketball to move, link, and uplift. Bryce Cotton, the pride of Sugar Hill, stands as a substantiation to the neighborhood's rich history and its ability to produce greatness.

Chapter 10

Tucson basketball today: The rise of Cisco and Marcus Llamas

In the heart of Tucson basketball today, two bright young stars are emerging; brothers Cisco and Marcus Llamas, both playing for Sahuaro High School. Cisco, a junior, and Marcus, a freshman, have already begun to leave their mark on the local basketball scene, drawing comparisons to the legendary Delano Price and Hoegie Simmons from their high school days. Much like Delano and Hoegie, the Llamas brothers are making waves in the community, with their undeniable talent and potential.

Cisco's journey began early, and his accolades speak for themselves. As a freshman, he earned the 2023 Defensive Player of the Year award in the 4A Kino, along with being named to the All-Section 1st Team and winning the Sahuaro High School Athletic Award. By his sophomore year, Cisco was named Conference Player of the Year and again earned All-Conference 1st Team and All-Section 1st Team honors. Now as a junior, Cisco is on the verge of a major milestone, having already surpassed 1,000 career points on March 3rd, 2024, with his eyes set on even greater achievements as the season continues.

Marcus, though just a freshman, has made an immediate impact, starting on the varsity team and showing flashes of brilliance. Despite his age, he leads the team in assists and has demonstrated a poise and playmaking ability that belies his years. One of his standout performances came when Cisco was sidelined with an injury in a game against Tanque Verde High School. Marcus stepped up, knocking down four three-pointers, along with a couple of impressive left-handed drives to the basket, scoring over defenders much bigger than him, showcasing his ambidexterity and fearless approach to the game.

Both brothers, though diminutive in size, play with a fierce defensive intensity and a wide array of offensive skills that rival anyone in the state of Arizona. Their relentless one-on-one defense and offensive versatility have made them standout players, and their basketball IQ is among the best in the region. Off the court, Cisco and Marcus are excellent students and high-character kids who come from a solid family foundation, supported by two loving and dedicated parents.

Delano and Márquez frequently attend games at both Tucson High and Sahuaro High, watching the Llamas brothers with a sense of nostalgia, seeing in them the same drive and talent that defined their own high school basketball experiences. The Llamas brothers represent the future of Tucson basketball, and their journey is just beginning. With their combination of skill and heart, it's clear that Tucson basketball is in good hands.

CHAPTER 11

HOEGIE SIMMONS: THE GOAT OF TUCSON HOOPS?

"I first encountered Hoegie Simmons when I was starting guard for Cochise College in Douglas. At the time, we were the talk of the Arizona JUCO scene, having surged to a 6-1 record and holding first place in the ACCAC. This was a dramatic turnaround for Cochise, which had suffered through a winless 0-52 record over the previous two seasons due to a short-sighted policy by the local college board that required the team to use only in-county players. When that rule was finally rescinded, a new coach came in, and we took off.

We traveled up to Tucson for a peculiar tournament format, playing two games just hours apart. In the first matchup, we edged out a tough University of Arizona squad featuring Timmy Marshall and Mitch Jones, avenging a loss to them earlier in the season. After a brief two-hour break, we returned to the court for our second game. However, the junior college team we were slated to play had canceled at the last minute, leaving the organizers scrambling. They called in a local city league team to fill the spot.

When this ragtag group took the court, we couldn't help but suppress laughter. Their jerseys didn't match, their trunks didn't match, and even their socks were mismatched; sometimes, not even on an individual basis. Two of their starters were aging hippies with long ponytails, and two others were lanky and weathered, carrying an air of oldness in their eyes and legs. The fifth starter was a short Black man who shuffled onto the court with stooped shoulders, making him appear even smaller than he already was.

I leaned over to one of my teammates and quipped, "Look at this, man. We're about to play Fred's Liquor Store."

He shook his head and replied, "Nah, this is Ernie's Pool Hall."

Our amusement vanished quickly when the little guy took center court for the jump ball, against our 6-foot-8 center, and outjumped him. From the moment the game began, he was unstoppable. He scored from anywhere and everywhere on the court: twisting jumpers, fearless drives, soft tip-ins. By halftime, our starting guard, Timmy Williams, who twice made ALL-ACCAC and later played at the University of Arizona, had fouled out trying to guard him. Desperation set in. We tried a box-and-one defense, then double-teams, but nothing worked. By the game's end, four of my teammates had fouled out, their only crime being unfortunate enough to share the same patch of hardwood with Hoegie Simmons in that fleeting instant.

Chapter 11

In the second half, we started riding the offensive boards and clawed back into the game, cutting their lead to just two points several times. But every time we did, Hoegie responded with another basket. Near the end of the game, he came down on a fast break. I was the only defender left. I met him at the top of the key, determined to cut him off. He circled down to his right, and I sprinted to the baseline, cutting off his path. He paused, smiled, and said, "Good 'D', man." Then, as casually as if he were alone in an empty gym, he executed a flawless 360-degree jumper that barely rippled the net.

Oddly, I felt a strange sense of pride in that moment.

I don't recall him missing a single shot that day, though the stat sheet said otherwise. Officially, he was 28 of 33 from the floor. He finished with 67 points, 15 rebounds, and 12 assists. No one else on his team even reached double figures, yet they beat us, 102-97.

That's my Hoegie Simmons story."

Writer's Note by Tom Danehy of the Tucson Weekly

As Michael Luke wrote in his 2013 article about Hoegie Simmons, titled "Was 'Hoegie' the City's Best? Decades Later, Legend Lives On,":

"Incarceration dashed any distant dreams he might have had of playing professionally, but it was no impediment to the expansion of Hoegie's legend. His dreams of playing in front of packed arenas dashed, Hoegie proceeded to captivate a literally captive audience.

'Some tall guys with basketball credibility in prison knew about me and wanted to play one-on-one,' Hoegie said. 'People

Chapter 11

would watch to see what would happen, and I beat down every guy I played.'"

After his release, Hoegie returned to Tucson and seamlessly jumped back into the recreational basketball scene, where his legend only grew stronger. For those fortunate enough to have seen him play, his skill set, and sheer will to dominate remain unmatched in Tucson's basketball lore.

"It was always going to be hard for him to get a fair chance, but I've never seen a player in Tucson with Hoegie Simmons' ability or will to win," said former classmate and long-time Palo Verde coach David Gin. "He was a once-in-a-lifetime-type player on the best team I ever saw."

Michael Luke, a renowned sports savant and southern Arizona hoops aficionado, continues to celebrate Tucson basketball history as the editor and host of the Arizona Wildcats station at PHNX Sports, ensuring that Hoegie's story remains alive and vibrant for future generations.

In the world of street basketball legends, players who electrified the courts without ever stepping into the NBA have carved a unique space in basketball lore. Figures like Earl "The Goat" Manigault, Demetrius "Hook" Mitchell, Pee Wee Kirkland, Raymond Lewis, Edward "Booger" Smith, and James "Fly" Williams achieved mythical status with their dazzling talent and larger-than-life stories. Each was a player whose name evokes reverence on asphalt courts and in gymnasiums worldwide. Tucson's own Hoegie Simmons belongs in this pantheon. His legend rivals the best of them, not only in skill but in the complexity of his life, which mirrors the tales of triumph and tragedy that define playground heroes.

Chapter 11

Earl "The Goat" Manigault

Earl Manigault's story is one of potential both realized and lost. Known for his unbelievable leaping ability, Manigault was a Harlem legend, performing feats like snatching coins off the top of a backboard although this has been widely debated. While the tales of Manigault's exploits border on mythical, his battles with addiction and time spent in prison add a layer of tragedy to his legacy. Manigault's raw ability drew admiration from NBA greats, including Kareem Abdul-Jabbar, who once called him "the best basketball player his size in the history of New York City."

Hoegie Simmons' own high-flying style and relentless scoring made him the "Manigault" of Tucson. Though smaller than many of his opponents, Hoegie dominated with sheer strength of will and skill. His uncanny ability to "float" to the rim or hit a 360-jumper over defenders drew comparisons to the playground creativity of Manigault. Like Earl, Hoegie's life was marked by choices that kept him from professional basketball, but his ability left those who witnessed him in wonder.

Demetrius "Hook" Mitchell

Demetrius "Hook" Mitchell from Oakland, California, is a prime example of untapped greatness. Standing just 5'10", Mitchell performed gravity-defying dunks, including his famous 360 dunk over a car, that left crowds speechless. Despite playing with NBA stars like Jason Kidd, Gary Payton, and Antonio Davis, Mitchell's academic struggles and eventual incarceration cut short a career that many believed could have rivaled the greatest in the NBA.

Similarly, Hoegie Simmons operated on a plane few could match. His quickness, vertical leap, and ability to score at will made him the talk of Tucson courts. While "Hook" Mitchell captivated the Bay Area, Hoegie reigned in Tucson, regularly dismantling defenders with his finesse and explosiveness. Both players shared a tragic arc: immense talent overshadowed by struggles with the law and life outside the court. Yet, like Hook, Hoegie's legend endures as a symbol of what could have been.

Pee Wee Kirkland

Pee Wee Kirkland is perhaps the most fascinating figure among playground legends. Known as much for his off-court life as his transcendent moves on the court, Kirkland turned down opportunities to join the NBA because he made more money as a drug dealer. Despite this, his incredible scoring ability and showmanship solidified his status as a streetball legend.

While Hoegie Simmons didn't live the same dual life to a level as Pee Wee, he did find himself immersed in Tucson's underground world, using the basketball court as both an escape and a battleground for his hustle. Like Pee Wee, Hoegie used his craftiness and confidence to outwit opponents and sometimes earn a quick payday. Both men proved that their dominance on the court was not just about athleticism but also a sharp mind for the game.

Chapter 11

Raymond Lewis

Raymond Lewis, a California basketball sensation, is often regarded as one of the most skilled players to never make it to the NBA. At Verbum Dei High School and later at Cal State LA, Lewis was an unstoppable scorer, averaging 39 points as a college freshman. Drafted by the Philadelphia 76ers, Lewis' career was derailed by contract disputes and clashes with management, keeping him from showcasing his talent on a larger stage.

Hoegie Simmons shares Raymond Lewis' underdog narrative. Both players were underestimated by those who hadn't seen them play and were revered by those who had. Hoegie's one-on-one domination and inexorable scoring evoke comparisons to Lewis, who was said to score on anyone, anywhere. Like Lewis, Hoegie's story is one of a talent too big to ignore yet confined to the arenas that couldn't fully contain it.

Edward "Booger" Smith

Booger Smith was a wizard on the court, known for his otherworldly dribbling and supernatural passes in the EBC basketball tournament at Rucker Park in New York City. A true point guard, Booger's creativity and court vision set him apart. Despite his talent, Booger never made it to the professional ranks but remains a revered figure in the streetball world.

Hoegie Simmons, while primarily known as a scorer, had a similar ability to impress with his handle and passing. His flashy moves and ability to read the court earned him a loyal following in Tucson, just as Booger did in Brooklyn. Both players turned ordinary games into performances that left spectators talking for weeks.

James "Fly" Williams

James "Fly" Williams was a scoring machine whose playground exploits became legendary in New York City. With a silky jumper and unmatched charisma, Fly once scored 100 points in a game at IS8, further cementing his place in basketball folklore. Despite brief stints in the ABA and professional leagues, Fly's career was marred by off-court issues, including gunshot wounds that prematurely ended his career.

Fly's scoring mastery and allure parallel Hoegie Simmons' authority on Tucson courts. Like Fly, Hoegie had the crowd in the palm of his hand, whether it was with a showstopping dunk or a buzzer-beater from deep. And like Fly, Hoegie's larger-than-life persona made him a legend.

Comparing Hoegie Simmons to the GOATs

The term "GOAT" (Greatest of All Time) is often debated in the basketball world, but in Tucson, the conversation inevitably circles back to Hoegie Simmons. While playground legends like Earl Manigault, Demetrius Mitchell, and others built their myths in larger urban centers, Hoegie's story is uniquely rooted in Tucson's Sugar Hill neighborhood. He brought the same voltage and mystique to Tucson courts that these legends brought to Rucker Park, Oakland, and Los Angeles.

Chapter 11

Hoegie's versatility, whether scoring 60 points in a city league game or schooling college athletes at Bear Down Gym, placed him in rarefied air. His ability to adapt to any opponent, any style, mirrored the radiance of legends like Manigault and Lewis. His vertical leap and dunking ability earned him respect akin to "Hook" Mitchell, while his street-savvy approach to the game evoked shades of Pee Wee Kirkland.

The greatest players in streetball history didn't need NBA credentials to define their greatness. They inspired generations through their talent, swagger, and stories. Hoegie Simmons, like his counterparts in New York, Oakland, and beyond, turned every court he stepped onto a stage. His legend has grown through those who watched him play and those who felt his impact in a game. In many ways, Hoegie embodies the spirit of street basketball: a love of the game, a defiance of expectations, and an ability to captivate.

When we ask if Hoegie Simmons is Tucson's GOAT, the answer may depend on who you ask. But among those who witnessed his reign on the court, the consensus is clear: Hoegie Simmons belongs in conversation with the greats, not just Tucson but of street basketball. His legacy, like theirs, isn't measured in numbers or trophies. It's the ingrained mark left on the game and those who love it.

Hoegie Simmons: The playground King

Hoegie Simmons ruled Tucson's playgrounds like a monarch. While others played with textbook precision, Hoegie brought artistry and unpredictability. His game was about scoring, he could drop 50 or 60 points in a heartbeat, but even more about creating moments. He could humiliate defenders with a crossover, rise for a seemingly impossible shot, or deliver a no-look pass that left both teammates and opponents inextricably perplexed.

Fat Lever, a legend in his own right, once shared a story about Hoegie while scouting for the NBA. During a meeting with another scout from New York, a conversation about playground legends arose. The scout, deeply familiar with New York's iconic streetball culture, asked Fat if he knew Hoegie Simmons. When Fat said yes, the scout remarked that Hoegie was every bit as good as the celebrated legends of New York. For a city synonymous with basketball greatness to recognize Hoegie's skill speaks volumes about his impact.

However, when it comes to overall basketball achievements at every level, high school, college, and the NBA, Sean Elliott and Lafayette "Fat" Lever stand as the two best players to emerge from Tucson. Their unparalleled success, both on and off the court, elevates them to a different stratosphere in basketball history.

CHAPTER 12

A REUNION OF LEGENDS

In the stillness of early mornings or the calm of late evenings, a phone call between Delano Price and Hoegie Simmons transforms into a symphony of laughter, reflection, and shared wisdom. For two men who once conquered the courts of Tucson and left an ineffaceable mark on their community, these weekly calls have become a ritual and bridge across time, tying together decades of friendship, rivalry, and shared triumphs.

Their voices carry the weight of their experiences; each word infused with the hard-earned lessons of their lives. Delano speaks with calm, steady wisdom that evokes his reputation as a leader both on and off the court. His words are measured and thoughtful, often punctuated by a knowing chuckle as Hoegie weaves his signature blend of wit and candor into their conversations. Hoegie's humor is infectious, but beneath it lies the unassuming nature of a man who has lived through storms and come out the other side with his spirit intact.

Their bond, shaped by the fiery vessel of competition and annealed by the passage of time, has grown only stronger in their golden years. These phone calls, once sporadic and fleeting, are now a weekly lifeline. A sacred thread that connects their present with a shared past.

Delano and Hoegie's conversations often meander like a game of pick-up basketball, shifting effortlessly from one topic to another. They reminisce about the glory days when their names reverberated through the gymnasiums of Tucson, their chemistry a spectacle that drew crowds and inspired young players. Hoegie teases Delano about a missed free throw; Delano counters with jabs about Hoegie getting his shot mashed to the ground by a defender who caught Hoegie from behind as he followed through for an attempted release. Their laughter is rich and genuine, echoing through the miles that separate them.

The two men have become ardent students of the modern game, dissecting college games and debating the NBA's rising stars. Delano admires the discipline and team-first mentality of players like Nikola Jokić, while Hoegie marvels at the raw athleticism and flair of Ja Morant. Their analysis is informed by their years of experience; each opinion steeped in the nuances of the game they know so well.

Occasionally, their conversations take a serious turn, touching on the changes in the basketball world and the societal challenges that accompany them. Delano reflects on the opportunities that today's young athletes have, chances that were scarce in their

Chapter 12

time. Hoegie, ever the realist, points out that while the game has evolved, the struggle for equity and recognition remains.

The impact of Delano and Hoegie's lives extends far beyond the hardwood. For those who know them, they are symbols of the imperishable spirit of Tucson. Their names are spoken with reverence in gyms and playgrounds, their stories passed down as inspiration for young athletes navigating their own journeys.

Delano, with his solid presence, became a mentor to limitless players, infusing in them not just the fundamentals of basketball but the values of solidarity, direction, and esteem. His influence can be seen in the success of players like Sean Elliott and Fat Lever, whose own journeys to greatness were nudged by Delano's guidance and example.

Hoegie, despite his turbulent path, has left a large mark. His story is a reminder that greatness is not defined solely by accolades or achievements but by the impact one has on others. To those who saw him play, Hoegie was a virtuoso on the court, a player whose talent and creativity defied convention. To those who know him now, he is a man who has faced life's challenges head-on, emerging with a renewed sense of reclamation for what was once squandered.

At the heart of Delano and Hoegie's bond is their shared love for basketball. Their weekly calls are peppered with discussions of plays and strategies, debates about the greatest players of all time, and predictions for the next championship.

Basketball, to them, is a metaphor for life. Delano often compares the discipline required on the court to the self-control needed to navigate life's challenges. Hoegie, with his characteristic wit, likens the unpredictability of a fast break to the twists and turns of his own journey. Together, they find meaning in the game they both love, drawing lessons that continue to guide them.

For Delano and Hoegie, these weekly conversations are more than just a way to pass the time. They are a source of strength, a reminder of where they have been and how far they have come. Through their banter and laughter, they find solace and connection, a sense of belonging that exceeds the years and the miles.

Their story is a testimonial to the enduring power of friendship, a reminder that even the most divergent paths can lead back to a shared beginning. Delano and Hoegie's reunion are a tie that continues to inspire those who are lucky enough to witness it.

As their conversations wind down and the phone call comes to an end, one thing is certain: the legends of Delano Price and Hoegie Simmons will continue, moved forward by the accounts they share, the lives they have touched, and the game they love. Their story, like the game itself, is timeless.

Joseph's Journey in Delano's Story

Delano Price stands as a figure of adaptability and firm resolve, embodying the principles of faith, perseverance, and leadership. His life mirrors the biblical story of Joseph. Like Joseph, Delano has faced the betrayals and challenges of life like disappointments, losses, and moments that could have shattered a lesser spirit. Yet, through it all, he has emerged stronger, guided by an unshakable faith in his purpose and an enduring commitment to his community.

Chapter 12

Joseph's story in the Bible begins with promise and potential. As the favorite son of Jacob, Joseph was marked for greatness, but his journey to fulfilling that potential was fraught with adversity. Sold into slavery by his jealous brothers, Joseph endured years of hardship, from serving in Potiphar's house to languishing in prison. Yet, through each trial, Joseph remained steadfast in his faith and purpose, ultimately rising to a position of power and influence as Pharaoh's trusted advisor.

For Delano, the correspondences are striking. As a young man, he showed great promise on the basketball court, his leadership and talent setting him apart. Yet life, like Joseph's brothers, presented obstacles that sought to derail his journey. The challenges of navigating systemic racism, the pressures of providing for his family, and the heartbreaks of personal setbacks tested Delano's resolve. But, like Joseph, he never wavered in his integrity or his belief.

Joseph's rise to prominence in Egypt came not through force but through service by interpreting dreams, managing resources, and providing for others in a time of need. Similarly, Delano's influence in Tucson's basketball community and beyond has been rooted in service. Whether coaching young athletes, mentoring aspiring players, or offering guidance as a father and husband, Delano has built a legacy defined by his unshakeable staunchness to others.

One of the hallmarks of Joseph's story is his ability to lead, even in the throes of adversity. In Potiphar's house, he was entrusted with great responsibility. In prison, he became a leader among the inmates. And in Pharaoh's court, he managed the resources of an entire nation during a time of famine. Joseph's leadership was marked by wisdom, veracity, and a focus on serving the greater good.

Delano's life has reflected these same qualities. As a coach, he was a teacher of basketball fundamentals, and he was a mentor who instilled discipline, confidence, and a sense of purpose in his players. Many of the young men he coached went on to achieve great things, not just in basketball but in life, carrying with them the lessons they learned under Delano's guidance.

His impact extended beyond the court. As a father and husband, Delano exemplified patience, strength, and love through action. His consistency and firm support created a foundation of stability for his family, even in challenging times. Much like Joseph, who provided for his brothers and their families despite their betrayal, Delano's capacity for understanding and transformation has been a basis of his character.

One of Delano's greatest challenges was navigating the intersection of his passion for basketball and his responsibilities to his family and community. While his talent could have taken him far, he chose to remain rooted in Tucson, dedicating himself to uplifting those around him. This decision, though not without sacrifice, became a defining aspect of his journey.

Hoegie's Return: The Prodigal Son

Hoegie Simmons' life has been a tapestry interlaced with vivid highs and sobering lows, a journey that embodies the parable of the Prodigal Son. Where Delano's path was marked by unvarying perseverance, Hoegie's life burned like a comet streaking across the sky; bright, unpredictable, and marked by moments of

Chapter 12

inventiveness and turmoil. His chronicle speaks to the power of a second chance.

In his youth, Hoegie was nothing short of a basketball extraordinaire. On the courts of Tucson, he was a living legend. Yet, Hoegie's talents extended beyond basketball. His charisma, charm, and larger-than-life personality made him a beloved figure in Tucson. People gravitated toward him, inspired by his self-confidence and mesmerism. But, as with the Prodigal Son, the temptingness of fast living began to overshadow his natural gifts. The streets offered enticements such as fame, quick money, and fleeting pleasures that pulled Hoegie away from a more grounded path.

Like the Prodigal Son who lavished his inheritance on reckless living, Hoegie found himself ensnared in the trappings of his own success. Streetball stardom came with its own dangers, and for Hoegie, the line between grandeur and self-destruction fogged together. While his peers and contemporaries pursued structured opportunities in college or professional basketball, Hoegie's choices led him down a path of instability.

The basketball court, once a sanctuary, became a fleeting escape. Poor decisions and the pull of the streets led to moments of sequestration and anguish. His time in prison marked the bottommost point of his odyssey, an unsympathetic reminder of the outcomes of straying too far from the values that once guided him. Yet even in these darkest moments, Hoegie's impregnable nature refused to be extinguished. Behind the walls of confinement, he continued to play, stunning even the most hardened skeptics. Fellow inmates would gather to watch him, rapt by his ability to vanquish any opponent.

Chapter 12

Like the Prodigal Son, Hoegie eventually reached a point of self-realization. Reflecting on the choices that had led him astray, he saw the need for change. His time in prison, though painful, became a crucible that forged a new understanding of himself and his purpose. Hoegie began to see his life not as a series of missteps but as an opportunity for redemption.

Hoegie's story is one of redemption not just in basketball but in life. His reunion with Delano, and his renewed presence in the community are testaments to the transformative power of forgiveness and self-reflection. Much like the Prodigal Son, Hoegie returned with an understanding of what truly matters; a sense of belonging, the love of community, and the opportunity to contribute to something greater than himself. His bond with Delano has played a pivotal role in this transformation. Delano, ever the fixed and compassionate figure, has provided Hoegie with the encouragement and perspective he has needed to move forward.

Together, their lives have interweaved a narrative of triumph, struggle, and the everlasting ascendancy of friendship, a record defined and forever rooted in the backcourt.

Chapter 12

The Backcourt- Hoegie Simmons and Delano Price

EPILOGUE

MÁRQUEZ PRICE

Delano Price has achieved an impressive array of accomplishments throughout his life, leaving an indelible mark on his community and beyond. A transformative figure, he is respected across diverse demographics who can easily attest to his contributions. These accolades are not just limited to his basketball achievements but extend to his role as a mentor and leader.

In 2011, Delano was inducted into the Pima County Sports Hall of Fame. That same year, he was hired as a consultant by the Pima County Office of Education, tasked with researching and assessing after-school childcare programs. His work helped identify areas for improvement and informed future decisions regarding the direction of these programs, ultimately benefiting the community's youth.

Delano's athletic journey began with a standout career as a basketball All-American. He captained Tucson High's 1969 state championship team and became an All-Conference player at Phoenix Community College. After returning to Tucson, Delano pursued both undergraduate and graduate degrees at the University of Arizona. He went on to make history as Tucson's first Black coach for boys' varsity basketball at Sunnyside High School and its first Black administrator at Sahuaro High School. Throughout his 33 years as a coach, teacher, and administrator in the Sunnyside and Tucson Unified School Districts, Delano became known as one of the community's most dynamic and respected leaders.

What truly sets Delano apart is his ability to connect with people. Whether as a coach or an administrator, he intuitively understands the nuances of everyone's personality, using his deep empathy and wisdom to guide his interactions. His speeches are often impromptu yet powerful, and he is recognized as a gifted orator. Despite all his professional accolades, Delano's greatest achievement, in my eyes, has been as a father.

One vivid memory from my childhood, when I was about six years old, exemplifies his protective nature. I had just received a new BMX bike, which I immediately became attached to, so much so that I kept it inside my room for a month. One afternoon, I met two brothers while riding around the neighborhood. They were eight and eleven years old, and we quickly became friends. But our interaction soured when one of them demanded that I give them my bike. When I refused, they both shoved me to the ground and rode off laughing.

What they didn't realize was that I had a powerful ally, my father. I rode home, walked into the bathroom where he was shaving, and explained what had happened. Without a second thought, he put down his razor and said, "Show me where they

Epilogue

live." We walked down the street together, and when we arrived at their house, I'll never forget the look on their father's face when he opened the door. My father stood there, a face full of Barbasol foam, wearing sweatpants, with a Jheri curl and shirtless. Despite his casual appearance, he was in peak physical condition, a look that rivaled Apollo Creed from Rocky, as he had been training religiously. The confrontation was brief, but powerful as those boys never bothered me again.

My father is a man of action. He didn't wait to clean up before addressing the situation. This is one of many examples where he demonstrated his unwavering support and protection. My sisters have their own stories of his interventions. I remember the time my oldest sister was bullied by a jealous family in high school. My father entered their living room, and with no hesitation, declared, "This stops today," using a more colorful expletive. And just like that, it stopped. On another occasion, when a kid hurled a racial slur at my other sister, my father confronted the boy's father, who was feared in the neighborhood, and demanded that the racial slurs cease. After that, my sister never faced such insults again.

Growing up, I didn't need to read statistics to understand the importance of a father's presence in a child's life. I could see the impact of absent fathers all around me. During the crack epidemic of the 80s, many Black fathers abandoned their families, leaving their children without the guidance they needed. I saw firsthand how many of my friends were raised without their fathers. But I was fortunate as my father was there every single day, teaching me invaluable life lessons that would shape my future.

My father gave me his time. He took me to the barbershop every other Friday and made sure I understood the importance of maintaining a positive reputation. When I got into trouble at school for defending myself, he stepped in and made sure my teacher didn't label me as "aggressive." He knew those types of labels contributed to the school-to-prison pipeline, something many Black boys fall victim to. I saw my father every morning when I woke up, and again when he came home, his tie thrown over his shoulder while preparing dinner.

Saturday mornings were for cleaning the house to the rhythm of classic soul and R&B. Sunday afternoons were spent doing yard work, where my father still cuts the grass with a push mower. He made sure that if I could recite rap lyrics, I could also recite my history lessons. My friends saw my father as a father figure, as most of them lacked that presence in their lives. He taught me the importance of investing not only in money, but in relationships and health. I watched him maintain a strict workout routine and eat healthy foods, setting an example I would follow for the rest of my life.

My father became my best friend. Our bond was like that of a backcourt duo—unspoken understanding, seamless teamwork, and a chemistry that couldn't be broken. As a child, I was taught that man was created in God's image, but at the time, I didn't fully understand what that meant. Now, I know that my father was that image to me. I revered him with a depth that only a son could understand.

When I was older, my father told me that being a Black man was demanding. I've carried that wisdom with me throughout my life. I thank God every day for having a father like mine as an example.

Epilogue

I also call Hoegie Simmons my "uncle" because, from birth to age 12, I spent countless hours with him and my father at the gyms they frequented. Hoegie's distinct voice, boisterous and full of life, was the first thing I'd hear before I even saw him. After going on the run for 20 years, I was overjoyed the day he reappeared, sitting in my parents' living room, greeting me with that familiar voice. He had always told my dad, "That boy's gonna be a star," and though I didn't get to see him witness my rise as a local legend, I could feel his pride.

Hoegie's influence in my life cannot be overstated. He introduced me to a world of experiences. There were many "firsts" I experienced with Hoegie, each one leaving a lasting imprint on my childhood. The first time I saw someone riding a motorcycle in person was Hoegie. He calls them "cycles" and, over the years, has owned around 200 of them. The sound of a motorcycle engine revving became synonymous with his presence. The first time I saw a Great Dane was also thanks to Hoegie. He had one named "Killa," a dog that patrolled his mother's backyard, and as a child, it looked to me like a horse. Hoegie's world was full of larger-than-life experiences, and it was in his presence that I first encountered these monumental "firsts."

Hoegie was also known for his distinctive car, which would play popular jingles as sirens, the kind you'd hear on a police car when he'd pull up to the gym. My favorite jingle was the "Pink Panther" theme, which only added to his unique presence. Hoegie had a penchant for candy, particularly Bazooka bubblegum, which he'd share with me generously. One time, while he went to the bathroom, I couldn't resist peeling open his gym bag to sneak a little more than my usual ration. What I discovered, however, was a Magnum revolver, tucked neatly inside the bag. He carried it to every gym in case someone couldn't handle the way he dismantled them on the court. It was also the tool he carried during his graveyard shifts in the streets.

On weekends, my dad and I would pick up Hoegie to head to the gym. I can vividly recall his mother, Miss Simmons, opening the door for us. I couldn't help but try not to laugh because, much like Hoegie, she had the same distinctive voice and Jheri curl. It was like looking at a reflection of Hoegie in a mirror. His basketball trophies were lofty and plentiful, scattered throughout his house. His walls were adorned with plagues, while thick scrapbooks housed newspaper clippings commemorating his basketball feats. For me, Hoegie's house was a home and shrine to his legacy as a player.

Each visit to Hoegie's world was a reminder of the larger-than-life presence he had, not just on the court but in the way he lived and the stories he shared.

I also remember our trips to the gym, where I would sit in the back seat between my dad and Hoegie. It felt like a scene from a movie, with the two of them reminiscing about the past while teaching me about the present and future of basketball. I watched them personify mastery over pickup games into their 30s and 40s, witnessing firsthand the legends they had become. It was like watching Superman and Batman play against mere mortals. As I grew older and heard stories about them from before my time, I realized just how special it was to witness their greatness up close.

Ultimately, it was a privilege to be part of their lives, to see the legacy of both men unfold, and to learn from their dichotomous paths and love for the game. The memories I carry from those formative years shaped who I am today, and I will always honor the impact Delano Price and Hoegie Simmons had on my life.

The author Márquez Price with a rim's eye view of the story.

EPILOGUE

DELANO PRICE

My story with Hoegie Simmons began in 1965 when we were both freshmen in high school. Hoegie had moved to Tucson from Louisiana with his mother and was living with his aunt on south Park. My family moved to Tucson from Gary, Indiana in February of 1959. Our story is a key component of a bigger story, the great black migration from the South.

On Friday, January 14, 1966, our freshman basketball team at Tucson High School played host to Pueblo High School's freshman team. We had heard talk around town about a phenom named Hoegie. During warmups, a figure emerged from the locker room that looked more like a caricature. He was all arms and legs. It was Hoegie.

He was everything that we had heard. He razzled and dazzled all game. One moment occurred during the game that I'll never forget. He dribbled up to our 6'5" center and shot a jump shot right in his face. Swish! Despite his size, I knew right then and there that he possessed the heart of a lion. Little did I know that one day we would form one of the top backcourts in Arizona prep basketball history and one of the top ten teams in state history.

During Hoegie's sophomore year, his mother purchased a house at 1118 E. Hampton Street, placing him in Tucson High's attendance zone. During my junior year, my parents purchased a house at 834 E. Linden Street. Even though we already resided in Tucson High's attendance zone having lived at 449 E. Lester in the Sugar Hill neighborhood, Hoegie and I were just five minutes away from each other.

The next three years would witness the formation of a friendship, a brotherhood and bond that endures to this day. We were inseparable. We would spend days walking to school, playing one on one at the YMCA and any other court that we could find and challenging other players to two-on-two games. By the time we were seniors, we operated on instinct. It was automatic.

The culminating event in our high school career was winning the state championship. Winning the championship was a life-changing event because it happened at Tucson High, the Home of Champions. At the time, Tucson High had won more championships in football, basketball and baseball than any high school in the Nation. We had made history. Reflecting on that magical year, I realized that winning the championship involved possessing talent and at times, a dose of luck. Hoegie, as it turned out, became the missing piece, that player that would complement Kenny Ball, Chuco Miranda and me. In my four years at Tucson High, Kenny Ball was the best player and in my humble opinion, the top player in the state of Arizona, our senior. He was the equivalent of a five-tool player. He was beautiful to watch. Chuco was the perfect teammate, always steady. His four epic games during the Southern Region and State Tournament were the bridge that we needed to win it all!

Following high school, Hoegie's and my path went in different directions. He enrolled at Glendale Community College where he became an All-Conference player and set several records. From there, he received a scholarship to Texas A & I where he became a legendary player setting several records that still stand to this day.

I attended Phoenix Junior College and became an All-Conference my sophomore year and was named team Most Valuable Player. Although I was recruited by the University of Kansas, I chose to transfer to the University of Arizona and completed my degree in Education. I had a young family, thus completing my degree and beginning my career became my priority. No regrets. I realized that I could balance my career and still pursue and participate in the game that I loved.

Over the years, Hoegie and I would reunite and perform the same magic that we had displayed on so many courts around Tucson. We hold our own with the best high school, college and professional players into our forties. I'm honored that players today still speak of us as legendary players and role models who influenced their lives.

Although there were periods in our lives when we were separated by circumstances beyond our control, I believe that we are the sum of our lives' decisions. Our love as brothers and for the game has withstood the test of time. Hoegie made his choices, and I made mine. The bottom line is that when reflecting over our lives we have endured. We will forever be joined as two kids who met and made history. I consider Hoegie Simmons to be the "Sugar Ray Robinson" of my basketball experience. He was pound for pound, the most phenomenal basketball player of his size that I've ever seen.

Special thanks to my son, Marquez, an author, poet, philosopher, scholar and basketball player in his own right. After conducting several interviews and engaging in hours of research, I realized that it was part of his calling to tell this story. It's his story, an eyewitness account. Marquez Price has given the Tucson community and beyond, a gift, a compelling story of two people whose story is our story. I'm forever indebted to Marquez Price (Doc).

www.ingramcontent.com/pod-product-compliance
Ingram Content Group UK Ltd.
Pitfield, Milton Keynes, MK11 3LW, UK
UKHW022238230426
12048UKWH00018BA/1325